Jesus' Amazing Miracles @ Work
365 Day Devotional

My Story/My Song

Selwyn B. Cox

Kingdom Journey Press
A Division of Kingdom Journey Enterprises

Copyright Instructions
JAMS (Jesus' Amazing Miracles) @ Work 365 Day Devotional (Revised)
Copyright 2018 and 2016 by Selwyn B. Cox

Unless a person is explicitly identified by name, the statements that are used should not be directly attributed to any specific person.

All rights reserved under the international copyright law. No part of this book may be reproduced or transmitted in any form or by any means, electronic or mechanical, including photocopying, recording, or by any information storage and retrieval system, without the express, written permission of the author. The exception is reviewers, who may quote brief passages in a review.

Unless otherwise marked, all scripture quotations are referenced from the New King James Version of the Bible.

ISBN-10: 0-9890878-4-0
ISBN-13: 978-0-9890878-4-1

Printed in the United States of America.

Published by Kingdom Journey Press
A Division of Kingdom Journey Enterprises
www.kjpressinc.com
Woodbridge, VA

Cover Design by:
Brandon Richardson
E-Mail: richardson.the@gmail.com

Brand U Inc.
Website: www.branduinc.com

Table of Contents

Dedication iii
Acknowledgements v
Devotional Introduction 1
My Story 3
My Song 9
"That's My JAM!" 11
How To Use This Devotional 13
Significant Dates and Definitions 15
Significant Dates Chart 18
My Playlist 20
January: Seeking God (Communication Through Prayer) 33
February: Sin (Conquered By Jesus) 67
March: Salvation (Forgiveness and Eternal Life) 100
April: Sanctuary (Attendance and Altar Call) 134
May: Support (Creating Stable Relationships Among Family andFriends) 167
June: Self-Esteem (Learning Self-Love, God's Way) 204
July: Satisfaction (Living Within God's Plan For Your Life) 238
August: Spirit (God's Holy Spirit Within) 272
September: Self-Preservation (Learning to Survive Crisis) 306
October: Serenity (Having Peace That Passes Understanding) 339
November: Service (To God and Others) 373
December: Surrendering (Letting Go) 406
About The Author 441
About Kingdom Journey Press 443

Dedication

This effort is dedicated to my Lord and Savior, Jesus Christ, and the great cloud of witnesses who have gone on before me, who are looking down from the balcony of heaven, cheering me on:

My parents, Arthur B. and Emma G. Cox; my grandmother, Lillian Faison; my brother, whom I resemble, Livy Bernard Cox; and my sister, Denise Cox (my big sister who passed away as a child).

Selwyn B. Cox

Acknowledgements

I could not have accomplished this goal without the influence of the following persons:

My siblings, who love me in spite of the "Selwyn Factor": Dallas Fowler (my father figure and mentor); Vincent Cox (the best trophy-winning sportsman I know); the twins, Vaughn Cox (Vonnie Boy) and Vanessa Cox (my one and only sister who is the wind beneath my wings); my aunt, Florence H. Faison-Carter (the "Lady of the House"); my uncle, Graham Faison ("Mr. Wonderful"); my nephews, Brian Fowler, Livy Bernard Cox II, Steven Cox, Derin Cox and Brandon Richardson (also my graphic artist); my nieces, Sonya Cox, Shantelle Coleman, Triesta Fowler-Lee, Nina Cox, Tia Cox, and Traci Cox; my "kissin" cousins, Stephanie Faison and Yvette Faison;

To the generation who made me "great" ~ my great-nieces, Parshia Fowler and Brielle Fowler; my great-nephews Donte' Lee, Devon Lee, Jabari Coleman and Zion Cox;

God-children Angela Speight, Goldie Brown, Idailyon Saladin Helm Jr., Jabari M. Rorie-Boyd, Justin L. Wheeler;

My Extended Family: Faison, Sampson, Thompson, Swinton, Robinson, Myrick, Moses, Dowell, Barber, Lewis, Vaughn/Fortune, Gardner, Morris, McCrae, Hamlin, Stokes, Hunt, Devine, Stratton, Arrendell, Witcher, Harvey, Hampton, Wheeler;

Thank you to my Pastor, Rev. Dr. Howard John Wesley, for excellent leadership and the divine wisdom you have imparted into me. I pray God's blessings on your ministry for many years to come. Also to my entire Alfred Street Baptist Church family;

To these great men and women of the gospel who have spoken into my life along the way:
The late, great Dr. John O. Peterson, Alfred Street Baptist Church; Reverend Dr. Faye Savage Gunn, Alfred Street Baptist; Reverend Dr. Dexter U. Nutall, New Bethel Baptist Church; Reverend Dr. Haywood A. Robinson, III, The People's Community Baptist Church;

Spiritual Advisors/Teachers: Reverend Beverly Moses, Reverend Marla Hawkins, Reverend Samuel Nixon, and Minister Rosalind Brooks, all of whom attend the Alfred Street Baptist Church; Reverend Carolyn Jackson, Galilee Baptist Church and Minister Joan McCarly, The People's Community Baptist Church;

Pastor Marcus and Co-Pastor Stacey Barber, Filled with the Holy Spirit Ministries, thank you for wise counsel and a timely prophetic Word;

The Jesus' Amazing Miracles at Work (JAMS @ Wk) Ministry members at EPA;

Special thanks to the following persons who comprised the editorial team for this effort:
Reverend Lisa Gillespie, Filled with the Holy Spirit Ministries; Deacon Donnell Hampton, Macedonia Christian Church; Minister Theresa Fleming-Blue, Alfred Street Baptist Church;

A host of others too numerous to name, whom I greatly appreciate with my whole heart.

Devotional Introduction

God inspired me to write this book. I was instructed to assemble a collection of devotions that would edify Christ each day and remind us of what God has done for us. We could never repay God for what He has done, is doing and will do, but we can spend our time trying until the day we are called to be with Him. The intent of each devotional is to cause a "spiritual paradigm shift" for the purpose of developing a deeper relationship with Jesus Christ.

Upon completing this book, you should experience a transformation of your devotional habits, such as:
- removing your devotion from man and giving it to God;
- reducing the level of importance you place upon material things;
- replacing bad habits of self-gratification with good habits that bring glory to God;
- replenishing your level of spiritual nourishment.

In short, your new habits will give credence to the fact that all glory, honor and praise belong to God. A Holy God wants a relationship with sinful man. This fact alone is amazing! Man's natural inclination is toward evil and without God, he would ultimately destroy himself. It seems that humans are simply "naughty by nature". Jeremiah 17:9 says "the heart is deceitful above all things, and desperately wicked; who can know it?"

Despite this fact, God longs for a meaningful spiritual connection with you. He wants to be everything to you and He is equipped to meet every need you will ever have. All you have to do is live according to His will for your life and there will be nothing that will be off limits to you.

The writings here reflect the influences I obtained from many recording artists. The titles inspired me to take a journey from the secular into the sacred. I have enjoyed converting each song title to reflect a spiritual connotation. The concept of converting the secular to the sacred was introduced to me by the late great Reverend James Cleveland when he remade a song called "The Best Thing That Ever Happened To Me" (also performed by R&B legendary artist Gladys Knight).

I believe the secular version was referring to a person, however James Cleveland's rendition was clearly talking about the Lord. Kirk Franklin often times takes a journey from the secular to the sacred in his method of rewriting songs, reaching many people who may not otherwise know or hear about Jesus. This book does not use or change lyrics but rather, uses titles to convey a spiritual message.

Each day's reading should cause us to reflect on the fact that we are amazing miracles and that God is still in the miracle-working business. Each entry contains a reflection of God's purpose for us in our daily lives and in our walk with Him. This daily devotional is a testimony — a little bit of country, rock and roll; a whole lot of gospel and a whole lot of soul.

After reviewing my musical collection, coupling song titles, certain television shows and quotes we have used in JAMS@WK, I have compiled a list that I pray will provide daily enlightenment. I am under the premise that people listen to music more frequently than they read the Bible. They enjoy music while working, driving, watching TV, relaxing or just as something to do. Our daily routine should include praying, reading the Bible, meditating on God's Word, loving and forgiving one another and living our lives intentionally, carrying out our individual God-ordained purpose.

This devotional should not take away from your daily Bible-reading. The Bible has been referred to as our "Basic Instructions Before Leaving Earth." It is the greatest book that God inspired man to write. My prayer is that something written in this devotional will cause you to get acquainted with God, draw nearer to Him and redirect your focus to Christ. Each entry is written in a universal fashion, so as to embrace people at their current stage in their spiritual walk.

My Story

In September 2000, there was an incident that changed the rest of my life. I had a near death experience and was admitted to Holy Cross Hospital. Lying in a semi-coma, I heard the voice of the Lord, telling me to change my life. Up to that point, I was not actively seeking God and had not surrendered my will and ways to the Lord.

Each night, there was a light outside the window that shined into my room and it illuminated a cross that hung on the wall. Seeing this made me feel like I was in the very presence of God. As the doctors worked to diagnose me, I repeatedly heard Psalm 23:6 which says, "Surely goodness and mercy shall follow me all the days of my life; And I will dwell in the house of the Lord forever."

While going in and out of consciousness, I was filled with the Holy Spirit. After regaining full consciousness, the nursing staff and my family members told me that I literally ran down the hospital corridor unclothed. I did not remember this incident; I just knew that I felt free.

This experience reminded me of the story in Acts, chapter 9, where Paul had a conversion encounter with Christ on the road to Damascus. Like Paul, prior to my encounter, I did things that were not pleasing in the sight of God. I had sinned and fallen short of God's glory. Brother Paul stated he was the chief sinner; I must share that I often begged to differ with him because I felt that phrase more accurately described me.

When talking with my sister about my condition, I told her many things that God shared with me, among which was the fact that my test results would be negative. I asked her if she believed the things I was sharing that God told me. She said yes, but that she was wondering, after running with Jesus for 16 years herself, why He had not talked to her like that!

I later discovered that the only reason I was brought into this situation in the first place, was for God to talk to me. Upon the conclusion of all the testing procedures, the doctors indeed confirmed the negative test results, which is what I had already told my sister. Upon hearing this, I surrendered to God's will for my life. Through grace, I joined the church, accepted the Lord as my Savior and embraced my calling to serve God's people.

My conversion experience was such a great feeling that I asked God why He had not come to me before then. He said He did come, witnessing through others, but I would not receive Him. He would send people to me, who would tell me that I did not belong in various places, but I was unwilling to hear them. Now, it was time for me to serve God.

As I think back now, I remember God speaking to me a few days before the hospital encounter. My sister, who is also my confidante, was spending the night at my home. I awakened her and told her that I could not sleep and that God was keeping me awake, convicting me and "kicking my behind." Through this encounter, the Lord got my attention.

Sometime later, my sister and I laughed about that night. She told me what I did that night by waking her at 2:00 am was "kicking her behind" because she normally gets up at 4:00 am to go to work!

Prior to accepting Christ, I was self-serving and materialistic. I had accumulated an array of possessions but was focusing more on the gifts rather than the Giver. Little did I know that I needed to practice the truth contained in Matthew 6:33, which says "But seek first the Kingdom of God and His righteousness, and all these things shall be added to you". I needed to stop praising things and start praising God.

I was also reminded of Mark 8:36, where it says "For what will it profit a man if he gains the whole world, and loses his own soul?" and Matthew 19:24, where it says "And again I say to you, it is easier for a camel to go through the eye of a needle than for a rich man to enter the Kingdom of God."

In addition to being materialistic, I had issues with unforgiveness. God made me aware of the importance of forgiving others so that I myself could receive forgiveness. There is no valid reason for holding on to unforgiveness; not even when your feelings get hurt. God let me know that no hurt was as great as the hurt that Jesus suffered on the cross for my sins. He told me that letting go of past hurts and offenses was vital to my spiritual growth.

Another area in which I struggled was with race relations. My experiences involving civil rights developed prejudices within me. God revealed that He was a God for all people and that His love is for everyone. God's love is blind and sees NO COLOR and this is how my love needed to be.

During this time, I was given instructions on how to prioritize my life by using what I would like to refer to as the "Believer's 12-Step Plan". Included in this book are daily devotionals where the theme at the beginning of each month is based upon one of the 12-Steps outlined. Readers can apply each of these steps to their own lives by following the prescribed formula shown below. Doing so walked me from an unsaved life without Christ into a saved life as a born-again believer. I will share these steps with you now:

1) **Seeking God** – *have you ever heard the voice of God?*
   Here is my encounter: God spoke to me through this analogy -- when boarding a plane, you rely on the pilot to take you to your destination. You don't attempt to fly the plane. You simply board, have a seat and buckle your seatbelt. God wanted me to follow these steps as it pertains to spiritual things. He wanted to be my pilot. I should simply buckle my seat belt, trust Him to take care of me and allow Him to take me to my destination (Proverbs 3:5-6).

2) **Sin** – *are you focused on the wrong things?*
   Here is my encounter: Prior to accepting Christ, the most important things to me were money, fortune and fame. God told me I needed to change my life and follow His plan rather than my own.

3) **Salvation** – *are you saved and/or do you desire a closer walk with God?*
   Here is my encounter: The Lord revealed to my aunt that I was unsaved. When she asked me about it, I told her I was not. Sometime later, I attended an evening service at a local church and while there, made a subconscious commitment to God that if I ever moved back to the Alexandria area, I would join this congregation. A few years later, I indeed moved back to Alexandria and God directed me to make good on my

word. I joined the Alfred Street Baptist Church and was baptized on September 21, 2000.

4) **Sanctuary** – *are you connected to a local congregation?*
Here is my encounter: I was not connected and did not go to church on a regular basis. God's message to me was that if He allowed me to do as I pleased for six days a week, then I should be willing to come to His house at least one day a week. Once there, I would receive a life-changing Word from the pulpit, have an opportunity to fellowship with like-minded believers and would be an example of obedience to those in my neighborhood.

5) **Support** – *do you give support to and receive support from family and friends?*
Here is my encounter: I was reminded of God's commandment in Exodus to "honor thy father and mother….." How you treat your parents is one very important indication of how well you love God. I was blessed with the privilege of caring for my mother during her illness prior to death. God also shared the importance of family and the necessity of having reunions in order to stay connected.

6) **Self-esteem** – *do you love yourself?*
Here is my encounter: I felt I was treated differently. I had low self-esteem and I struggled with being accepted by others. I had five brothers who were often complimented on their looks and athletic abilities for which they had received trophies, while I had none. People would comment that I was different and would not amount to much. God had other plans.

7) **Satisfaction** – *do you know your God-given purpose?*
Here is my encounter: I thought God created me to be an interior decorator because I had a talent for teaching others how to make the best use of spaces within their homes. This is one of my talents but not my divine purpose. God revealed to me that my purpose was my ability to speak and to tell my story for the benefit of others. So it appears that I'm an interior decorator after all; not only in the natural sense, but in the spiritual sense as well, leading people in the discovery of their inner beauty and gifts from God.

8) **Spirit** – *are you resisting the move of God's Holy Spirit?*
   Here is my encounter: People would tell me they had a message for me from God but I rejected them. As a result of that, God said some people would reject me but I still have to tell the story.

9) **Self-preservation** – *are you quick to discard others?*
   Here is my encounter: I had a habit of "cutting people off". At this stage of my life, I was good in my own eyes but God had to let me know that some people were called into my life by Him and I was not to discard them. I had to learn to allow God to protect my feelings and not try to protect them myself.

10) **Serenity** – *have you found your place of serenity?*
    Here is my encounter: I thought I could find peace in possessions, people and positions. God told me that I would only find peace in Him.

11) **Service** – *in what way are you serving God and others?*
    Here is my encounter: God told me I needed to have a ministry dedicated to Him, which is why you have this book! Then, He also gave me the vision for an online business, which is forthcoming. It is called the Chic Unique Boutique, and will showcase original designs and creations, along with a few of my favorite things.

12) **Surrendering** – *what stands between you and your total surrender to God?*
    Here is my encounter: It was time to make a choice. God told me I would either live for Him or die and come with Him! I prayed the "Hezekiah" prayer (Isaiah 38) asking for an extension of my life. God granted that request because I am now in my 16th year of life following that incident.

Today, I have been on this journey for more than 15 years, doing God's will for my life. Taking these steps was the beginning of my journey, crossing a spiritual bridge from the secular into the sacred. My relationship with God inspired me to change the way I thought about music. I discovered that I could take secular song titles and derive spiritual meanings from them.

I began by **SEEKING GOD** because the Holy Spirit pricked my conscience and let me know I could not make it on my own. That process led to repentance and the confession of my **SIN**, after which I accepted Christ as my personal Savior and Lord. Then I received **SALVATION,** which afforded me the gift of eternal life. I developed an understanding of the importance of going into God's **SANCTUARY**, for the purpose of fellowshipping with other like-minded believers in Christ.

I increased my ability to give and receive **SUPPORT** to and from my family and friends. This helped me develop greater **SELF-ESTEEM** because the more I was able to love and appreciate myself, the more I loved and appreciated others. My spiritual growth produced a deep sense of **SATISFACTION** within me. Soon, I was introduced to God's Holy **SPIRIT** and He has changed my life forever.

I no longer have to practice **SELF-PRESERVATION** because God takes good care of me. This fact alone produces a great deal of **SERENITY** within me and I no longer worry about the things that once consumed me. Now, I am living a life of **SERVICE** to my heavenly Father and continually **SURRENDERING** my life to Him. This was my personal journey through the "Believer's 12-Step Plan." Now, I invite you to read "My Song."

My Song

I have always had a tune on my lips and a song in my heart. Music was, is and will always be a big part of my life. I loved music, yet I could not sing. I had a longing to sing and often dreamed that I possessed that gift, but even to this day, I cannot hold a tune. When I grew up and accepted the Lord, I wondered how my love for secular music would fit into my saved life. I connected my conversion experience to an R&B song performed by Peaches and Herb called "Reunited" because I was reunited with the Father and the feeling was better than good!

One of the old clichés used in regards to music is "music has charms to soothe a savage beast." This proverb comes from the play "The Morning Bride" by William Congreve. By definition, this quote means that music has the power to influence the hardest heart. Likewise, music is universal and has the ability to bring people together, especially families. Back in the day, my siblings and I grew up with a love for music. We had a desire to become artists like The Jackson 5. I would often gather my siblings and we would put on talent shows for our mother. I developed routines for us to do during our shows.

Having this experience with my siblings birthed within me the desire to become a lead singer. To help me accomplish this task, I hired a vocal coach. Since I was now saved, I preferred to sing gospel music. Upon auditioning with the coach, she told me that I was tone deaf and refunded my money! That news presented a stumbling block but did not stop me from pursuing my love of and interest in music. Here is where I had to employ my ability to turn something negative into something positive.

I began to accept the fact that I would not become a famous, lead singer as I once believed. While I may not have had a singing voice, I had a voice nonetheless; and you have one as well. I became aware of a hit TV series called "The Voice" where aspiring singers auditioned for celebrity judges. There are four judges and at the bottom of all the chairs are the words, "I Want You". Among the chairs that turn indicating their interest in you, you are tasked with choosing a team on which to participate and you can only choose one team. Our spiritual life can be equated to these components.

Spiritually speaking, the four chairs would be called Self, Secular, Sin and Savior. The chair of Self would represent your personal desires; the chair of Secular would represent the world; the chair of Sin would represent satan and the chair of the Savior would represent Jesus Christ. As soon as life begins, each chair competes for your attention and desires to be chosen by you. It is up to you which chair to choose.

Once a chair is chosen, the contestant is known as a member of that particular team. To get the best out of your life and the plan that has been designed for you, allow me to recommend Team Jesus! If this show had been around when I was younger, undoubtedly, I would have auditioned. Because that was not the case, we will never know what the outcome would have been. That was then, this is now.

The life of the person who wins The Voice changes forever. This is a positive change. But every change in life is not positive. Sometimes, tragic events occur and there is also music that speaks to these situations. Situations change lives --- sometimes for the better; sometimes for the worse. Events affect what happens in the lives of people. All we have to do is look at our history. Even in the face of tragedy, music plays a part. The terrorist attacks of 911 brought us together in the midst of several tragic incidents. In these moments of crisis, we became a unified symphony of concern, love and togetherness. We were rescuing, praying for and comforting one another. We learned how to rally together for one purpose, which is our freedom. We also learned how to take care of one another, even if those we helped were not blood relatives.

The analogies used in reference to The Voice and the events of 911 sparked a desire in me to formulate a ministry that would serve a dual purpose – honoring God and serving man; that's my JAMS ministry!

"That's My JAM!"

Back in the day, when I used to hear a song I loved, I would say "that's my jam!" Speaking along the lines of purpose, I began to discover what God had birthed in me. He shared a ministry concept called "Jesus' Amazing Miracles @ Work (JAMs @ Wk)". In 2012, while working at the Environmental Protection Agency (EPA), I was led by the Holy Spirit to begin holding lunchtime Bible studies with my coworkers.

Although I knew I would not be a singer, God gave me another way to express my love for song through His Word. Our group meets once a month for one hour to study God's Word. During our "JAM sessions", we talk about our walk with God, express our fears and share our innermost thoughts and desires. Plainly put, "we be jammin" in the name of the Lord!

Because each one of us is an amazing miracle, we praise God for who He is and what He means in our lives. The miracle is in the fact that we live and breathe and were created by God. God created everything in six days and called it good and gave man dominion over His creation. The JAMs @Wk teachings and core values are the catalyst for this book. This ministry is a tool designed to nourish the souls of existing believers and to win new souls for Christ.

As believers, we are to govern ourselves according to Hebrews 10:25, "not forsaking the assembling of ourselves together, as is the manner of some, but exhorting one another, and so much the more as you see the day approaching." In other words, we are to attend church regularly. There is a God-inspired message, an opportunity to fellowship with like-minded believers and the chance to demonstrate a commitment to doing what God has requested. God makes it easy for us to do because these days, there are many churches with various denominational practices.

There is an urgency for us to attend church because when we do not, it makes satan happy and ecstatic because we are not doing the will of God. You don't have as much time as you think to find a place to worship and develop a close relationship with God. Our time here on earth is like sand through the hourglass, fleeing fast. Procrastination is the biggest enemy we have and has been the result of many unrealized dreams.

Likewise, cemeteries are full of unrealized treasure: unwritten books, unfulfilled dreams, unreceived wealth, careers never started and inventions never realized. For this reason, I would like to challenge you to begin doing what is needed to fulfill God's purpose for your life. My belief is there is a winner in you; a song in you; a book in you; even perhaps a movie in you. As a matter of fact, there is a new you in you, just waiting to be birthed. Now, let's look at How To Use This Devotional.

How To Use This Devotional

This devotional is intended to help you develop a deeper connection to and relationship with God. The holidays mentioned within reflect the dates they will fall upon during the year 2017 and forward (see Significant Dates/Definitions section). Guided by the power of the Holy Spirit, the theme for each month is based on one of the Believers 12-Steps. For this reason, each month begins with the letter "S", starting with seeking God in January and ending with surrendering to God in December. Each month is introduced with prayer asking for "Strength for the Journey" followed by a brief statement explaining the particular "S" word and the intended purpose for its use within that month.

A quote is listed under that to inspire your thought process and to prepare you to receive spiritual revelation and insight from God. Lastly, a scripture reference pertaining to the theme will be given for further consideration. Once you turn the page, you will see the daily entries. There are five elements to each entry, including a song title, a scripture, a *Spiritual Vitamin*, a prayer and reading references known as daily bread. Here is the breakdown of how these elements are intended for use:

The song **title** will serve as the theme of the day.

The **scripture** is a daily reference to the Word of God and can also serve as a memory verse. All scripture references will be from the New King James Version, unless otherwise noted.

The *Spiritual Vitamin* is a "life lesson" of sorts, something that I've learned and/or experienced in my personal walk, meant to nourish your soul and to feed your spirit as you walk with God each day. Take one a day or as often as needed. Many, but not all, of the *Spiritual Vitamins* will begin with thought-provoking questions.

The **prayer** is designed to aid you in formulating a daily connection to God.

The **Daily Bread** section contains scripture references from the Old Testament, New Testament, Psalms and/or Proverbs. If followed as written, it will enable you to read through the Bible in one year. Just as your physical body needs to be sustained by physical food, your spirit man or woman needs to be fed by the Word of God. You could approach the reading of the references as your spiritual breakfast, lunch and dinner; starting your day with the Old Testament reading; taking a midday break with the New Testament reading and ending the day with Psalms and/or Proverbs. What good is it to take a daily vitamin and not eat any food? God's Word is the Bread of Life.

I pray that you will enjoy each day's entries and experience a greater level of spiritual growth as a result of the material presented here. It is not intended to be interpreted from the perspective of a theologian, but rather from a more personal perspective as it relates to my experience with God. I invite you to take this journey with me. If you do, I believe God will be pleased by your decision to know more about Him. Are you ready? Let's take a look at my playlist and after you have finished this material, feel free to develop your own.

Significant Dates and Definitions

Dr. Martin Luther King Jr. Day is a federal holiday held on the third Monday of January. The holiday celebrates the life and achievements of Dr. Martin Luther King Jr., an influential American civil rights leader. Dr. King is most well-known for his campaigns to end racial segregation on public transportation and for racial equality in the United States. The King Holiday is a time when the nation pauses to remember Dr. King's life and work, but also to honor his legacy by making the holiday a day of community service, "a day on, not a day off.

Ash Wednesday is the first day of Lent in the Western Christian calendar. It occurs exactly 46 days before Easter (40 fasting days not counting Sundays). It can fall as early as February 4 and as late as March 10.

Women's Month is celebrated on March 1-31. We recognize International Women's Day each year on March 8th. It is a time of general celebrations of respect, appreciation and love towards women for their economic, political and social achievements.

National Sibling Day is observed on April 10. It is a day created to honor your brothers and sisters.

Palm Sunday is the day that Christians celebrate the triumphal entry of Jesus Christ into Jerusalem and occurs the week before his death and resurrection. For many Christian churches, Palm Sunday is often referred to as "Passion Sunday." Palm Sunday marks the beginning of Holy Week which concludes on Easter Sunday.

Maundy Thursday is an alternate name for Holy Thursday, the first of the three days of solemn remembrance of the events leading up to and immediately following the crucifixion of Jesus. The English word "Maundy" comes from the Latin mandatum, which means "commandment." As recorded in John's gospel, on his last night before his betrayal and arrest, Jesus washed the feet of his disciples and then gave them a new commandment to love one another as He had loved them (John 13:34).

Good Friday, also known as "Holy Friday," is the Friday immediately preceding Easter Sunday. It is celebrated traditionally as the day on which Jesus was crucified.

Easter is the most important and oldest festival of the Christian Church. Easter is the celebration of the resurrection of Jesus Christ. Easter falls on the first Sunday following the first full moon after the vernal equinox. If the first full moon occurs on the equinox, Easter is the following Sunday. Thus, Easter can fall anywhere between March 22 and April 25.

National Day of Prayer is an annual day of observance held on the first Thursday of May, designated by the United States Congress, when people are asked "to turn to God in prayer and meditation."

Pentecost Sunday is a commemoration and celebration of the receiving of the Holy Spirit by the early church. Pentecost Sunday depends on the date of Easter. Pentecost always falls 50 days after Easter (counting both Easter and Pentecost), but since the date of Easter changes every year, the date of Pentecost does as well.

Memorial Day is observed on the last Monday of May. It was formerly known as Decoration Day and commemorates all men and women who have died in military service for the United States. Many people visit cemeteries and memorials on Memorial Day and it is traditionally seen as the start of the summer season.

Independence Day, also referred to as the Fourth of July or July Fourth., is a federal holiday commemorating the adoption of the Declaration of Independence on July 4, 1776, by the Continental Congress declaring that the thirteen American colonies regarded themselves as a new nation, the United States of America, and no longer part of Britain.

Global Forgiveness Day is recognized on the 7th of July each year. Forgiveness Day is a day to forgive and be forgiven. Forgiveness Day is a chance to set things right. Put aside old differences, move beyond grievances and hurts and start afresh.

Labor Day, the first Monday in September, is a creation of the labor movement and is dedicated to the social and economic achievements of American workers.

Veterans Day is an official United States holiday, which is observed annually on November 11th. Veterans Day honors military veterans, persons who served in the United States Armed Forces.

Thanksgiving Day is a national holiday. It was originally celebrated as a day of giving thanks for the blessing of the harvest and of the preceding year. Thanksgiving is celebrated on the fourth Thursday of every year.

The Advent season is a season observed in many Christian churches as a time of expectant waiting and preparation for the celebration of the Nativity of Jesus at Christmas. The term is a version of the Latin word meaning "coming. Its length varies from 22 to 28 days, encompassing the next three Sundays, ending on Christmas Day.

Significant Dates Chart

Although this devotional was published in late 2016, the holidays are reflective of their respective dates beginning in 2017. With the chart below, this material will be relevant for years to come. The dates change from year to year. With that in mind, I have highlighted the holiday on the date it fell during the year of publication and provided you with dates for future reference from 2017 to 2028. I encourage you to read the corresponding devotional on the actual date for the current year, which is also highlighted in the Table of Contents. My intent is to have the JAMs@Wk devotional book tailor made for you.

Holidays	Year of 2017	Year of 2018	Year of 2019	Year of 2020
New Year's Day	January 1	January 1	January 1	January 1
Martin Luther King Jr. Day	January 16	January 15	January 21	January 20
Ash Wednesday	March 1	February 14	March 6	February 26
International Women's Day	March 8	March 8	March 8	March 8
National Sibling Day	April 10	April 10	April 10	April 10
Palm Sunday	April 9	March 25	April 14	April 5
Maundy Thursday	April 13	March 29	April 18	April 9
Good Friday	April 14	March 30	April 19	April 10
Resurrection Sunday	April 16	April 1	April 21	April 12
National Day of Prayer	May 4	May 3	May 2	May 7
Mother's Day	May 14	May 13	May 12	May 10
Pentecost Sunday	June 4	May 20	June 9	May 31
Memorial Day	May 29	May 28	May 27	May 25
Father's Day	June 18	June 17	June 16	June 21
Independence Day	July 4	July 4	July 4	July 4
Global Forgiveness Day	July 7	July 7	July 7	July 7
Labor Day	September 4	September 3	September 2	September 7
Thanksgiving Day	November 23	November 22	November 28	November 26
Advent Season	December 3	December 2	December 1	November 29
Christmas (Birth of Jesus)	December 25	December 25	December 25	December 25

Significant Dates Chart

Although this devotional was published in late 2016, the holidays are reflective of their respective dates beginning in 2017. With the chart below, this material will be relevant for years to come. The dates change from year to year. With that in mind, I have highlighted the holiday on the date it fell during the year of publication and provided you with dates for future reference from 2017 to 2028. I encourage you to read the corresponding devotional on the actual date for the current year, which is also highlighted in the Table of Contents. My intent is to have the JAMs@Wk devotional book tailor made for you.

Holidays	Year of 2021	Year of 2022	Year of 2023	Year of 2024
New Year's Day	January 1	January 1	January 1	January 1
Martin Luther King Jr. Day	January 18	January 17	January 16	January 15
Ash Wednesday	February 17	March 2	February 22	February 14
International Women's Day	March 8	March 8	March 8	March 8
National Sibling Day	April 10	April 10	April 10	April 10
Palm Sunday	March 28	April 10	April 2	March 24
Maundy Thursday	April 1	April 14	April 6	March 28
Good Friday	April 2	April 15	April 7	March 29
Resurrection Sunday	April 4	April 17	April 9	March 31
National Day of Prayer	May 6	May 5	May 4	May 2
Mother's Day	May 9	May 8	May 14	May 12
Pentecost Sunday	May 31	May 23	June 5	May 19
Memorial Day	May 31	May 30	May 29	May 27
Father's Day	June 20	June 19	June 18	June 16
Independence Day	July 4	July 4	July 4	July 4
Global Forgiveness Day	July 7	July 7	July 7	July 7
Labor Day	September 6	September 5	September 4	September 2
Thanksgiving Day	November 25	November 24	November 23	November 28
Advent Season	November 28	November 27	December 3	December 1
Christmas (Birth of Jesus)	December 25	December 25	December 25	December 25

Selwyn B. Cox

Significant Dates Chart

Although this devotional was published in late 2016, the holidays are reflective of their respective dates beginning in 2017. With the chart below, this material will be relevant for years to come. The dates change from year to year. With that in mind, I have highlighted the holiday on the date it fell during the year of publication and provided you with dates for future reference from 2017 to 2028. I encourage you to read the corresponding devotional on the actual date for the current year, which is also highlighted in the Table of Contents. My intent is to have the JAMs@Wk devotional book tailor made for you.

Holidays	Year of 2025	Year of 2026	Year of 2027	Year of 2028
New Year's Day	January 1	January 1	January 1	January 1
Martin Luther King Jr. Day	January 20	January 19	January 18	January 17
Ash Wednesday	March 5	February 18	February 10	March 1
International Women's Day	March 8	March 8	March 8	March 8
National Sibling Day	April 10	April 10	April 10	April 10
Palm Sunday	April 13	March 29	March 21	April 9
Maundy Thursday	April 17	April 2	March 25	April 13
Good Friday	April 18	April 3	March 26	April 14
Resurrection Sunday	April 20	April 5	March 28	April 16
National Day of Prayer	May 1	May 7	May 6	May 4
Mother's Day	May 11	May 10	May 9	May 14
Pentecost Sunday	June 8	May 24	May 16	June 4
Memorial Day	May 26	May 25	May 31	May 29
Father's Day	June 15	June 21	June 20	June 18
Forgiveness Day	June 26	June 26	June 26	June 26
Labor Day	September 1	September 7	September 6	September 4
Thanksgiving Day	November 27	November 26	November 25	November 23
Advent Season	November 30	November 29	November 28	December 3
Christmas (Birth of Jesus)	December 25	December 25	December 25	December 25

JAMS @ Work 365 Day Devotional

My Playlist

January ~ Seeking God (Through Communication and Prayer)
1. Hello, It's Me **(New Year's Day)**
2. All the Man I Need
3. Arms Wide Open
4. Can We Talk?
5. Ain't Nobody (Loves Me Better)
6. Can't Take My Eyes Off You
7. Do I Stand a Chance?
8. Don't You Forget About Me
9. Follow Me
10. When (Glory) Comes
11. God Only Knows
12. Good Life
13. Heaven Knows
14. Higher Ground
15. We Shall Overcome **(Martin Luther King Jr's Birthday)**
16. If Only You Knew
17. Love Story
18. I Will Always Love You
19. Love Will Lead You Back
20. You're the First, My Last, My Everything
21. Never Stopped Loving You
22. One Love
23. Remember Me
24. Saving All My Love
25. Sending You Forget Me Nots
26. Stay With Me
27. The Best Is Yet To Come
28. The Closer I Get To You
29. Use Me
30. Walk This Way
31. No Matter How High I Get

February ~ Sin (Conquered By Jesus)
1. With a Little Luck
2. The Big Payback

3. Say My Name
4. Dead and Gone
5. Don't Be Cruel
6. Don't Look Back In Anger
7. Don't You Worry 'Bout a Thing
8. For the Love of Money
9. (How Did You Get Here?) Nobody Supposed To Be Here
10. I Did It My Way
11. I'll Do For You
12. I Have Nothing
13. And I'm Telling You
14. I Want Your Love **(Valentine's Day)**
15. It's My Prerogative
16. Leave Your Lover
17. Never Gonna Get It
18. Once You Get Started
19. Rebellion Lies
20. Same Script, Different Cast
21. Secret Lovers
22. Stop In the Name of Love
23. Backstabbers
24. Fame
25. Through the Fire
26. Two Lovers
27. Upside Down
28. Use Somebody
29. Your Body's Here With Me

<u>March ~ Salvation (Forgiveness and Eternal Life)</u>
1. Ain't No Mountain High Enough **(Highlights Ash Wednesday)**
2. After the Love Has Lost Its Shine
3. Anyone Who Had a Heart
4. Always and Forever
5. Spend My Life With You
6. Angel of Mine
7. Can We Try?
8. Cherish the Love **(Highlights Women's Month)**

9. Don't Cost You Nothin'
10. Don't Stop Believing
11. Do You Know Where You're Going To?
12. The Greatest Love of All
13. How Deep Is Your Love
14. I'm Sorry
15. If I Could Turn Back Time
16. Life Keeps Moving On
17. Loving You (Is Easy Cuz You're Beautiful)
18. My Love Is Your Love
19. Oh Happy Day
20. For the Love of You
21. Power of Love
22. Real Love
23. Send for Me
24. I'll Still Love You More
25. Imagine (The World Will Be As One)
26. Time (Clock of the Heart)
27. Like Paradise
28. We Will, We Will Rock You
29. Who Will Save Your Soul
30. Why Can't We Be Friends?
31. Bridge Over Troubled Water

April ~ Sanctuary (Attendance and Altar Call)
1. A Joy To Have Your Love
2. All of Me
3. Somebody Told Me To Deliver This Message
4. At Midnight (My Love Will Lift You Up)
5. Easy Like Sunday Morning
6. Come and Talk to Me
7. I Believe
8. Endless Love
9. Signed, Sealed, Delivered (**Highlights Palm Sunday**)
10. I Can't Live, If Living Is Without You (**National Siblings Day**)
11. I Just Had To Hear Your Voice
12. If I Didn't Have You

13. I Don't Deserve Your Love **(Highlights Maundy Thursday)**
14. The Adventure **(Highlights Good Friday)**
15. It's My House
16. Rise Up **(Highlights Resurrection Sunday)**
17. Lean On Me
18. Run To You
19. Solid As a Rock
20. Sure Thing
21. That's the Way My Love Is
22. This Will Be
23. Be Intentional
24. Up Where We Belong
25. When I Found You (I Found Love)
26. You Are My Friend
27. You Are On My Mind
28. You Bring Me Joy
29. You Give Good Love
30. Your Love Keeps Lifting Me Higher

<u>May ~ Support (Creating Stable Relationships Among Family & Friends)</u>
1. What About the Children
2. Ain't Nothin' Like the Real Thing
3. As Days Go By
4. Say a Little Prayer **(Highlights National Day of Prayer)**
5. Come Together (Right Now)
6. Ordinary People
7. Everywhere You Look
8. I'll Be There
9. A Family Affair
10. Family Reunion
11. Grandma's Hands
12. Have I Told You Lately That I Love You?
13. I Believe In You and Me
14. I'll Always Love My Mama **(Highlights Mother's Day)**
15. I'll Stand By You
16. I Apologize
17. I Wanna Be Down

18. Let's Stay Together
19. Stand By Me
20. Time After Time
21. Walk With You
22. What Would We Do Without Us?
23. We Are Family
24. Just To Be Close To You
25. Why Do We Hurt Each Other?
26. You and I
27. Just the Two of Us
28. You'll Never Find
29. One Sweet Day **(Highlights Memorial Day)**
30. You Needed Me
31. You Remind Me

<u>June ~ Self Esteem (Learning Self-love, God's Way)</u>
1. Be Yourself
2. I Will Survive
3. Come As You Are
4. Make Me Over Again **(Highlights Pentecost Sunday)**
5. Got 2 Find Love
6. Fix You
7. Be Optimistic
8. I Believe I Can Fly
9. I'm Coming Out
10. I'm Here
11. Invisible (For the Last Time)
12. Looking For Love
13. Love Has Finally Come At Last
14. Man In the Mirror
15. Me Time
16. Hot-n-Cold
17. One In a Million
18. Dance with My Father **(Highlights Father's Day)**
19. One Moment In Time
20. Pocketful of Sunshine
21. Respect
22. Somebody Loves You

23. The Best of Me
24. The Great Pretender
25. To Be Real
26. Let's Talk About Love
27. Where Do Broken Hearts Go?
28. Winner In You
29. You Are So Beautiful
30. You've Got the Love

July ~ Satisfaction (Living within God's Plan for Your Life)
1. All My Life
2. All Right Now
3. At the Cross
4. Beautiful Life **(Independence Day)**
5. Better Life
6. Cloud Nine
7. Do It Till You're Satisfied **(Global Forgiveness Day)**
8. Do You Love What You Feel?
9. Good Times
10. Happy Days
11. I Can't Get No Satisfaction
12. In Your Eyes
13. Is It the Way You Love Me?
14. I Still Haven't Found What I'm Looking For
15. I've Been To Paradise But I've Never Been To Me
16. Take Time Out
17. Let's Chill
18. (God's) Masterpiece
19. Movin' On Up
20. New Attitude
21. Over the Rainbow
22. Practice What You Preach
23. Stir It Up
24. Tell Me Something Good
25. The Boss
26. This Time I'll Be Sweeter
27. Love Changes

28. Walking On Sunshine
29. When You've Been Blessed
30. Never Knew Love Like This Before
31. Nothing Compares To You

August ~ Spirit (God's Holy Spirit Within)
1. Amazing Grace
2. Ascension
3. Black or White
4. Blowin' In the Wind
5. Put Your Body In It
6. Breathe Again
7. Bustin' Loose
8. Circle of One
9. Daydreaming and Thinking of You
10. (Everything I Do) I Do It For You
11. Inseparable
12. Jesus Will
13. Just a Closer Walk With Thee
14. Let's Do It Again
15. Can You Feel It?
16. Perfect Gift
17. Power of Love
18. (I Need A) Refill
19. Seek and Ye Shall Find
20. Sending My Love
21. Shine
22. The Impossible Dream
23. The Spirit Is In It
24. This Too Shall Pass
25. To God Be the Glory
26. Unforgettable
27. War
28. Wind Beneath My Wings
29. Windows of Hope
30. You're All I Need To Get By
31. You Light Up My Life

September ~ Self-Preservation (Learning to Survive Crisis)
1. All Things Are Working For My Good
2. A Long Walk
3. Are You Gonna Go My Way?
4. Brand New Me **(Highlights Labor Day)**
5. Express Yourself
6. Found a Cure
7. Free Your Mind
8. Get Here
9. Gimme a Break
10. Give Me Some Time
11. 911 **(Anniversary of Terrorist Attack)**
12. Have You Ever?
13. I Can See Clearly Now
14. I Don't Love You Anymore
15. Satisfaction Guaranteed
16. I've Got Love On My Mind
17. Keep On Smiling
18. Let the Sun Shine In
19. You're So Vain
20. No More Tears
21. Real Love
22. Starting Over Again
23. Stop for Love
24. Victory Shall Be Mine
25. What's Going On?
26. Worth Fighting For
27. You Can't Always Get What You Want
28. Everything I Need
29. You're Gonna Make It After All
30. Lose My Mind

October ~ Serenity (Having Peace that Passes Understanding)
1. At Your Best (You Are Love)
2. Quiet Storm
3. Harvest for the World
4. Everything Will Be Alright
5. Finally

6. His Eye Is On the Sparrow
7. How Excellent Is Thy Name
8. How Sweet It Is
9. I Can't Stop Loving You
10. I Don't Feel No Ways Tired
11. I Love Your Smile
12. I Need Thee
13. It's Gonna Be Alright
14. It Is Well
15. Jesus Loves Me
16. Keep Smiling
17. Living On a Prayer
18. I Luh God
19. On the Ocean
20. What a Wonderful World
21. On Bended Knee
22. Paradise
23. Peace Be Still
24. Quiet Time
25. Remember the Time
26. Rhythms of Life
27. Sittin' Up In My Room
28. Take Me To the King
29. Walk By Faith
30. Yes We Can
31. When October Goes

November ~ Service (To God and Others)
1. A Different World
2. Close the Door
3. Don't Ask My Neighbor
4. Do You Love Me?
5. Every Praise
6. Got Me Working Day and Night
7. If I Can Help Somebody
8. If I Could
9. If You Asked Me To
10. If You Want Me To Stay

11. I Give Myself Away **(Veteran's Day)**
12. I'm On Your Side
13. In the Upper Room
14. I Pray
15. I See You Brave
16. It Takes Two
17. I Walk the Line
18. Love Is Like That
19. Love Is the Message
20. One-on-One
21. Reach Out and Touch
22. That's What Friends Are For
23. It's A Good Day **(Highlights Thanksgiving Day)**
24. This Little Light of Mine
25. Try a Little Tenderness
26. Wake Up Everybody
27. What a Friend We Have In Jesus
28. What Have You Done For Me Lately?
29. He's All I Need
30. You're Number One In My Book

<u>December ~ Surrender (Letting Go)</u>
1. All At Once **(World Aids Day)**
2. Bittersweet Symphony
3. Brokenhearted (It's Not Over) **Highlights Advent Season**
4. (A Wonderful) Change
5. Come What May
6. We Don't Say Goodbye
7. Don't Take It Personal
8. End of the Road
9. Everything Must Change
10. I Can't Make You Love Me
11. If Loving You Is Wrong
12. I Know I'll Never Love This Way Again
13. I Look To You
14. I Surrender
15. Kiss and Say Goodbye

16. Let It Be
17. (Sometimes You Gotta) Lose To Win
18. My Heart Will Go On
19. Nearer My God To Thee
20. Love Under New Management
21. On My Own
22. Precious Lord
23. Shaky Ground
24. Haven't You Heard?
25. The Only Hope We Have **(Christmas Day)**
26. The Beat Goes On
27. Ain't No Stopping Us Now
28. No More Drama
29. Time To Say Goodbye
30. Try Jesus
31. Let Go & Let God

Selwyn B. Cox

January: Seeking God (Communication Through Prayer)

Strength for the Journey

Heavenly Father,

As I embark on this new year of my life, I enter into it, seeking a deeper relationship with You, through prayer. You have shown me unconditional love but I have not always reciprocated that love to You. I confess and repent of my sins. Please forgive me and help me to begin putting You first --- on this day, continuing throughout this month and for the remainder of the year. I need You to help me obey the words recorded in Matthew 6:33 to, "seek You first, Your kingdom and Your righteousness." I decree and declare that I will not make another New Year's resolution. Instead, I will seek Your face with my whole heart, that You might give me a new **revelation** of Your plans for my life. I pray that You will take Your rightful place on the throne of my life. Your Kingdom come, Your will be done, in the name of Jesus, Amen.

January

Seeking God (Communication Through Prayer)

During the month of January, you will go on a journey, seeking God and communicating with Him through worship and prayer. When you seek something, there is an attempt or desire to obtain or achieve it. *Seeking* is different than just looking; seeking is on a higher level. When you seek something, there is a deeper motivation inside of you to find it and until you do, you will not take no for an answer. When you seek something, you put a great deal of effort into actually finding it. God wants to be pursued and discovered by you. If you haven't yet had a personal encounter with Him, perhaps you haven't sought after Him hard enough. It is my prayer that you will use this month's devotionals to aid you in learning how to communicate with God through prayer, thereby strengthening and deepening your connection to Him.

Quote: "Just because you are already saved and/or have a successful ministry, does not mean you should stop seeking God" --- Selwyn B. Cox

"I love those who love Me, and those who seek Me diligently will find Me."
~ Proverbs 8:17

Hello (It's Me)
January 1

Scripture: "For I know the thoughts that I think toward you", says the Lord, "thoughts of peace and not of evil, to give you a future and a hope."
~ Jeremiah 29:11

Spiritual Vitamin

Hello and Happy New Year! Today marks the beginning of a new chapter in your life. The old has gone, the new has come. This is a perfect time to say hello to God and to begin communicating with Him; seeking Him through meditation, study and prayer. The practice of prayer is a good habit to form on the first day of the year. *Before you decide to make plans for yourself, why not have a consultation with God to discuss His plans for you?* Jeremiah clearly states that God has a plan for you. *Do you want to know what His plans are?* Finding out what God wants you to do before going off on your own will save you a lot of time and trouble. Don't waste years of your life, fighting against the plan of God because in the end, His plan will prevail. You don't want to experience the dreaded feelings produced by wasted time, for the Word of God tells us in Matthew 6:33 to "seek first the kingdom of God and His righteousness, and all these things shall be added to you." Jesus said "..... Behold, I make all things new" (Revelation 21:5) and He's done that yet again. Hello! Happy New Year and happy new you! Take time today to accept God's divine plan for your life and then you can enjoy a bright, blessed and bountiful future!

Affirmation Prayer: Heavenly Father, thank You for a brand new year and another chance to live my life Your way. Thank You for this blessed, new beginning. Teach me how to appreciate Your provision, in the name of Jesus, Amen.

Daily Bread: Genesis 1 - 2; Matthew 1; Psalm 1:1-6

All the Man I Need
January 2

Scripture: "And God is able to make all grace abound toward you, that you, always having all sufficiency in all things, may have an abundance for every good work."
~ 2 Corinthians 9:8

Spiritual Vitamin

Does the title of this song bring anyone in particular to mind? Who and/or what is all you need? Is it your man, your woman, your child, your car or your home? What does this person provide that you feel you cannot live without? Do you feel that same way about God? He fits perfectly into the description of all the man you need. He is responsible for filling you with His precious Holy Spirit and He gives you everything you need to sustain your life. 2 Peter 1:3 says, "As His divine power has given to us all things that pertain to life and godliness, through the knowledge of Him who called us by glory and virtue." When it comes down to it, God is the only person in your life who will transcend time into eternity. The only way you will come to know God as all the man you need is if you take the time to nurture a personal relationship with Him; one in which constant prayer and intimacy exist. Remember, Jesus is amazing and through Him, God promises to "..... supply all your need according to His riches in glory (Philippians 4:19). You will not be able to experience God's power in this way if you have only a surface relationship. Take time today, through prayer, to get to know God in a more personal and intimate way. As Corrie ten Boom said, "you may never know that Jesus is all you need until Jesus is all you have."

Affirmation Prayer: Heavenly Father, I am weak and heavy laden because I have made others more important than You. I surrender all of my relationships to You and declare that You are my everything. Teach me how to recognize You as my source, in the name of Jesus, Amen.

Daily Bread: Genesis 3; Genesis 4:1-15; Matthew 2:1-15; Psalm 2:1-12

Arms Wide Open
January 3

Scripture: "Our Master Jesus has his arms wide open for you."
~ 1 Corinthians 16:23 MSG

Spiritual Vitamin

Do you talk to God on a regular basis? If not, who is the person you talk to the most during your daily routine? Jesus is standing with His arms wide open, waiting to spend some time with you. He wants you to surrender the busyness of your day in order to share some quiet time. It is His desire that you continually seek Him through regular worship and prayer. God has all the answers to all your questions. *Shouldn't you talk to Him the most? Is there someone in whose presence you feel safe, comfortable and welcome?* God wants you to feel this way with Him. He sent Jesus into the world to teach you that you have a loving, caring Father who desires to spend time *and* eternity with you. As a bridegroom waits for his bride, so Jesus waits for you, with "Arms Wide Open". He is your Bridegroom. Don't keep Him waiting at the altar. Surrender your will and run into the arms of the lover of your soul. Then God will welcome you into His family of believers. Take time today to accept the invitation extended by your Heavenly Father. He is waiting, just for you.

Affirmation Prayer: Heavenly Father, today I run into Your open arms and I lay down my life, surrendering all to You, so that You can purify my heart. Teach me how to let You have Your way in my life, in the name of Jesus, Amen.

Daily Bread: Genesis 4:16-26; Genesis 5 – 6; Matthew 2:16-23; Matthew 3; Psalm 3:1-8

Selwyn B. Cox

Can We Talk?
   January 4

Scripture: "Call to Me, and I will answer you, and show you great and mighty things, which you do not know."
~ Jeremiah 33:3

Spiritual Vitamin

Are you pretending to know God? It is not worth it to try and fool man when God knows the whole truth. He has a sincere desire to be in intimate fellowship with you. *When was the last time you called out to God?* Matthew 6:6 says, "But you, when you pray, go into your room, and when you have shut your door, pray to your Father who is in the secret place; and your Father who sees in secret will reward you openly." He is never too busy and will never turn you away. He created you for the purpose of fellowship with Himself and others. God desires to speak to you and to have you take the time to listen. *Do you desire to listen to God?* God is interested in and wants to talk about what's going on in your life. He issues an invitation to have "one-on-one" interaction with you and provides an opportunity for you to get to know Him better. God is nearer to you than you think and He has a question for you. The question, *"can we talk?"* Take time today to answer God's question with a resounding YES. Your yes will open the door to everything your Heavenly Father wants to give you, according to His will for your life.

Affirmation Prayer: Heavenly Father, please help me understand the importance of communicating with You on a daily basis. Teach me how to patiently wait for and listen to Your answers and not just run down my list of wants, in the name of Jesus, Amen.

Daily Bread: Genesis 7 – 8; Genesis 9:1-17; Matthew 4:1-22; Proverbs 1:1-7

Ain't Nobody (Loves Me Better)
January 5

Scripture: "Inasmuch as there is none like you, O Lord (You are great, and your name is great in might)"
~ Jeremiah 10:6

Spiritual Vitamin

Have you done the work that is necessary to put you in a position to be shown the deep things of God? There is so much He wants to share with you. *Do you have His Holy Spirit living on the inside of you?* If you do, then you know the sheer joy of being able to commune with an all-wise and loving God. There "ain't nobody" who can love you better than God. He is your Creator, Sustainer, Helper and Keeper. *Do you know Him this way?* If not, you're missing out on the benefits of your most valuable resource. God is accessible to you anytime of the day or night, is never too busy to hear what you have to say and will never turn you away. As written in 1 Chronicles 17:20, "O Lord, there is none like You, nor is there any God besides You, according to all that we have heard with our ears". There is no one greater than God. No one. Take time today to ponder on the fact that God loves you more than any other human being is capable of loving you and respond accordingly in prayer.

Affirmation Prayer: Heavenly Father, I have searched for love in all the wrong places. Nothing and no one has measured up to Your undying love for me. Please forgive me for even looking elsewhere. You have always been there, I was just too blind to see. I thank You for loving me in spite of myself. Teach me how to recognize your constant Presence, in the name of Jesus, Amen.

Daily Bread: Genesis 9:18-29; Genesis 10; Genesis 11:1-9; Matthew 4:23-25; Matthew 5:1-20; Psalm 4:1-8

Can't Take My Eyes Off You
January 6

Scripture: "I will instruct you and teach you in the way you should go; I will guide you with My eye."
~ Psalm 32:8

Spiritual Vitamin

Has something ever caught your attention and you found it hard to take your eyes off of what you were seeing? When something delights you, it is able to capture and keep your attention. It provides a sense of curiosity and may cause you to stare in wonder and amazement. It may be so captivating that you can't take your eyes off of it. God feels this way about you, to the point that He continually watches you and you are never out of His sight. *Does that resonate within your spirit?* God, the Creator of heaven and earth, the Omnipotent (all powerful), Omnipresent (everywhere at the same time), Omniscient (all knowing) God, loves you so much that He can't take His eyes off of you! Zephaniah 3:17, tells you that "…. He will rejoice over you with singing". God is watching you and He wants to spend some time with you. He wants you to seek Him and to commune with Him in prayer. *Will you step away from the busyness of life to spend some quality time with your heavenly Father?* Take time today to celebrate the fact that God's eyes are forever upon you. If He's watching the sparrow, then surely, He's watching you.

Affirmation Prayer: Heavenly Father, as You watch the birds in the trees and the beasts of the field, I know You never take Your eyes off me. You Lord, have continuously kept me through seen and unseen dangers. You are my joy and peace. I sometimes look to others and take my eyes off You; please forgive me. Teach me to never stop trusting and depending on You, in the name of Jesus, Amen.

Daily Bread: Genesis 11:10-32; Genesis 12 – 13; Matthew 5:21-42; Psalm 5:1-12

Do I Stand a Chance?
January 7

Scripture: "Being confident of this very thing, that He who has begun a good work in you will complete it until the day of Jesus Christ."
~ Philippians 1:6

Spiritual Vitamin

Have you ever done something wrong and needed another chance? It has been said that God is the God of a second chance. Actually, He's the God of unlimited chances. He gives you countless chances to be right and to do right, despite your endless mistakes and sins. The fact is, God still loves you, no matter how much you mess up. *Can you say that about anyone else you know?* It is the miracle of His grace that causes this response. This is less true of humanity. When humans hurt one another, they have a tendency to sever ties and go their separate ways. *Have you thrown someone away because of a mistake they've made in your relationship? Likewise, has someone thrown you way because of a mistake you have made?* You will never be thrown away by God. Because of His great love for you, you stand every chance of being forgiven and restored. This should cause you to gain a greater appreciation for the fact that God is not like man. Take time today to thank God in prayer for all the chances He has/is giving you to make a better choice.

Affirmation Prayer: Heavenly Father, I have made a conscious decision to make You first in my life. I am grateful for what You have done for me. Teach me how to ask for forgiveness and how to know that You have answered my prayer, in the name of Jesus, Amen.

Daily Bread: Genesis 14 – 16; Matthew 5:43-48; Matthew 6:1-24; Psalm 6

Don't You Forget About Me
January 8

Scripture: "Be careful not to forget the Lord, who rescued you from slavery in the land of Egypt."
~ Deuteronomy 6:12 NLT

Spiritual Vitamin

Are you doing what God has asked you to do? One of the ways to honor God is to do what He has commanded. While Jesus walked the earth, He obeyed everything God told him to do. When He was preparing to leave, He asked His disciples to remember Him by doing the things He taught them to do. Now, we are His disciples and it's up to us to carry the torch. In order to be fully rewarded by God, you must be fully obedient. There is no compromise when it comes to being obedient to God. You are either fully obedient or you are disobedient. It is within your control to obey God. He has said that He would give you the power to do all things. Keep your relationship with God vibrant and growing by staying in constant communication and fellowship with Him. This is the only way to fully know His will. Take time today to learn and obey the Word of God. Follow every command that He gives you so that you may experience increase and live the abundant life He promised you.

Affirmation Prayer: Heavenly Father, I am Your creation. I know that You'll never forget about me. I know that even when I fall short of Your glory, You are right there for me. Therefore, this day is the beginning of my rescue from the cares of this world. You have made me a priority. Teach me how to focus on You, the way You focus on me, in the name of Jesus, Amen.

Daily Bread: Genesis 17 – 18; Matthew 6:25-34; Matthew 7:1-20; Proverbs 1:8-19

Follow Me
January 9

Scripture: "Then He said to them, 'Follow Me and I will make you fishers of men.'"
~ Matthew 4:19

Spiritual Vitamin

Are you following Christ? God sent Jesus so that you would have someone to imitate, learn from and follow. Jesus is the door through which you gain access to God. *Have you walked through the door?* In His human experience, He taught you how to live a life that is pleasing to your Heavenly Father. He taught you how to communicate with God. You don't have to reinvent the wheel; all you have to do is follow the ways of Jesus. Sadly, this is not something many readily choose to do. Humanity would rather go its own way and only return when too many mistakes have been made. *Why go down this road?* If it is your desire to arrive at a certain destination to which you've never been, it is wise to ask for and follow directions. *Why not do the same concerning your life? Similarly why ask for directions that you have no intention on following?* Take time today to read God's Word, which is His instruction manual, and then follow what it says.

Affirmation Prayer: Heavenly Father, Your Word tells me that You will lead me in the paths of righteousness for Your name's sake. You have ordered my steps but oftentimes I have rebelled and gone the wrong way. Teach me how to firmly decide to follow You – without turning or looking back, in the name of Jesus, Amen.

Daily Bread: Genesis 19 - 20:; Matthew 7:21-29; Matthew 8:1-22; Psalm 7:1-8

When (Glory) Comes
January 10

Scripture: "And you said, 'Surely the Lord our God has shown us His glory and His greatness, and we have heard His voice from the midst of the fire. We have seen this day that God speaks with man; yet he still lives."
~ Deuteronomy 5:24

Spiritual Vitamin

Have you ever wondered what God wants with sinful man? God is Holy. God wants you because you are His creation and what He made is perfect. When sin entered the picture, man became vain and he developed a spirit of pride. This pride led him to desire to receive credit that does not belong to him. *Why does man want to take credit for what only God can do?* Only He is worthy of glory and honor. God deserves your reverence, your worship and your praise. As you get closer to God, you will understand that He alone deserves glory, not man. There is nothing you can do that is greater than what God can do. God has never failed, at anything. There is nothing He desired to accomplish that has not been done. Now, all we have to do is thank Him. Psalm 86:12 says "I will praise You, O Lord my God, with all my heart, And I will glorify Your name forevermore." Giving God glory is a privilege. It should not be viewed as an obligation but rather should be viewed by mankind as a pleasure. Take time today to give God glory for the great things He has done and is doing in your life.

Affirmation Prayer: Heavenly Father, I give You glory! All of my needs are continually met. I do not want for any good thing and I am not ashamed to bow down before You and worship You in spirit and in truth. I am not worthy of Your greatness. Teach me to be grateful for all you are doing for me, in the name of Jesus, Amen.

Daily Bread: Genesis 21 - 23; Matthew 8:23-34; Matthew 9:1-13; Psalm 7:9-17

God Only Knows
January 11

Scripture: "So God, who knows the heart, acknowledged them by giving them the Holy Spirit, just as He did to us."
~ Acts 15:8

Spiritual Vitamin

Do you believe that God knows everything? He gave His only Son, Jesus Christ, to provide a way for you to be in right relationship with Him. Once Jesus was taken up into Heaven, God knew you would be in need of comfort. In order to meet this need of yours, He provided His Holy Spirit to live inside of you, to give you that comfort, in a way that only He can provide. You have a caring and loving Father who has made it His business to take care of everything concerning your life and existence. Knowing this should bring you a sense of peace and comfort. There are certain aspects of your life that you will know how to handle and there are certain other aspects about which you will have no clue. Even when you know what to do, it is best to place your plans in the hands of God. When things don't work out as you planned, you must use your faith to navigate your way to a place of peace. In the end, everything will work out as God desires. Take time today, through prayer, to place your full confidence and trust in God's plan for your life. He alone knows what is best for you.

Affirmation Prayer: Heavenly Father, my heart and my hands are open to You. Show me Your ways, in the name of Jesus, Amen.

Daily Bread: Genesis 24; Matthew 9:14-38; Psalm 8:1-9

Good Life
January 12

Scripture: "When times are good, be happy; but when times are bad consider this: God has made the one as well as the other. Therefore no one can discover anything about their future."
~ Ecclesiastes 7:14 NIV

Spiritual Vitamin

Are you living the "Good Life?" As you very well know, everything that happens in life is not good. It has been said that even though everything is not good, everything works out for good in the end. In order for this to be true, you must be in right relationship with God. Then, you can be confident about what is happening to you. No matter what goes on in your life, in the end you will be alright. God is going to make sure of that. If you are walking within the will of God and have made Jesus the Lord of your life, then you realize that you don't have to be in control. You can rest upon the promises of God and wait for His instructions on what to do and how to do it. If you follow God's instructions, you can live the "Good Life" He created you to have. Under the influence of God's Holy Spirit, life will never be a guessing game for you. You can experience the abundant life He is waiting to give those who walk in His perfect will. Take time today to appreciate and honor God for the opportunity He has given you to live a good life and let nothing stop you from experiencing God's best for you.

Affirmation Prayer: Heavenly Father, in the midst of my good, bad and ugly moments, You never condemn me for my ways. Thank You for Your forgiveness. Help me to want to do Your will and teach me to do only what is pleasing in Your sight, in the name of Jesus, Amen.

Daily Bread: Genesis 25 - 26; Matthew 10:1-31; Proverbs 1:20-33

Heaven Knows
January 13

Scripture: "He has not dealt with us according to our sins, nor punished us according to our iniquities."
~ Psalm 103:10

Spiritual Vitamin

Have you ever tried to hide something from God? God has seen every day of your life. He knows about every mistake you will ever make and has decided to love you anyway. Despite all the wrong you have already done and will do, God has already made a way of escape for you. Why has God given this type of forgiveness --- "Heaven Knows" no one deserves it! God didn't base His love for you on how much you would love Him. He already knew how hard it would be for you to step down off of the throne of your life and let Him take first place. Perhaps you are still struggling with that decision. If so, spend some time in prayer, telling God how you honestly feel and what your fears are concerning the surrender of power and control. God rewards honesty and He will speak to your heart and calm your fears. God doesn't want the process to be needlessly painful for you. He wants you to rest on His promises. Take time today to have an honest conversation with God about what's in your heart. He understands you better than you think!

Affirmation Prayer: Heavenly Father, You bring me comfort. You are compassionate and caring. I have thought some things, said some things and done some things that are not in line with Your plan for my life. But because of Your grace, I have a new attitude. Teach me how to bless Your name at all times, in the name of Jesus, Amen.

Daily Bread: Genesis 27 - 28; Matthew 10:32-42; Matthew 11:1-19; Psalm 9:1-5

Higher Ground
January 14

Scripture: "If then you were raised with Christ, seek those things which are above, where Christ is, sitting at the right hand of God. Set your mind on things above, not on things on the earth."
~ Colossians 3:1-2

Spiritual Vitamin

Do you know that God is calling you to Higher Ground? The Bible repeatedly challenges you and calls you upward to a higher place, asking you to turn your back on the petty, trivial, superficial and unworthy things that so often command your attention. You are called to take the high road of uncompromising integrity and to stand on higher ground with the One who Himself is high and lifted up. There are unfortunate circumstances in every person's life but in each situation, you can choose to be the bigger person and allow God's plan to prevail. You never have to settle the score. God has promised to do that for you. His Word says that vengeance belongs to Him. You don't have to stoop to the enemy's level. All you have to do is give the offense to God, pray for and release the offender and keep moving forward. As you obey God's Word, He elevates you to "Higher Ground". Take time today to praise God for being willing to handle the adverse situations and circumstances in your life. That will free you up to press toward the goal for the prize of the upward call of God in Christ Jesus.

Affirmation Prayer: Heavenly Father, You know my intents and the thoughts I think in my mind. What a relief to be able to share everything with You. In spite of knowing my thoughts, You have set me free to press toward Your goal. Teach me how to go higher in You, in the name of Jesus, Amen.

Daily Bread: Genesis 29 – 30; Matthew 11:20-30; Psalm 9:6-12

We Shall Overcome
January 15

Scripture: *"These things I have spoken to you, that in Me you may have peace. In the world you will have tribulation; but be of good cheer, I have overcome the world."*
~ John 16:33

Spiritual Vitamin

God is the Father of every living being. All races, creeds and colors have the privilege of choosing Kingdom citizenship. We are one nation under God. There are those who would rather continue living under the spirits of bondage, oppression and racial division. But with the help of our living, loving God, "We Shall Overcome". When faced with issues of racial injustice and division, simply pray to your Savior, Jesus Christ. In John 16:33, Jesus plainly states that He "... has overcome the world". Jesus knows how you feel because He Himself was tempted in every way you are now, yet He never gave up or gave in. He continued pressing forward until He won! He never surrendered to the pressure of hatred in any form. It is God's desire that no matter what color we are or what racial background we come from, that we become united in Christ and seek Him for peace and racial unity. Make this, Martin Luther King Jr.'s birthday, a day of service: "a day on, not a day off!" In the words of Dr. King, "Everbody can be great ... because anybody can serve. You don't have to have a college degree to serve. You don't have to make your subject and verb agree to serve. You only need a heart full of grace. A soul generated by love." Take time today to pray that God would remove any form of racial injustice/prejudice within you and replace it with a love for all mankind.

Affirmation Prayer: Heavenly Father, thank You for the power You have given me to overcome the world. I cherish it and bless You for it. Teach me how to use it properly, in a way that will bring glory to You, in the name of Jesus, Amen.

Daily Bread: Genesis 31:1-55; Matthew 12:1-21; Psalm 9:13-20

If Only You Knew
January 16

Scripture: "For God so loved the world that He gave His only begotten Son, that whoever believes in Him should not perish but have everlasting life."
~ John 3:16

Spiritual Vitamin

Do you know how much God loves you? If you really knew the depth of God's love, it would change your life. You would not be the same person you are at this present moment. You would not behave as you now behave. You would treat others with more love and kindness than you did in the past. You would forgive everyone you were ever angry with and seek to restore a sense of peace and harmony with your fellow man. You would more readily walk within God's will for your life. His will for you would become your priority and you would seek to do what pleases Him. Everything you say and do would reflect this knowledge. You would stop struggling with every decision and rest on the promises found in God's Word. Your life would become one of peace, favor and grace. Everyone around you would benefit from your newfound perspective. *So, are you willing to take the necessary steps to walk in this type of newfound freedom?* Take time today to ponder on these things and allow God to change your heart and mind so that you can live life more abundantly.

Affirmation Prayer: Heavenly Father, I will focus on the promises that You have given me and I will enjoy the benefits of your blessings. Please change my heart and mind, so that I may experience the best life possible, in the name of Jesus, Amen.

Daily Bread: Genesis 32 – 33; Matthew 12:22-45; Proverbs 2:1-11

Love Story
January 17

Scripture: "He who does not love does not know God, for God is love."
~ 1 John 4:8

Spiritual Vitamin

Have you been changed as a result of God's love for you? The Bible tells you all about this great love. *Have you read it?* It is the greatest love story there is. It shares details of how our Creator and Father made us and the world in which we live. It gives details of the things God had to do in order to prepare the world for the arrival of mankind. It also discusses the fact that God's greatest creation, at some point in time, decided to rebel against Him, rejecting the love and provision that He so graciously provided. After man's rebellion, God did not give up on him. God's love runs deep and the love He has for man is beyond a human level of understanding. Once you experience it in a meaningful and authentic way, you will never be the same. There are billions of people in the world, yet God is able to love and care for you as if you were the only one. That is an amazing fact. Take time today to seek God's face and experience His love for yourself. It will change your life.

Affirmation Prayer: Heavenly Father, I have come to understand that You want all or nothing. Giving You a piece of myself is just not enough. I have decided to surrender and to believe all of Your Word. Teach me how to love You, in the name of Jesus, Amen.

Daily Bread: Genesis 34 – 35; Matthew 12:46-50; Matthew 13:1-17; Psalm 10:1-9

I Will Always Love You
January 18

Scripture: "And the Lord, He is the One who goes before you. He will be with you, He will not leave you nor forsake you; do not fear nor be dismayed."
~ Deuteronomy 31:8

Spiritual Vitamin

What criteria do you use when deciding to love someone? In human relationships, love must be earned. We don't just give love in an unconditional fashion, on equal levels to everyone around us. We have our favorites; there are those we like and those we don't. But God is not like man. As you study the scriptures and develop a more meaningful relationship with Jesus Christ, you learn that God's love toward you is everlasting, unending and eternal. You did nothing to earn or deserve it; He gave it to you as a result of His own decision to do so. This should cause a stirring in your spirit. At one time or another, you have felt unloved and have behaved in an unlovely manner. But God's love has rescued you and fulfilled the very longing of your soul. Remember, you are one of Jesus' amazing miracles and His love for you validates that fact. Take time today to share this knowledge with someone else, in an effort to allow it to change their life in the same way that it has changed yours.

Affirmation Prayer: Heavenly Father, thank You for Your undying love for me. I realize that it is the most priceless treasure I own. Help me to freely accept it and act accordingly, in the name of Jesus, Amen.

Daily Bread: Genesis 36 – 37; Matthew 13:18-35; Psalm 10:10-18

Love Will Lead You Back
January 19

Scripture: "Or do you despise the riches of His goodness, forbearance, and longsuffering, not knowing that the goodness of God leads you to repentance?"
~ Romans 2:4

Spiritual Vitamin

What will it take to lead you back to God? God created a perfect man and enjoyed a perfect relationship with the man He created. Then sin entered the picture and through acts of disobedience, man strayed away from God. When that happened, God designed another way to recapture the love and devotion of His creation. What God did was nothing short of a miracle. He gave a ransom for your sin so that you would never have to pay. Although you were guilty, you would never bear the punishment for your wrongdoing. Jesus was given as a ransom for your sin. Now all you have to do is accept what the ransom provided and you can go free. Now that is love and that kind of "love will lead you back" into a right relationship with God. There was never a question about whether you would stray away from God. Knowing that you would, He provided Jesus, so that you could be vindicated and accepted upon your return. Take time today to allow the love of God to lead you back to Him.

Affirmation Prayer: Heavenly Father, You thought enough of me to send Jesus to die for me. He paid the ultimate price; all of it, so that I could be free. Thank You for loving me unconditionally. Teach me to accept and appreciate the sacrifices You've made on my behalf, in the name of Jesus, Amen.

Daily Bread: Genesis 38 – 39; Matthew 13:36-58; Psalm 11

You're The First, My Last, My Everything
January 20

Scripture: "And when I saw Him, I fell at His feet as dead. But He laid His right hand on me, saying to me 'Do not be afraid; I am the First and the Last'"
~ Revelation 1:17

Spiritual Vitamin

Where is your treasure? Rarely can you find something that can qualify as the first, the last and everything, all rolled up into one. God meets this qualification. Before time, He was. In time, He is. After time and into eternity, He will be. God has no beginning and He has no end. He just is! What an amazing piece of knowledge. The human mind cannot comprehend this, yet it doesn't cease to be true. God has proven Himself worthy to be your first, your last and your everything. *Will you give Him that honor?* Before time began, God had you in mind. Before you were born, He made provisions for every day of your life and for that, deserves your love, loyalty and devotion. *Is there something else in your life holding the spot that God desires to occupy?* God is solely responsible for your existence and deserves first place. *How many layers does God have to sift through to get to your heart?* Don't put God on the back burner. He has earned the right to be first. Take time today to make Him first and let go of anything that gets in the way of that.

Affirmation Prayer: Heavenly Father, I acknowledge You as El Shaddai, the God who is more than enough. You are my all and all. Your love engulfs me and I surrender myself to You. Teach me how to let go of anything that attempts to come between us, in the name of Jesus, Amen.

Daily Bread: Genesis 40; Genesis 41:1-36; Matthew 14:1-21; Proverbs 2:12-22

Never Stopped Loving You
January 21

Scripture: "For I am persuaded that neither death nor life, nor angels nor principalities nor powers, nor things present nor things to come, nor height nor depth, nor any other created thing, shall be able to separate us from the love of God which is in Christ Jesus our Lord."
~ Romans 8:38-39

Spiritual Vitamin

Has someone you wanted in your life forever stopped loving you? Has that individual exited your life by choice or by death? In either case, you may be left with questions and broken pieces. This may be something you never saw coming and you feel like you have nothing left, but there is hope. You have a God who will never stop loving you. Although you were once apart from God, He never stopped loving you. No matter what you're going through, what troubling circumstances you're in or what your condition may be, nothing can separate you from the love of God in Christ Jesus. *Does that mean anything to you?* God never intended for you to love anything more than you love Him. It is never too late to begin that process. His love is a guarantee and the privilege will never be revoked. Take time today to accept the provision extended to you and enjoy the benefits for a lifetime and beyond.

Affirmation Prayer: Heavenly Father, the keys to eternal life are loving You, accepting Jesus as Lord and Savior, loving my neighbors and obeying Your Word. Thank You that You will never stop loving me. Teach me how to accept what You've done for me, in the name of Jesus, Amen.

Daily Bread: Genesis 41:37-57; Genesis 42; Matthew 14:22-36; Matthew 15:1-9; Psalm 12:1-8

One Love
January 22

Scripture: "one Lord, one faith, one baptism."
~ Ephesians 4:5

Spiritual Vitamin

Did you know there are different kinds of love? There is Eros, which is romantic love; there is Phileo, which is friendship and fondness; Storge, which is family loyalty and Agape, which is unconditional love and is the kind of love that God has for His creation. While there are many different kinds of love, they all originate from one God. Human love cannot and does not understand God's kind of love. Your finite mind will never understand the depth of the kind of love that God has for you. The good news is there is no requirement for you to understand God's love in order to accept and receive it. Just open your heart and embrace the love of your Heavenly Father. It is a free gift that you never have to work for to earn or maintain. As a matter of fact, there is nothing you can do to earn God's love. He has simply decided to give it to you. His decision holds true when you behave and even when you do not. This is when grace is also needed. Take time today to share God's love --- one world, one God and one people.

Affirmation Prayer: Heavenly Father, I often ask myself the question "what's love got to do with it?" I have concluded in my heart that love has everything to do with it, because YOU are love. Thank You for being my lover, my Father, my Savior and my friend. Teach me how to love others the way You love me, in the name of Jesus, Amen.

Daily Bread: Genesis 43 – 44; Matthew 15:10-39; Psalm 13:1-6

Remember Me
January 23

Scripture: "And when He had given thanks, He broke it and said, 'take eat this is my body which is broken for you. Do this in remembrance of Me'".
~ 1 Corinthians 11:24

Spiritual Vitamin

Do your actions and behaviors show evidence that you remember the Lord? When speaking to His disciples during the Last Supper, Jesus asked them to continue the tradition and each time they did, to do it in remembrance of Him. He's asking us to do the same. If you value what Jesus did for you on the cross, there will be some evidence of that in the way you live your life. Your actions will contain proof that you are living a life that is controlled by the power of God's Holy Spirit. Love will rule your every thought and cause you to behave in a loving manner towards those you serve. Once you have had an intimate experience with God, you will never forget it. You will do whatever is necessary to have this type of encounter every day of your life. Things that hold special significance stay in your heart and mind. *What are you doing in remembrance of Christ?* Allow your light to shine, that it may draw those who are currently living in darkness. Take time today to become a consistent witness for Christ and demonstrate that you remember what He's done for you through what you do for others.

Affirmation Prayer: Heavenly Father, at times, my mind gets overloaded with the cares of the world. I sometimes live as though I have forgotten Your mandate for me. My life should point people to the cross. You died for me and I desire to live for you. Teach me to never forget my responsibility as a witness for You, in the name of Jesus, Amen.

Daily Bread: Genesis 45 – 46; Genesis 47:1-12; Matthew 16:1-20; Psalm 14

Saving All My Love
January 24

Scripture: "with all lowliness and gentleness, with longsuffering, bearing with one another in love, endeavoring to keep the unity of the Spirit in the bond of peace."
~ Ephesians 4:2-3

Spiritual Vitamin

Are you saving your love for a particular group of people? Love is meant to be shared. It's meant to be given away, freely and generously; like a gift. God commands it in His Word. *Are you withholding love from someone? Is it because you feel they don't deserve your love? If that is the case, I have a question for you. Do you deserve God's love?* God is love. His very nature and essence is love. Romans 5:8 says "But God demonstrates His own love toward us, in that while we were still sinners, Christ died for us." There is enough love for everyone and you don't have to withhold love from some in order to have enough for others. God loves everyone; those who accept Him and those who do not. There is no qualifier. Our inability to love as commanded cannot interfere with God's decision to love us. God loves man because He has decided to do so, point blank, period. *Can you accept and appreciate that and allow it to change the way you love those in your life?* Forgive any offenses that have occurred in your life and decide to freely share love with everyone whom you encounter. That's the only way to have a life of peace. Take time today to unlock the place you've been storing your love. God wants you to give it all away and in the measure you give, that is the measure in which you will receive.

Affirmation Prayer: Heavenly Father, thank You for Your limitless love for me. Teach me how to freely receive it from You so that I can pour it out onto others, in the name of Jesus, Amen.

Daily Bread: Genesis 47:13-31; Genesis 48; Matthew 16:21-28; Matthew 17:1-13; Proverbs 3:1-12

Sending You Forget Me Nots
January 25

Scripture: "Beware that you do not forget the Lord your God by not keeping His commandments, His judgments, and His statutes, which I command you today."
~ Deuteronomy 8:11

Spiritual Vitamin

God uses nature to display His power to mankind. A beautiful morning sunrise, a colorful evening sunset, the waves of the ocean, snow-capped mountains and rainbows are all ways in which we get a glimpse of the handiwork of God. God is a master artist but you must be attuned with nature to really appreciate its beauty. We are taught that God is the most powerful Being known to mankind but it seems that sometimes we forget. It is in those moments when God will send a reminder, in a way that He knows will capture your attention. When He does this, He is "sending you forget me nots", so that you will remember His great love for you. God should not need to use outward signs to prompt you to remember Him, but He knows the fickle nature of man. Your deep connection and personal relationship with Him should prompt you to do that. Take time today to allow God to show you how to stay connected to Him and then follow His lead --- pray to Him without ceasing!

Affirmation Prayer: Heavenly Father, day by day, I behold the beauty of Your glory. Thank You for the things so important to me like life, health and strength that only You can provide. Thank You for all the ways in which You remind me of Your love. Teach me to never take these things for granted, in the name of Jesus, Amen.

Daily Bread: Genesis 49 – 50; Matthew 17:14-27; Matthew 18:1-9; Psalm 15:1-5

Stay With Me
January 26

Scripture: "Stay with me, and I am in you. Just as the branch cannot yield fruit by itself unless it remains on the vine, so neither do you unless you stay with me."
~ John 15:4 (Aramaic version)

Spiritual Vitamin

It is the enemy's desire to pull you away from God. It is God's desire for you to stay with Him. God is all you need for a blessed and fulfilled life. The enemy knows how fulfilling life with God can really be. After all, he was once living with God, until he allowed pride to overrule his senses. Now, because he has been evicted from the very Presence of God, he will use the thing that trapped him in an effort to try and trap you. The world will appeal to your senses in an effort to draw your attention to your carnal side and away from your spiritual nature. *When this happens, will you be able to remain focused on the things of God?* Prayerfully, your connection with God is deep enough to withstand this level of pressure. *What do you value the most? Is it something connected to the natural you or the spiritual you?* God is a Spirit and He must be worshiped in spirit and in truth. Take time today to determine ways to defeat the spirit of carnality and to grow in your faith and belief in the power of God.

Affirmation Prayer: Heavenly Father, help me to be grounded and rooted in Your Word. Give me the desire to stay with You. No matter what temptations may come my way, teach me to remain focused on and connected to You, in the name of Jesus, Amen.

Daily Bread: Job 1 – 3; Matthew 18:10-35; Psalm 16:1-11

The Best Is Yet To Come
January 27

Scripture: "But as it is written: eye has not seen, nor ear heard, nor have entered into the heart of man, the things which God has prepared for those who love Him."
~ 1 Corinthians 2:9

Spiritual Vitamin

As it pertains to your life, do you believe that the best is yet to come? Giving your life to Christ will create something wonderful to look forward to; eternity in heaven with God! Once your earthly experience has come to an end, your spirit will cross into eternity with your heavenly Father. *Isn't that good news?* You are not on earth to remain forever. You are destined for a greater home. Acceptance of Jesus Christ as your Savior and Lord will secure your future. If you think your life on earth is delightful, just wait until you get to heaven because the best is yet to come. If you think you're having an awesome time now, just wait until you get into the Presence of God. You will be free of worry, concern and care. Your only responsibility will be to give thanks and praise to God. No more hustle and bustle or hurry up and wait. You will be free to take it all in; the beauty and essence of God Himself. Take time today to prepare yourself to spend eternity with God. It's the best decision you will ever make.

Affirmation Prayer: Heavenly Father, thank You for something glorious to look forward to — heaven. You are preparing my entrance into heaven through the sanctification process. By it, I look more and more like You. Because You've prepared this special place, the best truly is yet to come. Teach me how to prepare to spend eternity with You, in the name of Jesus, Amen.

Daily Bread: Job 4 — 7; Matthew 19:1-15; Psalm 17:1-5

The Closer I Get To You
January 28

Scripture: "Draw near to God and He will draw near to you."
~ James 4:8a

Spiritual Vitamin

As the end of the month draws near, I want to encourage you to continue seeking God through communication and prayer. Ask Him for the desire to remain close to Him. When you want to be close to someone, you make an effort to communicate with that person. You become intentional about your desire to spend time with them. You let them know of your desire and take the necessary steps to make it happen. The same is true with God. The closer you get to God, the closer He gets to you. As you develop a hunger and thirst for His Word, your life will transform and it will become evident that you are connected to Him. Your habits will change and those close to you will begin to see a difference in how you operate. There will be evidence that you are actively seeking Him and that He is guiding you. You will increase in your knowledge of Him and happily conform to His will for your life. Those close to you may even inquire as to what's going on. Feel free to share your newfound faith. Testify and tell them about the goodness of the Lord. Take time today to call out to God for a closer walk with Him. When He grants your request, tell somebody.

Affirmation Prayer: Heavenly Father, the closer I get to You, the more I am able to see Your provision for me. Teach me how to live in a continual state of worship and praise, in the name of Jesus, Amen.

Daily Bread: Job 8 – 10; Matthew 19:16:30; Proverbs 3:13-20

Use Me
January 29

Scripture: "Also I heard the voice of the Lord, saying: 'Whom shall I send, And who will go for Us?' Then I said, "Here am I! Send me.'"
~ Isaiah 6:8

Spiritual Vitamin

Do you have a desire to be used by God? Will you allow Him to make an example of you for His glory? Can He use you in His service? In the human sense, being used can have a negative connotation. But when it comes to the things of God, the thought of being used becomes an honor and a privilege. Ephesians 2:10 says "For we are His workmanship, created in Christ Jesus for good works, which God prepared beforehand that we should walk in them." What God has placed within you is needed for the resolution of certain situations and circumstances in the earthly realm. The spiritual gifts you have been given were placed in you so that you can use them to light the way for someone who may still be in darkness. *Will you allow your light to shine?* When you are used by man, it can make you feel hurt and betrayed. But when you are used by God, you feel grateful, privileged and rewarded. You know that it is nothing but the grace of God that would allow Him to want to use someone who knows he/she is not even worthy of His grace. Take time today to thank God for deciding to use you before you were even born into this world. Let Him shine His light and love through you.

Affirmation Prayer: Heavenly Father, I surrender myself to You. My desire is to be used by You. Use me in any way that glorifies You, in the name of Jesus, Amen.

Daily Bread: Job 11 – 14; Matthew 20:1-19; Psalm 17:6-12

Walk This Way
January 30

Scripture: "And your ears shall hear a word behind you saying, 'This is the way, walk in it', when you turn to the right or when you turn to the left."
~ Isaiah 30:21 (ESV)

Spiritual Vitamin

Are you willing to walk in the ways of God? God has a plan for your life. I'm sure you have one too. *The question is whose plan will you follow, yours or His?* In order to achieve God's desired results, you must follow His plan. Sometimes, life can cause you to feel like you are all alone. When Jesus is Lord of your life, this is never the case. You will never be left to figure things out on your own. With Jesus as your guide, you cannot lose. God is always listening to hear your voice cry out to Him. Whether in praise or in need, His ear is attuned to your cry. He stands ready to lead you, whenever you are having trouble figuring out which way you should turn. His greatest desire is for you to come to Him. God's Word lights the way; it is a lamp for your feet and a light for your path. Take time today to listen to the words of God and the wisdom He shares therein. Then, decide for yourself that the best thing you can do is walk on the path God has established for you; the only one that leads to victory.

Affirmation Prayer: Heavenly Father, as I sit in my tent door, my prayer closet or my room, I clearly hear Your instructions concerning the path for my life. Teach me how to "walk Your way" and to obey the things You've said, in the name of Jesus, Amen.

Daily Bread: Job 15 – 18; Matthew 20:20-34; Psalm 17:13-15

No Matter How High I Get
January 31

Scripture: "For I say, through the grace given to me, to everyone who is among you, not to think of himself more highly than he ought to think, but to think soberly, as God has dealt to each one a measure of faith."
~ Romans 12:3

Spiritual Vitamin

Are you humble? It is God who gives you the power to get wealth and all promotion comes from Him. Often times, after something is attained, we allow the enemy to cause us to think that we've achieved the prize according to our own merits and intellect. This is never the case. You can't do anything without God. You must guard yourself against the spirit of pride. Pride is what caused Lucifer to be expelled from the Presence of God. He wants nothing more than for this same thing to happen to you. Don't let it happen. Stay in close communication with God and He will keep you humble. Don't allow the temptation to toot your own horn to cause you to become self-absorbed. Don't get caught up in status and titles. No matter how high you get, you will still have to look up to God. Ultimately, the best title you can ever obtain is "child of God." Riches and wealth cannot buy you a place in the Kingdom of God. Don't let the things of the world interfere with your devotion and commitment to God. Take time today to humble yourself, pray and seek a closer walk with Him. Nothing else will do!

Affirmation Prayer: Heavenly Father, because of You, I have accomplished many things. The world's way is to become arrogant and to take credit for what You alone have done. Please keep me humble under your Mighty hand. Remind me that no matter how high I get, there is still a need to look to You, in the name of Jesus, Amen.

Daily Bread: Job 19 – 21; Matthew 21:1-17; Psalm 18:1-6

MONTHLY REFLECTIONS

February: Sin (Conquered By Jesus)

Strength for the Journey

Heavenly Father,

You and You alone know my sins, past and present --- those that I have openly committed and those that I have committed in secret. You even know the sins I will commit in the future. Father, please have mercy on me. I cannot hide or cover up my sin because Psalm 139 lets me know that You have "searched me" and You know my ways. Please help me to put on the whole armor of God so that I can be "dressed to kill" when that mean old devil comes to me with his tricks and deception. Because of the death of Jesus Christ, sin has been conquered. Create in me a clean heart and continuously renew a right spirit within me. I pray that You will cover my sins with the blood of Jesus and wash me clean. Hear my cry of repentance, in the name of Jesus, Amen.

February

Sin (Conquered By Jesus)

During the month of February, you will go on a journey, learning about sin, its consequences and the deadly effects it will have on your life. Sin is defined as an immoral act considered to be a transgression against divine law. Sin did not have power over Jesus the way it has over humanity. Jesus was in every way tempted as every other human being, yet He never bowed to the controlling forces of sin; instead Jesus conquered sin. He showed us that it is possible to overcome and defeat sin by living a life that is totally submitted to God. When confronted by the enemy, Jesus defeated him with the words "It is written" and then quoted the Word of God, thereby causing the enemy to flee. Because of Jesus' victory, you have the right to use the Word of God against the enemy and win. It is my prayer that you will use this month's devotionals to aid you in the process of conquering sin in your own life.

Quote: "While it is not possible to be sinless, it is possible to sin less!" --- Author Unknown

"But if we walk in the light as He is in the light, we have fellowship with one another, and the blood of Jesus Christ His Son cleanses us from all sin. If we say that we have no sin, we deceive ourselves, and the truth is not in us. If we confess our sins, He is faithful and just to forgive us our sins and to cleanse us from all unrighteousness."
~ 1 John 1:7-9

With a Little Luck
February 1

Scripture: "My sheep hear My voice, and I know them, and they follow Me."
~ John 10:27

Spiritual Vitamin

Do you believe in luck? Luck is defined as success or failure apparently brought by chance rather than through one's own actions. Those who believe in God are taught that there are no coincidences; nothing just happens. *Which is true for you? Do you believe that God is in total control of every aspect of your life?* If so, then you know that there is no place for luck. The principle of luck is contrary to the principles of our Lord and He gives power to those who have faith in Him. Today's scripture points out that God's sheep know His voice and that they follow Him. In order to know someone's voice, you would need to have regular conversations with that person. Because God desires to fellowship with you on a regular basis, you have the opportunity to learn His voice. You don't have to live your life by chance or luck. You can allow faith to be the guiding force and the deciding factor. Because of a deeply rooted faith and trust in God, you don't need to rely on luck because you are blessed. Take time today to evaluate your belief system and make the decision to trade in luck for faith.

Affirmation Prayer: Heavenly Father, I ask that You help me to cease from my own labors and instead to have faith in You. Cause me to enter into Your divine plan for my life and not to rely on luck. Empower me to hear Your voice when You speak and to obey, in the name of Jesus, Amen.

Daily Bread: Job 22 – 24; Matthew 21:18-32; Proverbs 3:21-35

The Big Payback
February 2

Scripture: "Beloved, do not avenge yourselves, but rather give place to wrath; for it is written, "Vengeance is Mine, I will repay", says the Lord."
~ Romans 12:19

Spiritual Vitamin

Have you ever felt the need to get back at someone? When humans feel wronged, they also feel the need to get revenge. When you feel cheated or betrayed, the normal, fleshly response is anger and the desire to get even. Once you decide to live for Christ, you will learn that it is not wise to give in to the desires of the flesh. James 4:7 says, "Submit yourself then to God, resist the devil and he will flee." If Jesus is Lord of your life, you don't have to take matters into your own hands. You have a God who will fight for you. He knows how to deal with your enemies. Do what God has commanded you to do; pray for them, release the animosity and learn to forgive. With a great and powerful GOD on your side, you don't have to give into negative emotions because you are the apple of God's eye. He takes great delight in you. Take time today to ask God to strengthen your inner man (woman) so that you will be equipped to handle adversity.

Affirmation Prayer: Heavenly Father, please help me to let go of all bitterness, resentment and vengeance. You are the One who binds up wounds and heals the brokenhearted. Teach me to receive Your anointing that breaks and destroys every yoke and bondage, in the name of Jesus, Amen.

Daily Bread: Job 25 – 29; Matthew 21:33-46; Matthew 22:1-14; Psalm 18:7-15

Say My Name
February 3

Scripture: "Nor is there salvation in any other, for there is no other name under heaven given among men by which we must be saved."
~ Acts 4:12

Spiritual Vitamin

Are you ashamed of God? Today's devotional deals with deception and secrecy. When you have a deep and loving relationship with someone, there is evidence of this in the way you behave. You are not afraid for others to know about your relationship. You willingly and freely speak of the person you are fond of. God wants this type of relationship with you. He wants you to be free to say His name. These characteristics are not in line with a life that is surrendered to God. A God-centered life walks in the light of transparency. There are no secrets; only testimonies and evidence of the power and promises of God. Truth is the order of the day. Your utmost desire is to have clean hands and a pure heart, so that you can be used as an instrument by God. *Are there areas of your life where you're still hiding your Godly connection?* A relationship with God is not something you need to hide. Take time today to honestly evaluate where you are in your walk with Him. Ask God to reveal areas that need improvement and allow Him to do the work that is required in you.

Affirmation Prayer: Heavenly Father, it is by the name of Jesus that I am saved. In His name, I have power. What I bind and loose on earth shall be bound and loosed in heaven. I ask You to help me walk in the light of Your power. I declare here and now that I am not ashamed of the Gospel of Jesus Christ. Teach me to walk uprightly, knowing that I don't have to worry, in the name of Jesus, Amen.

Daily Bread: Job 30 – 32; Matthew 22:15-46; Psalm 18:16-24

Dead and Gone
February 4

Scripture: "Therefore, if anyone is in Christ, he is a new creation; old things have passed away; behold, all things have become new."
~ 2 Corinthians 5:17

Spiritual Vitamin

Is the old sinful nature still vibrant and alive in you? It has been said that death is a part of life. You experience symbolic death when getting baptized, where going down into the water represents dying to sin and being raised out of the water represents new life in Christ. It is designed for conversion to come along with new life, but this process must be intentional. You must have the desire to allow God to change you, removing your old sinful habits and replacing them with new, Godly ones. You must have the desire to "grow up" in the things of God and put away childish things. 1 Corinthians 13:11 says, "When I was a child, I spoke as a child, I understood as a child, I thought as a child; but when I became a man, I put away childish things." *Have you been converted?* If so, then the person you once were is dead and gone. You are living a new life with Jesus Christ at the center. Your hands are clean and your heart is pure. Your ultimate desire is to serve and please Almighty God. Jesus Christ left a legacy for us to follow. *What legacy will you leave and who will remember you after death?* Live your life in such a way that those who know you will have a desire to know the God you serve. Take time today to bury the old you and consider the memories being created by the life you are currently living.

Affirmation Prayer: Heavenly Father, I declare that I am a maker of long lasting memories. I was created to serve You and to worship You in spirit and in truth. You are my shield and buckler (significance is protection). Teach me to model my life so that I will be remembered for loving, trusting, leaning and depending on You, in the name of Jesus, Amen.

Daily Bread: Job 33 – 34; Matthew 23; Psalm 18:25-36

Don't Be Cruel
February 5

Scripture: "Don't be greedy, merciless and cruel as wolves, tearing into the poor and feasting on them, shredding the needy to pieces only to disregard them."
~ Proverbs 30:14 MSG

Spiritual Vitamin

What does it cost to be nice? Some people have not properly processed the stages of pain and disappointment and because there is unforgiveness resting in their hearts, they have become hard-hearted and mean. This is not God's way. A loving God expects His creation to behave in loving ways. As an ambassador of Jesus Christ, you have a responsibility to show compassion, kindness and love to a dying and sin-sick world. It seems that it would be easier and would take less effort to be nice than to be cruel. Being nice yields a harvest of good things in return, while being cruel yields a harvest of unfortunate and hurtful situations and circumstances. The laws of sowing and reaping work; you really do reap what you sow. If you sow seeds of love and kindness, you will reap a harvest of love and kindness in return. Likewise, if you sow seeds of cruelty and discord, you will reap a harvest of cruelty and discord in return. *Which would you prefer?* Take time today to reflect and determine if there is someone you have been cruel to who can use an apology from you.

Affirmation Prayer: Heavenly Father, please allow the blood of Jesus to wash over my mind so that I am nice rather than nasty. Please blot out all thoughts and feelings that would not show kindness. Open doors that need to be opened for proper vision. Please help me with my thoughts and words, in the name of Jesus, Amen.

Daily Bread: Job 35 – 37; Matthew 24:1-31; Proverbs 4:1-9

Don't Look Back in Anger
February 6

Scripture: "Be angry, and do not sin": do not let the sun go down on your wrath."
~ Ephesians 4:26

Spiritual Vitamin

Are you still angry over something that happened a long time ago? To some, it is justifiable to remain angry over things that have happened in their lives. The mistake often made is allowing the anger to lead to other crippling emotions like bitterness and unforgiveness. *When thoughts of some of the things in your past come across your mind, do you find that you're still angry or have you been able to move forward?* It is not wise to hold on to anger because it can lead to health problems and even mental and emotional issues. Jesus has invited you to tell Him your concerns. If you do this, you can look back over your life with gratitude for the things that have occurred whether they were good or bad. You will understand that the good was designed to bless you and the bad was designed to break and rebuild you. It is important to give God praise and thanks for allowing you to overcome that which was designed to destroy you. God has a better plan for you than you have for yourself. *Will you embrace His plan?* Take time today to pray and ask God to enable you to release any negative feelings that would keep you from enjoying the life He designed you to have.

Affirmation Prayer: Heavenly Father, I pray that You help me not to be the accuser of the brethren but to teach others in gentleness, to be a help in season, to edify, to exhort and comfort others. Help me not to be angry but agreeable to obeying Your Word, in the name of Jesus, Amen.

Daily Bread: Job 38 - 39; Matthew 24:32-51; Matthew 25:1-13; Psalm 18:37-45

Don't You Worry 'Bout a Thing
February 7

Scripture: "Therefore I say to you, do not worry about your life, what you will eat or what you will drink; nor about your body, what you will put on. Is not life more than food and the body more than clothing?"
~ Mathew 6:25

Spiritual Vitamin

Are you worried about something that's going on in your life? Worry is created by distrust, fear and doubt. Where trust is present, worry cannot exist. Where faith is present, fear cannot exist. Where belief is present, doubt cannot exist. *Can you trust God enough not to worry about the concerns in your life?* Jesus very clearly tells you to cast your cares on Him because He cares for you. He will handle everything concerning you but you have to willingly release what you're holding on to and believe in His promises in order for Him to do His work. *What is easier, to worry about the outcome of a situation or to rest on the promises of God?* God truly knows what He is doing. After all, He created an entire universe without the help of man. *Why do we think He needs our help to manage what He didn't need our help to make?* God really does have it all in control. In the end, you will be overjoyed with the outcome and also pleasantly surprised at the blessings you will receive. Take time today to release your cares to our Heavenly Father and allow Him to work out all the details.

Affirmation Prayer: Heavenly Father, I pray that my eyes of understanding will be enlightened so that I will not worry. I realize that Your exceeding greatness and power has taken care of the things that will occur in my life. Release me from the bondage of worry. Thank you Father, in the name of Jesus, Amen.

Daily Bread: Job 40 – 42; Matthew 25:14-46; Psalm 18:46-50

For the Love of Money
February 8

Scripture: "For the love of money is a root of all kinds of evils. It is through this craving that some have wandered away from the faith and pierced themselves with many pangs."
~ 1 Timothy 6:10 ESV

Spiritual Vitamin

What are you willing to do for money? Some people will do just about anything for money. Money in and of itself is not evil but the love of it is what creates the problem. The miracles of God have nothing to do with money. God's power comes from within Him and cannot be purchased for any price. The gifts of God are supernatural and God gives them to whomever He decides. The best way to use your money is in obedience to the principles of God. You can do this in several ways — through tithing (obedience); first fruits (generosity); alms (compassion) and seed (faith). Stewardship is very important to God. *He promises to give seed to the sower, but if you are not a sower, why should He give you seed?* Everything you own ultimately belongs to God. When you grasp the proper realization of this fact, it will become easier for you to obey His commands concerning giving. Obey God and send the enemy on his way. He will have you to believe that you cannot afford to tithe, when in actuality, you can't afford not to. Take time today to create a spiritual "spending plan" that will assist you in obedience to what God requires and watch God bless your life beyond measure!

Affirmation Prayer: Heavenly Father, I walk in Your faithfulness and denounce my failure to depend on You financially. I know that if You feed the birds and the bees, You will feed, clothe, comfort, and take care of me. Help me to keep reminding myself that my money does not buy me health, happiness or eternal life with You. Help me to be a cheerful steward, in the name of Jesus, Amen.

Daily Bread: Exodus 1 — 3; Matthew 26:1-30; Psalm 19:1-6

(How Did You Get Here?) Nobody Supposed To Be Here
February 9

Scripture: "Love suffers long and is kind; love does not envy; love does not parade itself, is not puffed up; does not behave rudely, does not seek its own, is not provoked, thinks no evil; does not rejoice in iniquity, but rejoices in the truth; bears all things, believes all things, hopes all things, endures all things."
~ 1 Corinthians 13:4-7

Spiritual Vitamin

Are you afraid to love? Have you been hurt and now you've decided that you won't let anyone else into your heart? This is not God's design for love. 1 Corinthians 13:13 says, "Now abide faith, hope, love; these three; but the greatest of these is love." It is possible to be hurt and to forgive and recover but this must be your desire. Forgiveness is a choice. You can choose to hold on to hostility and anger or you can choose to forgive and move forward, continuing to experience the peace and blessings of God. Unforgiveness creates a barrier between you and your future blessings. *Who is worth giving up all that God has designed for you to have?* Don't be afraid to let others into your heart. *If you practice love on a daily basis, there will be many fruitful relationships in your life and you won't have to ask anyone to whom you're connected "how did you get here?"* You will know how they got there because it will be as a result of the love that you've shared with them. Take time today to examine where your forgiveness is needed and be willing to extend it genuinely and completely.

Affirmation Prayer: Heavenly Father, You have assured me that You love me unconditionally. I will abide in Your love and live in it. It is only because of the love You have for me that I can do this. Teach me how to love others, in the name of Jesus, Amen.

Daily Bread: Exodus 4 – 5; Exodus 6:1-13; Matthew 26:31-46; Proverbs 4:10-19

I Did It My Way
February 10

Scripture: "But we are all like an unclean thing, And all our righteousness are like filthy rags; We all fade as a leaf, And our iniquities, like the wind, Have taken us away."
~ Isaiah 64:6

Spiritual Vitamin

Do you want to be right about everything? One of the biggest struggles of humanity is the desire to have one's own way. Having your way is contrary to the will of God. Psalm 128:1 says "Blessed is everyone who fears the Lord, who walks in His ways." Plainly stated, God wants you to do things His way. He deserves this desire to be met; after all, He created everything that exists, including you. If you could ever get to a point of total surrender in God, many of the problems you now have would disappear. When Jesus is Lord of your life, you no longer seek to do things your own way. You become submitted under His leadership and His lordship and as a result, you are eager to follow His instructions. Your ultimate goal is to please Him. The desires of God and His will for your life become the driving force behind everything you say and do. You become an agent of change, sharing with everyone who will listen, the miraculous saving power of Almighty God. You have the desire to share how He has changed your selfish nature into one of complete surrender and compassion. Take time today to gauge where you are on your journey toward total surrender to God and become willing to do the work of the Lord; performing His will and walking in His way.

Affirmation Prayer: Heavenly Father, I plead the blood of Jesus over my thoughts, over my mind, will, emotions, ego, imagination and all subconscious areas that will bring doubt about who You have made me to be. Forgive my sins, for my own good deeds are nothing but filthy rags. Teach me to receive instruction, direction and correction, in the name of Jesus, Amen.

Daily Bread: Exodus 6:14-30; Exodus 7 – 8; Matthew 26:47-68; Psalm 19:7-14

I'll Do For You
February 11

Scripture: "But God demonstrates His own love toward us, in that while we were still sinners, Christ died for us."
~ Romans 5:8

Spiritual Vitamin

Do you only do things for people who can do things for you in return? Depending on who you're dealing with, in order to get something from someone, you sometimes have to do something for that person first. Most people do not live under the banner of performing "random acts of kindness" on a continuous basis. Most often, only people you know and are close to will do things for you without expecting something in return. *Aren't you glad God doesn't treat you that way?* Before you were even walking within the will of God, He gave you a gift that only He could give — the gift of His Son, Jesus Christ. Now, all you have to do is accept the gift. For some, this acceptance comes easy. For others, not so much. *What is holding you back from accepting God's gift of Jesus Christ?* His whole purpose for coming to earth was to provide a way for you to get back to God. Sin separated you from God and He wanted you back; so He sent Jesus. He offers you salvation and you must accept His offer in order to see our Heavenly Father. Take time today to examine where you are within this process. If you have accepted the gift, welcome to the family of God. Celebrate your salvation and bring others to Him. If not, *will you do so today?*

Affirmation Prayer: Heavenly Father, You are my Savior. Please help me to be dependent only on You. Take a thorough examination of my intents, thoughts and desires and help me to receive and give without expectation. I want to be like You. You freely gave Your Son's life for me. Help me to realize that Your love doesn't come with a price tag; it's priceless! Teach me to model You and demonstrate Your ways, in the name of Jesus, Amen.

Daily Bread: Exodus 9 — 10; Matthew 26:69-75; Matthew 27:1-10; Psalm 20

I Have Nothing
February 12

Scripture: "But without faith it is impossible to please Him, for he who comes to God must believe that He is, and that He is a rewarder of those who diligently seek Him."
~ Hebrews 11:6

Spiritual Vitamin

I have nothing – this is a very empty phrase. *Have you ever said this or felt this way before?* This could not be further from the truth. What you view as the most important need in your life most likely is not. *Who is the most important person to you?* Everyone has something or someone in their life they feel they can't live without. This should not be true regarding things or people because God is the only One you really can't live without. He can turn what seems to be nothing into something. Everything in your life, outside of God Himself, is temporary and will remain in the earthly realm. Tangible things will not be eligible to go with you into eternity. If you don't have a solid and productive relationship with God, then you have not tapped into the greatest resource that is available to you. It's true; apart from God, you have nothing. But with Him, you have everything you will ever need to navigate your way through this thing called life. Luke 1:37 says "For with God nothing will be impossible." Take time today to deepen your relationship with God and take advantage of all the benefits that come along with a yielded and surrendered life.

Affirmation Prayer: Heavenly Father, while I have so much, I really have nothing without You. Thank You for being my Source and Resource, my Father and my friend. I am rich because of You. Keep me in a position of gratitude, in the name of Jesus, Amen.

Daily Bread: Exodus 11 – 12; Matthew 27:11-44; Psalm 21:1-7

And I'm Telling You
February 13

Scripture: "Be strong and of good courage, do not fear nor be afraid of them; for the Lord your God, He is the One who goes with you. He will not leave you nor forsake you."
~ Deuteronomy 31:6

Spiritual Vitamin

God is the best man you could ever know. *Do you agree?* I know a lot of people and you probably do as well. Because of that, I have gained a greater appreciation for God and His ability to love everyone the same. Human nature dictates that we have our favorites but God doesn't discriminate. God loves all of His creation, flaws and all. As humans, we have a tendency to choose whom we will love and we base our level of love on their behavior and actions toward us. God does not love like that. His Word says that He doesn't want any of His children to perish. We can do nothing to earn His love; it comes as a result of His decision to freely give it. God has promised never to leave you and He's not going to, *but the question is, will you leave Him?* Take time today to examine God's place in your life so that you can make the declaration back to Him "and I'm telling You, I'm not going --- I will serve You all the days of my life."

Affirmation Prayer: Heavenly Father, I commit my total allegiance to You and I'm telling You I'm not going to continue living a life of sin. As I think back over my life, You are now and have been in the past, the best thing that ever happened to me. Teach me to continue trusting You with my future, in the name of Jesus, Amen.

Daily Bread: Exodus 13 – 14; Matthew 27:45-66; Proverbs 4:20-27

I Want Your Love
    February 14

                           Scripture:
"For God so loVed the world
    that He gAve His
        onLy
            bEgotten
    SoN,
      thaT whoever
believes In Him should
          Not perish but have
        Everlasting life."
              ~ John 3:16

              Spiritual Vitamin

Today, we celebrate love. Happy Valentine's Day! Many mark the occasion with the giving of cards, gifts and candy to their significant others. People give items to their significant other, asking them to "Be Mine" and expressing sentiments of love. God has been extending this offer since the beginning of time. He wants you to enter into a loving relationship with Him. He loves you unconditionally and desires you to accept His love. The love God offers is not like human love; it is a divine love and is available only from Him. No one can love you like your Heavenly Father. There is nothing that can separate you from the love of God. Your relationship with God is meant to be eternal and everlasting. It should bring you great comfort to know that there is someone who is willing to love you forever and that nothing you can ever do will change His mind. Even if you don't have a significant other, recognize and appreciate the Presence of God in your life on this day. Don't allow the lies of the enemy to convince you that you are alone; you're not, because God is with you. Take time today to celebrate the love God has for you. Once you grasp how deep His love really is, it will change how you love yourself and the people in your life.

Affirmation Prayer: Heavenly Father, Your rightful place is on the throne of my life. Help me never to waiver in knowing that You are with me even until the end of the earth. Thank You for sending Your Son Jesus to die for my sins and for being the author and finisher of my faith, in the name of Jesus, Amen.

Daily Bread: Exodus 15 – 16; Matthew 28; Psalm 21:8-13

It's My Prerogative
February 15

Scripture: "Or do you not know that your body is the temple of the Holy Spirit who is in you, whom you have from God, and you are not your own?"
~ 1 Corinthian 6:19

Spiritual Vitamin

Do you feel that you can do whatever you want to do? The verse for today makes it clear that you don't belong to yourself; you belong to God. You have the ability to make your own choices and decisions but you do not have ownership or rights over your life. *The question then becomes, how much control do you really have?* We are limited in our ability to control. Even as it pertains to eliminating waste from our bodies, it dictates to us the frequency of when it will occur. Once you become saved and have undergone the process of conversion, you realize that you are no longer in full and total control of your choices and decisions because you have willingly given that control over to God. He is now ruler over your life, so it's no longer your prerogative, but God's. Jesus Christ becomes your Lord and Savior and you live a submitted life to Him, under the power of God's Holy Spirit. God does not wish to exercise a hostile takeover of man. He wants you to willingly submit. *Will you do it?* Take time today to examine how submitted and yielded you are to the will of God for your life. After that, let God make the necessary changes according to His divine will.

Affirmation Prayer: Heavenly Father, I acknowledge You as Creator, Father, Savior and Lord. Because of this, I am not in control. What happens concerning me is really Your prerogative, not mine. I am not my own. Help me to surrender and submit all areas of my life to You, in the name of Jesus, Amen.

Daily Bread: Exodus 17 – 18; Mark 1:1-28; Psalm 22:1-11

Leave Your Lover
February 16

Scripture: "(for you shall worship no other god, for the Lord, whose name is Jealous, is a jealous God),"
~ Exodus 34:14

Spiritual Vitamin

Are you in a relationship that does not honor God? God is a jealous God and He will not share His glory. If you love something or someone more than you love Him, God is asking you to leave this love in order to become involved in an intimate and loving relationship with Him. God's love affords all of humanity the opportunity to experience perfect love. If you are honest, you can admit that at some point in your life, there was something you loved more than you loved God. But upon accepting God's offer of salvation, you are given the opportunity to leave something that may have been superficial for something true and authentic. You became united and joined to God in a loving, life-saving relationship through Jesus Christ. The more time you spend in God's Presence, the more you come to know that in His Presence is where you belong. *Is there some other lover you need to leave?* Take time today to examine where you are in terms of your relationship with God. Leave behind anything or anyone that you've placed above God. You owe it to yourself and certainly, you are worth it!

Affirmation Prayer: Heavenly Father, please help me to abort any feelings of loving anything more than You. This includes but is not limited to worldly possessions, people and practices that would rob me of my devotion to You. Cause me to be agreeable to leaving anything that stands to damage my relationship with You, in the name of Jesus, Amen.

Daily Bread: Exodus 19 – 20; Mark 1:29-45; Mark 2:1-17; Psalm 22:12-21

Never Gonna Get It
February 17

Scripture: "You shall walk in all the ways which the Lord your God has commanded you, that you may live and that it may be well with you, and that you may prolong your days in the land which you shall possess."
~ Deuteronomy 5:33

Spiritual Vitamin

Are you living within the will of God? You belong to God. Your body, soul and spirit belong to Him. Every part of you is His. In order for you to live the abundant life He created for you, you must come to grips with these facts. Once you do that, you become willing to yield to Him and accept the lordship of His Son, Jesus Christ. If you don't accept the saving work of Christ on the cross, you will never get what God has for you. His Word clearly states that He has plans for you. The mistake humanity often makes is that we make our own plans. Many times, those plans are not within the will of God for our lives, so they are rarely realized. James 1:22 says "But be doers of the Word, and not hearers only, deceiving yourselves." Ask yourself an important question. *Why would you want to live your life without experiencing the promises of God?* His plans are for peace, an abundant future and hope. These are things you cannot provide for yourself. You need God's help to attain victory while going through your earthly experience. God never intended for you to create your own plans. His desire is for you to embrace the plan He had in mind when He created you. Take time today to get on board with God's plan for your life. You will never get what He's planned for You until you totally surrender to Him. You will be oh so glad you did!

Affirmation Prayer: Heavenly Father, I know that I know that I know that I belong to You. I am unique from all others. You have a plan for my life but the evil one desires my devotion. I declare that satan will never get my soul because I am Yours forever. Teach me ways to display my loyalty and gratitude, in the name of Jesus, Amen.

Daily Bread: Exodus 21 – 22; Mark 2:18-27; Mark 3:1-30; Proverbs 5:1-14

Once You Get Started
February 18

Scripture: "Therefore we also, since we are surrounded by so great a cloud of witnesses, let us lay aside every weight, and the sin which so easily ensnares us, and let us run with endurance the race that is set before us."
~ Hebrews 12:1

Spiritual Vitamin

What kinds of habits do you have? All creatures have habits. Some habits are good, some habits are bad. There is a saying that old habits die hard. Some habits should not even be started, because once you get started, it can be very hard to stop. *Are your habits ones that promote your well-being and natural and spiritual health? Or are they habits that are hurting you, both naturally and spiritually?* Do yourself a favor and take good care of you. You have one shot at having a fulfilling earthly experience. You should do everything in your power to make it all God designed it to be. *Are there things in your life that seem to have control over you and you find it difficult to break free from their influence?* 1 John 1:9 says, "If we confess our sins, He is faithful and just to forgive us our sins and to cleanse us from all unrighteousness." God's Holy Spirit has the power to help you stop bad habits and start good ones. There is something in your life today that needs your attention and the desire for improvement. Take time today to replace bad habits with good ones and see how much better your life becomes.

Affirmation Prayer: Heavenly Father, I know You have the power to turn lives around because You have worked wonders in me. I am guilty of not destroying my bad habits and I need Your help. Please help me day by day, in the name of Jesus, Amen.

Daily Bread: Exodus 23 – 24; Mark 3:31 -35; Mark 4:1-29; Psalm 22:22-31

Rebellion Lies
February 19

Scripture: "For rebellion is as the sin of witchcraft, and stubbornness is as iniquity and idolatry. Because you have rejected the word of the Lord, He also has rejected you from being king."
~ 1 Samuel 15:23 (the conversation of the prophet with King Saul)

Spiritual Vitamin

Are you rebelling against God? Rebellion is a dangerous thing. When you rebel, you refuse. You refuse to listen to what is being said and you refuse to do what is being asked. You have the power to comply but you just choose not to do so. All human beings are born into a sinful state. To remain in that state is to refuse the offer to spend eternity with God through accepting Jesus Christ as your Savior and Lord. Continuous rebellion hardens your heart and makes you unable to hear the voice of God or to receive the promises He has offered to you in His Word. When you operate under the spirit of rebellion, you are following the plan of the enemy rather than the plan of God. God has so much to give you but your ability to receive His gifts are contingent upon your willingness to surrender to His will. Becoming a child of God is the best decision you will ever make. Do yourself a favor and put an end to your days of rebellion. Stop rebelling against God. Take time today, not to rebel against Christ but to become a rebel FOR the cause of Jesus Christ!

Affirmation Prayer: Heavenly Father, I know at some point and time in my life, I have rebelled. I now understand that my open resistance and opposition is not pleasing in Your sight. Help me to openly denounce my mistake of rebellion and cause me to cease and desist from sin, in the name of Jesus, Amen.

Daily Bread: Exodus 25 – 26; Mark 4:30-41; Mark 5:1-20; Psalm 23

Same Script, Different Cast
February 20

Scripture: "That which has been is what will be, that which is done is what will be done, and there is nothing new under the sun."
~ Ecclesiastes 1:9

Spiritual Vitamin

Do you find yourself practicing repeated patterns of sin? Sin was introduced into the world through Adam and Eve in the book of Genesis. Ecclesiastes says there is nothing new under the sun. The "script" of sin was instituted back then and is still being lived out in today's time. The Bible characters of old are no longer here but have been replaced by individuals today who are walking in their footsteps. Those alive today are now facing the same situations and circumstances as those in Bible days. *Which Bible character is your life most like?* When you are experiencing difficulty and hardship, you can glean from the wisdom of someone in the Bible who faced a similar problem. Read and study what that person did to bring closure to their issue. Find the wisdom and courage you need to be an overcomer. By consulting God's Word, you will find encouragement and instructions on how to navigate your way into God's next blessing. Take time today to confess and repent of your sins. Consider what God has to say about your current condition and follow His instructions.

Affirmation Prayer: Heavenly Father, I declare that I am like Paul, having a thorn in my flesh. My thorn has not been removed but neither has Your presence. Please destroy all of the old things that hindered me, all of the current things trying to hinder me and deliver me from any future things that would attempt to hinder me from complete obedience to You. Help me to rely on You rather than my own strength, in the name of Jesus, Amen.

Daily Bread: Exodus 27 – 28; Mark 5:21-43; Mark 6:1-6; Psalm 24

Secret Lovers
February 21

Scripture: "People who conceal their sins will not prosper, but if they confess and turn from them, they will receive mercy."
~ Proverbs 28:13 NLT

Spiritual Vitamin

Is there something you're trying to hide from God? With God, there is no such thing as a secret. When you are in the right kind of love relationship, it doesn't have to be a secret. God's truth and His light go together. John 4:24 says "God is Spirit, and those who worship Him must worship in spirit and in truth." God is inviting you to live and walk in the light. God's love is pure and anything pure has no need to be hidden. Living in God's love will bring you out of the darkness, where secrets live, into the marvelous light. Things that have to be hidden have nothing to do with truth and light. God wants to have a loving relationship with you; a relationship that is not a secret but a wonderful tale of His grace and glory. He wants others to know about your relationship with Him, so He gives you an abundance of blessings by which you can share your story. When you are in love, it shows. There is a glow about you that makes others ask or inquire as to what it's about. Take time today to surrender any secret sins you currently have and share your story of deliverance with someone who may not yet know Him. Then, they can begin their personal journey to deliverance.

Affirmation Prayer: Heavenly Father, You are a shield about me. Because of You, there is no need to hide or live in guilt or shame. You are the lifter of my head. Help me to denounce any hidden thing and to walk uprightly, knowing I am forgiven, in the name of Jesus, Amen.

Daily Bread: Exodus 29 – 30; Mark 6:7-29; Proverbs 5:15-23

Stop In the Name of Love
February 22

Scripture: "If you love me, keep my commandments."
~ John 14:15

Spiritual Vitamin

Have you ever cried out to God from the depths of your soul? God desires a true and loving relationship with you. If you give Him your whole heart, there is nothing He won't do for you. He watches over you with a deep and intense sense of love, care and concern. He looks out over every detail of your life and when you have a need, He is aware. He asks that you cry out to Him. Bartimaeus did. He was blind and in need of healing. He knew his condition required something beyond natural circumstances and power. In Mark 10:46 – 52, he cried out to Jesus. His cry caught Jesus' attention and Jesus stopped to minister to his need. Jesus stopped in the name of love. His love for Bartimaeus caused him to interrupt His plans and to focus His attention solely on the one who cried out to Him. He will do the same for you. Cry out to God with your needs. He's closer than you think. There is no difference between you and others whom God has helped. He loves all of us the same. What He does for one, He will do for all. Take time today to cry out to God. He'll be glad to stop, in the name of love, just because you took the time to call.

Affirmation Prayer: Heavenly Father, You have established me as holy. You promised that as I keep Your commandments and walk in Your ways, You will bless me. You are the lover of my soul. Help me to be faithful and true to You, in the name of Jesus, Amen.

Daily Bread: Exodus 31 – 32; Mark 6:30-56; Psalm 25:1-7

Backstabbers
February 23

Scripture: "But Jesus said unto him, 'Judas, betrayest thou the Son of man with a kiss?'"
~ Luke 22:48

Spiritual Vitamin

Are you loyal to those within your inner circle? Loyalty must be proven over time. When you meet someone, it takes time to get to know that individual. The only way to prove whether someone's motives are pure is to allow yourself to be open and honest with them and to agree to spend time in their presence. From this process, you will gain friends as well as enemies. The only problem is that you won't immediately know who is who. God does not expect us to put our trust in man. He expects us to put our trust in Him. He is the only One who can truly be trusted with the intimate details of our lives. It is never wise to share deep, intimate information with people you barely know. You cannot expect a high degree of loyalty from people who do not have a high degree of integrity and strong, solid morals. You were never asked to trust people. You are expected to love people and to trust God. You cannot go wrong with this principle. When you don't place unrealistic expectations on people, you won't have to experience the disappointment of being let down. Sometimes, you will be let down but never use that as an opportunity to belittle or betray others. Follow James 4:11(a), which says, "Do not speak evil of one another, brethren. He who speaks evil of a brother and judges his brothers, speaks evil of the law and judges the law." Do not gossip for Proverbs 16:28 says "A perverse person stirs up conflict and a gossip separates close friends." Take time today to evaluate areas where there is backbiting and gossiping in your own life. Then, pray for the strength to replace these ungodly habits with compassion and grace.

Affirmation Prayer: Heavenly Father, I surrender ALL. I forbid myself to hold grudges or to have ill feelings because of anything that has occurred in my life. You are my way-maker, my mentor, my leader, and I will follow Your instructions. Help me to stand still and trust in You no matter what comes my way, in the name of Jesus, Amen.

Daily Bread: Exodus 33 - 34; Mark 7; Psalm 25:8-15

Fame

February 24

Scripture: And they said, "Come, let us build ourselves a city, and a tower whose top is in the heavens; let us make a name for ourselves, lest we be scattered abroad over the face of the whole earth."
~ Genesis 11:4

Spiritual Vitamin

Do you love to be praised and exalted by others? It is very important to understand that God alone deserves the credit for anything man is able to do. *Do you take the credit for things that God enables you to accomplish without giving any thanks, praise or glory to Him?* You must not give in to the temptation to rely on your own abilities or to accept credit for what only God can do. When confronted with situations where your assistance is requested, the first thing to do is pray and ask God how He wants the situation to be resolved. Do not give in to the enemy's promptings to try and figure out a solution on your own. If you are going to do the work of God, you must employ the help of the Holy Spirit and operate in the name of Jesus. Don't get caught up and let pride enter the picture and convince you that you are smart enough to handle the issue alone. Pride is a destructive sin; one that you must actively work to avoid. God can use you to do a mighty work, but you must remain in close contact with Him in order to receive the needed instructions and the power to obey. You need God's help to successfully complete the mission. Make sure that what you're doing has been approved by God. Take time today to honor God and to give Him glory for your accomplishments, rather than seeking fame and taking credit for yourself.

Affirmation Prayer: Heavenly Father, please keep me protected from the spirit of pride. Help me to turn away from the need to have fame and glory for myself and give me the desire to always give You the praise in all things, in the name of Jesus, Amen.

Daily Bread: Exodus 35 – 36; Mark 8:1-12; Psalm 25:16-22

Through the Fire
February 25

Scripture: "When you pass through the water, I will be with you; and through the rivers, they shall not overflow you. When you walk through the fire, you shall not be burned, nor shall the flame scorch you."
~ Isaiah 43:2

Spiritual Vitamin

Do you know anyone who will risk everything for you? God will. He has proven this kind of love through the sacrifice of His Son Jesus, who gave up everything to have a relationship with you. As the end of the month draws near, I want to encourage you to continue to walk with Jesus, who has already conquered sin. Offer your repentance and seek His forgiveness for your sins. Allow Him to conquer the sin in your life. Often, when you have been in trouble, you needed the support of those who said they love you. *Did you receive that support?* In these days and times, it's hard to find people who are willing to make this type of sacrifice on behalf of someone else. You may never find the "sacrificial" kind of love in another human being, but you will find it in God. Seek His face and He will share with you the mysteries of the depth of His great love for you. This God-kind of love should stir you; it should cause a change in you. As a result of that change, you should become more loving and accepting of others. Take time today to ask God to walk with you wherever you go, even when you go "Through the Fire"; allow Him to change you from the inside out.

Affirmation Prayer: Heavenly Father, thank You for being with me through the hard times. Thank You for supporting me in my times of trouble. Please make me more accepting of others and more sympathetic to their needs. Help me to be more willing to provide strength and comfort to others in their time of need, in the name of Jesus, Amen.

Daily Bread: Exodus 37 – 38; Mark 8:13-38; Proverbs 6:1-11

Two Lovers
February 26

Scripture: "He is a double-minded man, unstable in all his ways."
~ James 1:8

Spiritual Vitamin

Are you trying to serve God with a divided heart? God wants your total and complete devotion. He wants your whole heart to belong to Him. *Do you love something or someone more than you love Him?* Matthew 6 says "you cannot serve two masters." God wants a solid, strong, loving relationship with you and He wants to be the one you love the most. God is a jealous God and is not willing to share His glory with anyone. *Who has your devotion and loyalty?* God wants and deserves first place in your life. He shouldn't have to compete with anyone or anything to spend time with you. You should be willing to make yourself available for this purpose. He gave His only Son so that you could have the right to live an abundant life and to be able to spend eternity with Him. Take time today to consider who is first in your life and think about changing your priorities around so that God can be first.

Affirmation Prayer: Heavenly Father, how excellent is Your name. I plead for Your loving kindness and tender mercies to shift my priorities from the things of this world, so that I may always have You as first place in my life. Teach me to appreciate Your love and dedication to me, in the name of Jesus, Amen.

Daily Bread: Exodus 39 – 40; Mark 9:1-32; Psalm 26:1-12

Upside Down
February 27

Scripture: "You turn things upside down, as if the potter were thought to be like the clay! Shall what is formed say to the one who formed it, 'You did not make me?' Can the pot say to the potter, 'You know nothing?'"
~ Isaiah 29:16 NIV

Spiritual Vitamin

The enemy will use you until you are all used up. Under his negative influence, you will be instructed to do things that are not only harmful to your body, but ultimately to your soul. Once you have allowed him to wreak havoc in your life, he will then move on to the next victim, leaving you all alone to deal with the consequences of all your bad choices and decisions. The desired goal of satan is to turn your life upside down. The good news is that you don't have to yield to the influence of the enemy. On the contrary, you can decide to become an instrument that is fit for the Master's use. You can listen to God and carry out the instructions He gives you through His Holy Spirit. Let God use you and you won't go wrong. Make a firm decision that God's gifts will not go unused but that you will share what you've been given with the Body of Christ in a way that brings blessings to everyone. Take time today to stop giving the enemy your consent to turn your life upside down. Instead, choose abundant life in Christ.

Affirmation Prayer: Heavenly Father, my life has been like a whirlwind. I have been tossed and driven by letting the enemy take control. But then You came along and turned my life upside down and because of it, I have landed right side up! Help me to continue to be grateful for Your rescue. I am no longer under the reigns of satan. Thank you, Father, in the name of Jesus, Amen.

Daily Bread: Leviticus 1 – 3; Mark 9:33-50; Mark 10:1-12; Psalm 27:1-6

Use Somebody
February 28

Scripture: "A man's gift makes room for him, and brings him before great men." ~ Proverbs 18:16

Spiritual Vitamin

Have you ever felt used? From a humanistic perspective, being used has a negative connotation. But when you look at it from a spiritual perspective, it takes on an entirely different meaning. Being used by God is a wonderful thing. It's actually an honor and a privilege that the Creator of the universe even has a use for humanity. God has taken the time to place spiritual gifts inside each one of His creation. He knows what He placed on the inside of you when He created you. That was His investment and He's expecting a return. Never allow yourself to be used by your fellow man for ungodly purposes. Instead, present yourself to God and allow Him to shine through you so that others can see Him in your life; in a way that will make them want Him in their lives. God desires for humanity to become one body and for each part of the body to function in its intended capacity. Take time today to present yourself to God, so that He can use you for His glory.

Affirmation Prayer: Heavenly Father, in my world, I have a community of people who help me. I depend and count on my barber/beautician, on my coach, on my doctor and so many others. But Lord, it was not until I learned that I could count on, depend on and rely on You, the King of Kings and Lord of Lords, that I was able to fully surrender. Thank You for letting me know that I could use someone like You in my life, in the name of Jesus, Amen.

Daily Bread: Leviticus 4 – 6; Mark 10:13-52; Psalm 27:7-14

Your Body's Here With Me
February 29

Scripture: "I beseech you therefore, brethren, by the mercies of God, that you present your bodies a living sacrifice, holy, acceptable to God, which is your reasonable service. And do not be conformed to this world but be transformed by the renewing of your mind, that you may prove what is that good and acceptable and perfect will of God."
~ Romans 12:1-2

Spiritual Vitamin

"Yes, you come to My house. You are sitting here in the assembly of the saints, but you're not completely, 100% here with Me. You're thinking about all the other things you want and need to do. Your mind is not completely on Me. You are not thinking about all that I do to sustain your life. Your heart is divided and you are not totally focused on Me". This is something God could say to all mankind. At some point, each of us has been guilty of not focusing on God and not putting Him first. We have been guilty of having divided hearts as it pertains to the things of God. We must make the decision to completely surrender to God so that He can get the glory out of our lives. *Will you yield to the voice of God today?* The next time you go to God's house to worship, be completely there. Allow your mind to be present in the assembly along with your body. Keep your mind focused on Jesus. If you do, He will keep you in "perfect peace". Give God what He so rightly deserves --- your time and your attention. Take time today to be wholly present with the Lord, so that He can minister to the total you.

Affirmation Prayer: Heavenly Father, united We (You and I) stand but divided I fall. I cannot make it without You. You are my El Shaddai, the God who is more than enough. I will not waiver, bend, or break. Help me to stand firm and to give You my time and my full attention, in the name of Jesus, Amen.

Daily Bread: Proverbs 6:12-19

MONTHLY REFLECTIONS

March: Salvation (Forgiveness and Eternal Life)

Strength for the Journey

Heavenly Father,

You are the Creator of the universe. Your name is above every name. There is no other name by which men can be saved. Thank You for forgiveness and eternal life. How great You are! Because of You, I have the opportunity to receive salvation and I am in awe of this. Thank You for salvation, forgiveness and eternal life. You have extended an open, eternal invitation to me to live with You forever. I accept, believe and receive it, in the name of Jesus, Amen.

March

Salvation (Forgiveness and Eternal Life)

During the month of March, you will go on a journey, learning about God's great gift of salvation. Salvation is defined as deliverance from the power of sin and its consequences. Along with that deliverance comes redemption, based on Jesus' death and resurrection. The benefits of salvation include eternal life, reconciliation with God, forgiveness of sins and assurance that you will spend eternity in heaven. The path to salvation is as simple as A-B-C-D: **Admit** that you're a sinner and that you need a right relationship with God (Romans 3:10); **Believe** that Jesus is God's only begotten Son and that God raised Him from the grave (Romans 5:8); **Confess** your sins and ask Jesus into your heart (Romans 10:9); and **Dedicate** yourself as a fully devout follower of Christ, receiving God's gift of forgiveness through Jesus Christ. It is my prayer that you will use this month's devotionals to celebrate your salvation.

I will not assume that you have already accepted God's gift of salvation. If not, are you ready to take these steps? If so, pray this prayer with me:

Father God, please forgive me for I have sinned against you. Today I repent of my sins. I believe that Jesus was born of a virgin, crucified for my sins and raised from the dead by our Heavenly Father. He is alive today, sitting on the right hand of God, pleading the forgiveness of my sins. Right now, I receive You as my Lord and Savior and dedicate my life to following You. Thank You for saving me in Jesus' name, Amen!

> "Then He said to them all "if anyone desires to come after Me, let him deny himself, and take up his cross daily, and follow Me."
> ~ Luke 9:23

Ain't No Mountain High Enough
March 1

Scripture: "So Jesus said to them, "Because of your unbelief; for assuredly, I say to you, if you have faith as a mustard seed, you will say to this mountain, 'Move from here to there,' and it will move; and nothing will be impossible for you."
~ Matthew 17:20

Spiritual Vitamin

Ash Wednesday signifies the beginning of the Lenten season. It can fall as early as February 4 and as late as March 10. For many Christians, this is a time of self-denial, moderation and fasting. This is necessary due to the inescapable sinful nature of man. Although God is aware of this sinful nature, you will never be too far away that His love cannot bring you back. But you must choose to surrender to the lordship of Jesus Christ. You can never be out of God's reach and He waits to hear you cry out to Him. God wants to hear about your problems; things that might look like mountains to you are miniscule to Him because His power supersedes that of anything known to man. God made you "an amazing miracle" and He has already provided everything you will ever need in your earthly experience. If you need God, call out to Him and no matter where you are, He will come to provide a way of escape for you. There is never a delay when you call His name. He comes quickly and you will never have to worry about whether He is able to save you because no mountain is too high to be moved by God, if you will only believe. Take time today to ask God to move any mountains in your life; things such as doubt, fear and unforgiveness. He's waiting to hear from you.

Affirmation Prayer: Heavenly Father, when I look at Your glory and Your beauty, I want to run to You. Show me that I am Your creation and help me to be determined that nothing and no one can keep me away from You, in the name of Jesus, Amen.

Daily Bread: Leviticus 7 - 8; Mark 11:1-26; Psalm 28

After the Love Has Lost Its Shine
March 2

Scripture: "But the path of the just is like the shining sun, that shines ever brighter unto the perfect day."
~ Proverbs 4:18

Spiritual Vitamin

Is your love for God still exciting and new? From a human standpoint, when love is new, it brings an element of excitement. The longer the love relationship lasts, there is a chance that the level of excitement can die down, leaving behind feelings of boredom and emptiness. The longer the relationship lasts, the more familiar it becomes. In order to maintain love from a human perspective, you must perform certain tasks and responsibilities. God's love is not like human love. God's love for His creation is undying and everlasting, which is the sole purpose for salvation. It is not contingent on something you do or don't do because there is nothing you can do to earn God's love. He has decided to freely give it to you, with no strings attached. *Isn't it comforting to know that His love will last forever?* Maybe you have lost someone you thought would be in your life forever. You know how much that hurts. With God, you will never have to experience this type of loss and His love for you will never lose its shine. It has the ability to remain forever new. Take time today to bask in the light of God's love for you; it is unending and everlasting.

Affirmation Prayer: Heavenly Father, Your Word says that I am the light of the world and the salt of the earth. I am well-seasoned in You and will never lose my flavor. Teach me to share my savor with others, in the name of Jesus, Amen.

Daily Bread: Leviticus 9 – 10; Mark 11:27-33; Mark 12:1-12; Psalm 29

Anyone Who Had a Heart
March 3

Scripture: "Let nothing be done through selfish ambition or conceit, but in lowliness of mind let each esteem others better than himself. Let each of you look out not only for his own interests, but also for the interests of others. Let this mind be in you which was also in Christ Jesus."
~ Philippians 2:3-5

Spiritual Vitamin

Do you have a heart for others? God has given each individual the capacity to demonstrate compassion on behalf of others. *Do the needs and circumstances of other people move you to act on their behalf?* God wants you to do for others what you would want them to do for you, in any given situation. God expects you to love someone other than yourself and to allow that love to push you into action and service. He declares that love is greater than faith and hope. That is a powerful declaration. God's Word says that what is within you will come out. If you have clean hands and a pure heart, your actions will demonstrate that to others. Compassion comes from God and is available to all who seek Him. Don't help others so that you can brag about how great you are. Help them out of the kindness of your heart. God's heart for us caused Him to sacrifice the life of His Son, so that we could receive salvation. After you have helped someone, don't continue to bring up what you've done for them in an effort to keep them beholden to you. Take time today to have a heart for others; showing them compassion, care and concern.

Affirmation Prayer: Heavenly Father, help me to not only think of my family and my friends but to have a heart for the least, the lost and the left out, in the name of Jesus, Amen.

Daily Bread: Leviticus 11 – 12; Mark 12:13-27; Psalm 30:1-7

Always and Forever
March 4

Scripture: "Therefore He is also able to save to the uttermost those who come to God through him, since He always lives to make intercession for them."
~ Hebrews 7:25

Spiritual Vitamin

Have you always been able to feel God's love for you? God has always loved you. You have lived in the light of God's love every day of your life. Even through the bad times, God's love was there to guide you through. *Did you take advantage of it?* His love is set in stone and can never be changed. No one can change God's mind about loving you. That is because He wants to be with you always and forever. His love will follow you into eternity. When you become certain that you have this kind of love, it changes you. You can't fully accept and receive this kind of love and remain the same. It makes you free; free to be the person you were created to be. You are no longer desperate for human validation and approval because you realize that the love of God is much more priceless and valuable. Learning how much you are loved and valued by God teaches you how to love yourself even more; from there you learn how to pass that love on to others. You no longer struggle with low self-esteem. Take time today to appreciate the privilege of having this kind of love from your Heavenly Father.

Affirmation Prayer: Heavenly Father, Your love is more precious than silver and more costly than gold. Nothing I desire can compare to it. Thank You for loving me before I was even aware of Your presence. Help me to value and appreciate Your love, in the name of Jesus, Amen.

Daily Bread: Leviticus 13; Mark 12:28-44; Proverbs 6:20-29

Spend My Life With You
March 5

Scripture: "If you love Me, keep My commandments."
~ John 14:15

Spiritual Vitamin

Who do you love spending time with? Maybe it's your husband, wife or significant other. *What feelings do you look forward to experiencing during your time with this person?* God wants you to have a deep longing and desire to be with Him; He wants to be the love of your life. Just as you have that special someone with whom you long to spend time, you *are* that special someone to God. He wants to spend time with you because He loves you more than you will be able to understand with the human mind. It's not a temporary love; it's eternal. That means it will last forever. God's love will follow you from earth to heaven. Hebrews 13:8 says "Jesus Christ is the same, yesterday, today and forever." What you have with God is consistent and firmly established. There is no second guessing or wondering about the validity of what He has said. If you haven't already done so, take time today to spend some quiet moments with God. Seek Him with your whole heart and receive all that He has for you.

Affirmation Prayer: Heavenly Father, I now see differently. I see Your love as a shadow and it covers me and follows me everywhere I go. Forgive me for not paying attention to it as often as I should, in the name of Jesus, Amen.

Daily Bread: Leviticus 14; Mark 13:1-31; Psalm 30:8-12

Angel of Mine
March 6

Scripture: "Do not forget to entertain strangers, for by so doing some have unwittingly entertained angels."
~ Hebrews 13:2

Spiritual Vitamin

How do you treat strangers? Are you kind to people you do not know? Common courtesy dictates a few things. *When you walk down the street, do you look into the eyes of those who may be walking toward you or do you look away as if they don't exist?* Saying hello to strangers and acknowledging their presence doesn't cost a thing. It is not difficult to make someone else feel special. When you acknowledge other people, you give them the message that they matter. You make them feel as if they are important. This is something God wants us to do. He asks us to esteem others better than ourselves. He wants us to honor those we do not know, because in so doing, we could be in the company of angels. If you knew for sure that you were in the company of an angel, you would be on your best behavior. *Why not just do that anyway?* Take time today to focus on showing kindness to everyone you meet and treat them as if they are angels in disguise. Who knows, they really may be!

Affirmation Prayer: Heavenly Father, please help me to stay conscious of the fact that every time I meet a stranger that I could be meeting an angel without knowing it. Help me to treat them like I would treat You, in the name of Jesus, Amen.

Daily Bread: Leviticus 15 – 16; Mark 13:32-37, Mark 14:1-16; Psalm 31:1-8

Can We Try?
March 7

Scripture: "Therefore let us pursue the things which make for peace and the things by which one may edify another."
~ Romans 14:19

Spiritual Vitamin

Are you patient in relationships when things aren't going well? When it comes to relationships, there are some people who are quick to throw in the towel when things don't go as planned. Once they have been offended, they build a fortress around their hearts in an effort to keep people at a distance. This does not leave room for forgiveness and reconciliation. It is inevitable to avoid conflict when dealing with others, but you don't have to allow conflict to cause a permanent breach between you and the other party. When sin entered the picture, there was a breach between us and God. But through salvation, the breach has been repaired. When communication breaks down in a relationship, you don't have to go your separate ways. You can try to work things out. If you apply the Word of God and relax your rules of engagement, it is quite possible to come to an understanding and ultimately solve the problem. Don't be so rigid and demand that things go your way all the time. Take into consideration the feelings of the other person. It is possible that they are as hurt as you are, maybe more. Pray for them and ask God to soften your heart to receive them in love. Take time today to try to work on a difficult situation in your life. God may surprise you with the results.

Affirmation Prayer: Heavenly Father, I have experienced a lot of pain at the hands of others. One day, they love me and the next day, they hate me. Help me to be consistent and give love to those who despitefully use and abuse me, in the name of Jesus, Amen.

Daily Bread: Leviticus 17 – 18; Mark 14:17-42; Psalm 31:9-18

Cherish the Love
March 8

Scripture: "But you are a chosen generation, a royal priesthood, a holy nation, His own special people, that you may proclaim the praises of Him who called you out of darkness into His marvelous light."
~ 1 Peter 2:9

Spiritual Vitamin

Women's Month is celebrated from March 1 – 31. In different regions, the focus of the celebrations range from general celebrations of respect, appreciation and love towards women for their economic, political and social achievements.

Whose love do you cherish? Is it someone from your past? God loves you more than any other human being ever could. He demonstrates that love on a daily basis. After all, God gave Jesus to die for our sins and Jesus offers us salvation. *Can you see a demonstration of God's love in your life?* For starters, He wakes you up every morning and blesses you with the ability to see and experience a brand new day. He provides food, clothing and shelter and a means by which you can receive the assistance you need to meet your responsibilities. God did not only plan your present, He's also planned your future. Jesus is your bridegroom and you are His bride. The bridegroom cherishes the bride. The marriage covenant is designed to last until death. God's love is even greater because it accompanies you into eternity. *Do you cherish the love God has for you?* If you do, there is evidence of it in the way you live your life. You are kind, compassionate, loving and generous. You place the needs of others before your own. You take care to protect the reputations and interests of those who are close to you. Take time today to cherish God's love and reflect on the depth of it and how it has changed your life.

Affirmation Prayer: Heavenly Father, I see so many relationships failing. I see fathers against sons, mothers against daughters and husbands against wives. Please help me to make a difference where I am able and to cherish Your true and undying love toward me, in the name of Jesus, Amen.

Daily Bread: Leviticus 19 – 20; Mark 14:43-72; Proverbs 6:30-35

Don't Cost You Nothin'
March 9

Scripture: "For by grace you have been saved through faith, and that not of yourselves; it is the gift of God, not of works, lest anyone should boast."
~ Ephesians 2:8-9

Spiritual Vitamin

Have you heard that salvation is free? On one hand this is true, on another it is not. There was a price for salvation but you were not the one who had to pay. The cost for salvation was high and humanity did not qualify to pay. Jesus made the ultimate sacrifice that was required and He paid the cost for you to receive the gift of eternal life. He freely laid down His life so that you could have the right to live eternally with God. *Do you understand the depth of that kind of love?* Stop what you're doing right now and really think about this. Before you were even born, someone made provisions to take care of you and to forgive every sin that you would ever commit. Now, that's love. In terms of cost, your payment won't demand the use of money. It will however, demand that you surrender your will for the will of God. It will also demand that your loyalties transfer from man to God. This is not too much to ask. Take time today to share your gratitude with others regarding what Jesus has done for you through the shedding of His blood.

Affirmation Prayer: Heavenly Father, when I think about how You gave Your life for me and paid it all on Calvary, I just want to declare how grateful I am. I'll never be able to repay you but I'm going to "die trying" to please You and bring glory and honor to You, in the name of Jesus, Amen.

Daily Bread: Leviticus 21 – 22; Mark 15:1-32; Psalm 31:19-24

Don't Stop Believing
March 10

Scripture: "But without faith it is impossible to please Him, for he who comes to God must believe that He is, and that He is a rewarder of those who diligently seek Him."
~ Hebrews 11:6

Spiritual Vitamin

No matter what it looks like, God is still in control. Things in your life might not look like they're working out. In fact, they might seem to be getting worse instead of better. But you have to believe that the opposite is true. You must decide to live by faith. In order to live by faith, you must believe that God is always working on your behalf. Just because you can't see what God is doing, doesn't mean that He's not moving. There are many coined phrases that people like to repeat such as, "God is good — all the time; I'm blessed and highly favored and I'm blessed by the best". While all those phrases are true, they will do absolutely nothing for you if you don't really believe the meaning behind them. God IS good all the time. You really ARE blessed and highly favored and you are definitely blessed by the best. *Knowing this, how can you worry about anything?* Let me repeat this, God will never stop working on your behalf. He will never stop taking care of you. *The question is, can you believe in Him enough to rest upon that promise?* Take time today to exercise strong faith in God, regardless of your circumstances, because He always performs His Word.

Affirmation Prayer: Heavenly Father, I have come to the realization that I have to believe ALL of the Word of God or none of it at all. Help me to believe it all, in the name of Jesus, Amen.

Daily Bread: Leviticus 23 - 24, Mark 15:33-47; Psalm 32

Do You Know Where You're Going To?
March 11

Scripture: Thomas said to Him, "Lord, we do not know where you are going, and how can we know the way?" Jesus said to him, "I am the way, the truth, and the life. No one comes to the Father except through Me."
~ John 14:5-6

Spiritual Vitamin

Where will you spend eternity? Your earthly existence is temporary. Just as you have an earthly home, you also have an eternal one and you must choose. It is up to you where you will spend eternity and a decision must be made. God desires for your eternal home to be with Him but the final choice rests with you. In order for you to live eternally with God, you must accept His Son Jesus Christ as your Lord and Savior. You must be born again and baptized into the family of God. You must turn away from sin and agree to take on the character of Jesus Christ. Your highest goal must be to please God and to bring glory to Him by the way you live your life. Acceptance into the Kingdom of God requires action on your part. Jesus paid a high price to afford you this opportunity. As a matter of fact, He goes so far as to say "I am the way, the truth and the life. No man comes to the Father except through Me." This means that Jesus is the only door you can use to get to God. Entry into heaven is not automatic and the only way in is through Jesus Christ. *Have you claimed your place in eternity?* When your earthly life ends, do you know where you're going to? Take time today to make sure you have done what is necessary to secure your entry into the Kingdom of God.

Affirmation Prayer: Heavenly Father, I look forward to the eternal life You have promised me. Please take away fear and doubt and help me in my preparation to enter Your Kingdom. Keep me certain that I am secure in You, in the name of Jesus, Amen.

Daily Bread: Leviticus 25 – 26; Mark 16; Psalm 33:1-11

The *Greatest Love of All*
March 12

Scripture: "Greater love has no one than this, than to lay down one's life for his friends."
~ John 15:13

Spiritual Vitamin

Have you experienced the "Greatest Love of All"? Accepting God's great love within yourself will enable you to extend great love to others. You will be equipped to handle situations differently than you currently do and you will have more tolerance for the shortcomings and mistakes of others. *From whom do you receive the greatest love?* I'm sure you have someone in mind. As much as that person loves you, God loves you even more. Another human being cannot pour God's kind of love into you. Only God can do that. If you haven't already discovered it, you will one day find out that His love is the greatest love of all. 1 John 3:16 says "By this we know love, because He laid down His life for us. And we also ought to lay down our lives for the brethren." Nothing you know at this present time can match or supersede the love God has for you. No one you know can love you more than God does, no matter how close the relationship. You can't even love yourself more than God loves you. How amazing is that? Drink it in. Soak it up. It's available for you. Take time today to receive love from God, then go and share that love with others.

Affirmation Prayer: Heavenly Father, I have experienced true love upon accepting You. The joy and satisfaction of Your love for me is truly the greatest love of all. Help me to always celebrate that, in the name of Jesus, Amen.

Daily Bread: Leviticus 27; Luke 1:1-25; Proverbs 7:1-8

How Deep Is Your Love?
March 13

Scripture: "Oh, the depth of the riches both of the wisdom and knowledge of God! How unsearchable are His judgments and His ways past finding out!"
~ Romans 11:33

Spiritual Vitamin

When it comes to God, "How Deep Is Your Love"? God has proven how deep His love is for you by giving you His Son. He's gone to lengths greater than you can imagine. *Have you personally acknowledged what He's done?* He has planned your whole life from start to finish and has taken care of every single detail. You will never experience a day that God has not already seen and planned for. Your worst moment has already been taken into account and dealt with. All He's waiting for now is for you to submit to His will for your life, so that He can open the windows of heaven and pour His blessings and His wisdom upon you. God has proven how deep His love is for you. The question is, *how deep is your love for Him? What are you willing to sacrifice for the cause of Christ?* There should be nothing in your life that is more important than your relationship with God. If there is, it's time to rearrange your priorities. Take time today to show the depth of your love for Christ through your thoughts, words and deeds.

Affirmation Prayer: Heavenly Father, I am aware that I can't stoop too low for You to pick me up. I can't get too high that You can't reach me. While my sins are ever before me, Your love for me is so amazing. Thank you for it, in the name of Jesus, Amen.

Daily Bread: Numbers 1 – 2; Luke 1:26- 38; Psalm 33:12-22

I'm Sorry
March 14

Scripture: "And be kind to one another, tenderhearted, forgiving one another, even as God in Christ forgave you."
~ Ephesians 4:32

Spiritual Vitamin

Are you sorry for your sins? Every person alive owes God an apology because man is born into sin. Because of this, there is something we must do to change the natural course of our lives. *What is that?* It is to take the necessary steps to receive Jesus Christ as Savior and to surrender to His lordship. *Have you taken these steps?* It was not the sin of Jesus Christ that took His life. It was the sin of mankind that led Him to the cross. Jesus was perfect in every way and knew no sin, yet because of God's great love for man, Jesus decided to take man's sin upon Himself. Since your sins were forgiven by a sinless Savior, surely you can find it within your own heart to forgive those who have transgressed and offended you. Have you apologized to God and accepted the gift of salvation, freely offered to you by Jesus? You have not yet begun to live if you are still outside of the will of God. He has so many wonderful things to give you, but you must yield to His way. If you already have, great! If not, consider asking God for His forgiveness for your sins. Take time today to examine your current relationships and to say "I'm sorry" to those whom you may have offended.

Affirmation Prayer: Heavenly Father, I read in Your Word that I could ask anything in Your name and You would answer. I am sorry for my sins, please forgive me, in the name of Jesus, Amen.

Daily Bread: Numbers 3; Luke 1:39-56; Psalm 34:1-10

If I Could Turn Back Time
March 15

Scripture: "Brethren, I do not count myself to have apprehended; but one thing I do, forgetting those things which are behind and reaching forward to those things which are ahead, I press toward the goal for the prize of the upward call of God in Christ Jesus."
~ Philippians 3:13-14

Spiritual Vitamin

Is there something in your life that you wish you could do over? What was it about that particular time that made you so happy? God is a redeemer of time. If you are longing to go back to a particular place in time because you want to choose differently than you originally did, know that God's grace had already created a space for any mistakes you've made. Not only does God redeem time, but He can also restore anything of value that you believe you have lost as a result of a poor decision. God's supernatural ability supersedes the abilities of man. You don't have to try to turn back the hands of time because your time is in God's hands. Don't waste the time you have left by being upset or worrying over the time you think you've lost. Make the most of the present moment and those yet to come. God can use you at every stage of your life. It is not too late to bring your gifts and talents for Kingdom use. Take time today to link up with a local church body and begin to work out your soul's salvation.

Affirmation Prayer: Heavenly Father, I have had some good days and some hardships. However, upon accepting You as Lord and Savior, I have not turned back and I never want to. Keep me from living in regret over things that have happened in my past. Thank You for leading me in the path of righteousness, in the name of Jesus, Amen.

Daily Bread: Numbers 4 - 5; Luke 1: 57-80; Psalm 34:11-22

Life Keeps Moving On
March 16

Scripture: "Not that I have already attained, or am already perfected; but I press on, that I may lay hold of that for which Christ Jesus has laid hold of me."
~ Philippians 3:12

Spiritual Vitamin

Do you ever wish you had more time? There are only 24 hours in a day. No matter what happens during the course of your days and nights, life continues on. It has been said that time waits for no one. The one thing in life that you can be certain of is change. You will have ups and downs as you journey through your time on earth. Trials and tribulations are sure to happen in everyone's life and they can make you stronger if you look to Jesus. He has promised to be there to help you through the ups and downs of life. Even when things are not going as you wish, keep pressing forward and moving ahead, knowing that God is walking beside you. God will never go back on His promise to take care of you. If He looks after the sparrow, surely He will provide for you. No matter how bad today may seem to be, there's always tomorrow. Activate your faith and begin to believe that God is working behind the scenes to make things better for you. He will work everything out. Just have faith. Take time today to give God praise and thanks that no matter what happens in life, He will always be there for you.

Affirmation Prayer: Heavenly Father, each day from our birth, we bloom in preparation for the grave. Life never stops for me and I am so grateful that You never stop providing for me. Help me to never abandon my purpose, in the name of Jesus, Amen.

Daily Bread: Numbers 6; Luke 2:1-20; Proverbs 7:6-20

Lovin' You (Is Easy Cuz You're Beautiful)
March 17

Scripture: "In this is love, not that we loved God, but that He loved us and sent His Son to be the propitiation for our sins."
~ 1 John 4:10

Spiritual Vitamin

When you accept Christ, people will be drawn to you because His light and love will flow through you. As people look upon you, they will be able to see Him in you. The old, unlovable you will no longer be seen. Only the version of you that shows the personhood of Christ and His attributes. You were once unlovely and undesirable. But because of the love of God through Jesus Christ, you are now easy to love. Now, others are drawn to you because of the warmth of your spirit. You cannot take credit for this. The credit belongs to God alone. Your personality once repelled others. Now, it draws others to you and to God. No matter how good or how bad you were, God decided to love you. He didn't need your permission or approval. His decision was made before you were even born. *Now that you know this, aren't you grateful for what He's done?* Take time today to express your appreciation to God for all the ways in which He shows His love toward you.

Affirmation Prayer: Heavenly Father, I have experienced love on different levels, but after loving You, I have reached my plateau. Teach me how to love You. Help me to always remain true to You, in the name of Jesus, Amen.

Daily Bread: Numbers 7; Luke 2:21-40; Psalm 35:1-10

My Love Is Your Love
March 18

Scripture: "In this the love of God was manifested toward us, that God has sent His only begotten Son into the world, that we might live through Him."
~ 1 John 4:9

Spiritual Vitamin

God has a special gift for you. *Do you want it?* It's a gift you can only get from Him. It's priceless and rare. It is not for sale and cannot be bought for any price. *What is this precious gift you ask?* It is His love. God is offering His love to you, with no strings attached. His love for you is so deep that it prompted Him to pursue you, even when you turned your back on Him and chose another road instead. Time can't separate you from God and there is no place you can go where His love cannot reach you. He is waiting to hear your cry. Many times, it takes a crisis or some type of painful situation to cause you to cry out for God's love. This doesn't have to be the case. You can experience God's love at any time of the day or night, at any point in your life. Even eternity can't break up your relationship with God because in His Presence is where He wants you to be. *Are you living in the safety of the love of God?* His love is for you. Take time today to accept it, live in it and allow it to change your life.

Affirmation Prayer: Heavenly Father, I know I really can't live my life without You. You are the center of my joy and nothing can ever separate our love. Thank You for never letting me go. Teach me how to live in Your love, in the name of Jesus, Amen.

Daily Bread: Numbers 8; Luke 2:41-52; Psalm 35:11-18

Oh Happy Day
March 19

Scripture: "This is the day the Lord has made; we will rejoice and be glad in it."
~ Psalm 118:24

Spiritual Vitamin

When was the happiest day of your life? Was it the day you received a promotion at work? Maybe the day you became a parent or the day you got married? Or was it the day you received salvation? At some point in your life, the day you receive salvation will without a doubt become the happiest day of your life. This will not occur until you realize the full meaning of what Jesus did for you when He died on the cross for your sins. Jesus was absolutely sinless and did nothing wrong, especially nothing worthy of death. Yet, He agreed to take on the punishment that would have been yours to bear because of the sins you have committed. Jesus willingly agreed to take your place in death. The mistakes and wrong-doings of mankind cost Jesus His life. All He asks in return is for you to agree to be willing to live your life for Him. In exchange for what He's done for you, that is not too much to ask. Take time today to rise to the occasion and commit your ways to God. Your happiest days are on the way.

Affirmation Prayer: Heavenly Father, I have enjoyed good, fun times in my life. I have enjoyed many happy days. There has been laughter and smiles. However, the happiest day was when I accepted Jesus as Lord and Savior of my life. Teach me how to serve You so that You are pleased, in the name of Jesus, Amen.

Daily Bread: Numbers 9 – 10; Luke 3:1-22; Psalm 35:19-28

For the Love of You
March 20

Scripture: "And we have known and believed the love God has for us. God is love, and he who abides in love abides in God, and God in him."
~ 1 John 4:16

Spiritual Vitamin

Humanity should desire to live for the love of God. *Whose love do you desire? Is it your spouse, your child, your parent? What is it about that person's love that gives you feelings of wonder and excitement?* God's love so far surpasses the love of another human being that it is almost difficult to even comprehend. The depth of His love is unexplainable. As Christians, we should be living for the love of God; willingly and excitedly participating in church programs and ministry activities, serving our fellow man and demonstrating our love for God in ways that others can see. Although one cannot really explain the depth of the love of God, the fact of it was proven and demonstrated in the death of Christ upon the cross. *After all, who else do you know who would willingly give up their life for yours? That being said, are you living for the love of God?* Take time today to examine whose love means the most to you. If your answer is anyone other than God, consider a change of heart and mind.

Affirmation Prayer: Heavenly Father, You have assured me of Your true love for me by the finished work of Jesus on the cross. I am thankful for You and the love we share, in the name of Jesus, Amen.

Daily Bread: Numbers 11 – 13; Luke 3:23-38; Luke 4:1-13; Proverbs 7:21-27

Selwyn B. Cox

Power of Love
March 21

Scripture: "A new commandment I give to you, that you love one another; as I have loved you, that you also love one another."
~ 1 John 13:34

Spiritual Vitamin

Did you know that love has the power to heal? God's Word says that love covers a multitude of sins and nothing can outweigh the power of love. To prove this point, the power of God's love caused Him to call for the life of His only Son. This is why the enemy fights so hard against successful relationships because he knows that if he can keep you at odds with others, you will remain stuck in a rut. But if you would only realize the power of love and forgiveness, you will be set free. You will no longer live under the curses of anger, bitterness and unforgiveness. You will be able to bask in the light of God's love for you which will in turn give you the desire to share His love with those around you. There is power in the love of God and if you accept His love, it will equip you to love others. Everyone will be the better for what you are learning and experiencing. Love has power and can transform the hardest heart. No one can resist the power of true love because it's the very thing the heart craves most. Take time today to reflect on the ways in which God has shown you the power of love.

Affirmation Prayer: Heavenly Father, Your umbrella of love has helped me to recover from the storms in my life. It was always open to keep me from drowning. You have an awesome power to love and I thank You for it. Teach me to love that way, in the name of Jesus, Amen.

Daily Bread: Numbers 14; Luke 4:14-37; Psalm 36:1-12

Real Love
March 22

Scripture: "For God so loved the world that He gave His only begotten Son, that whoever believes in Him should not perish but have everlasting life."
~ John 3:16

Spiritual Vitamin

Have you been hurt by someone who told you they loved you but failed to show that love in tangible ways? Once they hurt you, they caused you to doubt the power of love. God's love is not like man's love. Everything authentic has a counterfeit substitute. So it is with love. Love is an action word. Love is not something you say, it's something you do. The enemy has taken the purity of God's love and attempted to twist and distort it, somehow trying to turn it into something of lesser value than originally intended. If you allow God's love to rest in your heart and if you take the time to experience it for yourself, you will learn that it will never disappoint. Once you receive God's love, the void that was once inside you will disappear, along with the need for anything less than what you are worth. Spend time in the Presence of God so that He can show you genuine love and then teach you how to share it with others. Take time today to show everyone around you how it feels to know real love.

Affirmation Prayer: Heavenly Father, some things are real and some are imitations. Coca Cola uses the slogan "it's the real thing!" When speaking of You, I use those same words. They are referring to their product; I am referring to Your love. What a difference! Your love is truly the real thing. Help me to taste and see that You are good, in the name of Jesus, Amen.

Daily Bread: Numbers 15 – 16; Luke 4:38-44; Luke 5:1-16; Psalm 37:1-9

Send For Me
March 23

Scripture: "Behold, I send an Angel before you to keep you in the way and to bring you into the place which I have prepared."
~ Exodus 23:20

Spiritual Vitamin

Have you made the necessary arrangements to enter the Kingdom of God? You must be intentional about this process. Everyone has an appointed amount of time to live in the earthly realm. Once that time has expired, a transition occurs. When God gets ready, He's going to send for you and have you come to live with Him. Some of those who will inhabit the Kingdom of God have already departed; others still remain. Whether through physical death or in the rapture, those who belong to God will go to live eternally with Him. One day, God is going to send for you. *The question is, will you be ready to go?* You must make a decision to follow the plan of God and take the steps He laid out for your salvation to take effect. It is necessary for you to get prepared and ready, for when God calls, you will have no choice but to answer. *What will your answer be?* Take time today to ensure that you've made adequate preparations for the time when God sends for you.

Affirmation Prayer: Heavenly Father, prepare me for the time of my departure so that I am ready when you send for me, in the name of Jesus, Amen.

Daily Bread: Numbers 17 – 18; Luke 5:17-32; Psalm 37:10-20

I'll Still Love You More
March 24

Scripture: So when they had eaten breakfast, Jesus said to Simon Peter, "Simon, son of Jonah, do you love Me more than these?"
~ John 21:15a

Spiritual Vitamin

How do you measure love? What standard defines the level of love you are willing to share with others? God's love is immeasurable and no matter how much you think you love Him, He still loves you more! God has gone to great lengths to demonstrate His love to you. For starters, He gave His only Son, Jesus, to die for your sins. If that were not enough, He has made provision to care for and love you for the entire duration of your life. Many people measure love through deeds. *If that were the only measure to use, how well would you measure up?* If you feel there is a shortfall, here is a chance for you to do more for those around you. Please don't think that you need to earn God's love because you don't. But God has work for you to do to assist Him in the up-building of His Kingdom here on earth. At the altar is where you may experience an inpouring of the love of God. As you spend time in the sanctuary, your burdens will be lifted and you will be relieved of the cares of this world. Then, once your life on earth is through, His love is waiting to carry you into eternity with Him. His great love runs deep and you won't find a deeper love for you in any heart other than God's. In reality, you can't live one day without Him and all of your thoughts should be about Him. Take time today to consider and appreciate the great love of God, the One who loves you more!

Affirmation Prayer: Heavenly Father, there's nothing that can keep me from loving You. No matter what comes into my life, attempting to steal my devotion from You, I'll still love you more than anything else. Please let nothing come between us, in the name of Jesus, Amen.

Daily Bread: Numbers 19 – 20; Luke 5:33-39; Luke 6:1-11; Proverbs 8:1-11

Imagine (The World Will Be As One)
March 25

Scripture: "Now to him who is able to do immeasurably more than all we ask or imagine, according to His power that is at work in us."
~ Ephesians 3:20

Spiritual Vitamin

Can you imagine yourself free? Free from struggle, free from trouble, worry and stress? If you have accepted the saving work of Christ on the cross, then you have been made free. *Are you living within that reality?* Proverbs 23:7 says "For as he thinks in his heart, so is he." *So, how are you thinking? What are you thinking about? Are you experiencing thoughts of victory or thoughts of defeat?* If you are a born-again Christian, you must begin to think like Christ. Allow your thoughts to be pure, positive and productive because you were created in the image of God. There is no weakness in God. Focus and concentrate on His power within you, His purpose concerning you and His promises to you. This way, you will never be allowed to remain in a state of discouragement, disappointment and/or defeat. Not only can you imagine yourself as free, you can actually walk in that freedom and live the life you were created to live. Take time today to imagine all the possibilities of becoming all that God created you to be.

Affirmation Prayer: Heavenly Father, thank You for setting me free. With You by my side, I am on the winning team. I cannot lose for I am more than a conqueror. Teach me that because of You, I am the head and not the tail, above and not beneath, in the name of Jesus, Amen.

Daily Bread: Numbers 21 – 22; Luke 6:12-36; Psalm 37:21-31

Time (Clock of the Heart)
March 26

Scripture: "I must work the works of Him who sent Me while it is day; the night is coming when no one can work."
~ John 9:4

Spiritual Vitamin

As the end of the month draws near, I want to encourage you to continue working out your soul's salvation, focusing on forgiveness and the gift of eternal life. Each person has a set time to be born and a set time to die. God has seen every day of your life from beginning to end. He alone knows what's going to happen over the course of your time here on earth. Time is God's gift to mankind. God is ageless and He existed before time began. There is time allotted in this life to do everything God intends for you to do. There's even a time to accept Christ as your Lord and Savior. God has given man free will to decide how he will spend his time. *How will you use your time? Will you be a wise steward over the days, weeks and months that God gives you or will you squander them away as if there is no end in sight?* You are not too young or too old to surrender to God. He has made provision to receive you at your point of surrender. Since God is a redeemer of time, it will never be too late for you to decide to do the right things. Take time today to evaluate your relationship with "time". *Are you spending time or wasting it?*

Affirmation Prayer: Heavenly Father, I realize that time can be used as a trick of the enemy. He comes to rob me of my life but Lord, You have already numbered my days. I am not on satan's time clock but on Yours. I shall live and not die a second before You have preordained. Help me to spend time rather than waste it, in the name of Jesus, Amen.

Daily Bread: Numbers 22 – 23; Luke 6:37-49; Luke 7:1-10; Psalm 37:32-40

Like Paradise
> March 27

Scripture: And Jesus said to him, "Assuredly, I say to you, today you will be with Me in Paradise."
~ Luke 23:43

Spiritual Vitamin

What is your idea of paradise? Is it blue water, white sand and palm trees? Or is it being in the very Presence of God? Jesus offers you a chance at paradise. *Will you accept His offer?* There are certain things you must do in order to partake in the blessing of spending eternity in paradise with your Creator. You must first accept Jesus as your Lord and Savior and then turn your back on the sinful ways of this world. *Do you want to share your life with God?* You don't have to wander aimlessly through life, suffering and questioning the point of your existence. Just surrender to the plan of God for your life. Jeremiah 29:11 says "For I know the plans I have for you says the Lord, plans to prosper you and not to harm you, plans to give you hope and a future." Once you decide to live within the will of God, when it's time to transition from time into eternity, Jesus will allow you too, to be with Him in paradise. Take time today to accept the provisions He's made and to secure your eternal place in paradise.

Affirmation Prayer: Heavenly Father, when I think of being in a state of bliss and felicity, I delight myself in knowing that You have promised me eternal life. Experiencing Your love for me is like paradise. Help me live a life that is worthy of Your provision, in the name of Jesus, Amen.

Daily Bread: Numbers 24 – 25; Luke 7:11-35; Psalm 38:1-11

We Will, We Will Rock You
March 28

Scripture: "Then Jesus said to him, "Away with you, Satan! For it is written, You shall worship the Lord your God, and Him only you shall serve."
~ Matthew 4:10

Spiritual Vitamin

Do you acknowledge Christ's victory over sin and death? With the death, burial and resurrection of Jesus Christ, God gave humanity the victory over sin, death and the grave. The enemy thought he had stopped God's plan when Jesus died; little did he know that it was all a part of the plan of God to raise Jesus from the dead. With the resurrection of Christ, God obtained victory over satan. This however, did not stop satan's desire to have you. Jesus' resurrection rocked the plan of the enemy. Now, there's a war going on and as a born-again believer in Jesus Christ, you are on the front line. You must decide whose side you're going to be on. There are only two forces in the world, good and evil. *Will you do what is right and stand on the Lord's side? Will you fight for your rights as a Kingdom citizen? Or will you allow the enemy to be victorious with his evil tactics?* You have the power to win but you must decide to use it. Don't sit idly by and let the enemy win. Fight for the victory that is already yours. Take time today to stand, with the Lord on your side, against the fiery darts of the evil one.

Affirmation Prayer: Heavenly Father, I am comforted in knowing that You are my rock and my protection. Help me to stand strong in the face of adversity, knowing that You are with me, in the name of Jesus, Amen.

Daily Bread: Numbers 26 – 27; Luke 7:36-50; Proverbs 8:12-21

Who Will Save Your Soul?
March 29

Scripture: "that if you confess with your mouth the Lord Jesus and believe in your heart that God has raised Him from the dead, you will be saved."
~ Romans 10:9

Spiritual Vitamin

Have you confessed Jesus as your Lord? There is only One who can save your soul; He is the Lord Jesus Christ. He is the Son of Almighty God. Every human being must make a decision regarding the final resting place for his soul. Your body is destined to return to the ground while your soul is destined to return to God. Flesh will die, spirit will live forever. Salvation is a requirement needed to enter the heavenly realm. The method of salvation is discussed in the book of Romans. God says that you must confess Jesus as well as believe in Him, that God has raised Him from the dead. Once you do that, you will be saved. It is so comforting to know that you have an opportunity to spend eternity with God. *Are you willing to take advantage of such an awesome gift?* When you repent and turn away from sin, you are forgiven by a faithful and loving God. You are released from the penalty of what you've done wrong. Jesus took your sins to the cross and they were covered by His blood. Take time today to offer your thanks to God, for giving Jesus as your Savior.

Affirmation Prayer: Heavenly Father, I have learned my ABC's. I've **admitted** that I am a sinner, **believed** that Jesus is my Savior and **confessed** my need for Him. I have hidden Your Word in my heart that I may not sin against You. Thank You for saving my soul, in the name of Jesus, Amen.

Daily Bread: Numbers 28 – 29; Luke 8:1-18; Psalm 38:12-22

Why Can't We Be Friends?
March 30

Scripture: "A man who has friends must himself be friendly, but there is a friend who sticks closer than a brother."
~ Proverbs 18:24

Spiritual Vitamin

Is there someone in your life you used to be friends with but are no more? What happened to sever the relationship? Regardless of who was at fault, can you extend forgiveness and possibly restore the relationship? Even if restoration is not possible, forgiveness is still necessary. In most cases, pride keeps you from doing what you know you should -- forgive. You replay the situation in your mind over and over, in an attempt to become justified in your anger. Love is meant to be everlasting. If you once loved someone, but don't love them anymore, examine what it was that caused your love to grow cold. God's love will never grow cold. He will never allow you to be out of His reach unless you do not accept His Son as your Savior. If there is someone in your life who has hurt you, consider applying God's grace to the situation and allowing everyone involved to benefit from His mercy. Take time today to evaluate who needs your forgiveness and freely offer it to them.

Affirmation Prayer: Heavenly Father, You are a friend that sticks closer than a brother, sister, mother or father. I thank You for being my best friend forever (BFF). Help me to display an attitude of sincerity so as to draw others unto You, in the name of Jesus, Amen.

Daily Bread: Numbers 30 – 31; Luke 8:19-39; Psalm 39:1-13

Bridge Over Troubled Water
March 31

Scripture: "Greater love has no one than this, than to lay down one's life for his friends."
~ John 15:13

Spiritual Vitamin

Have you needed a friend lately? Life will not always be easy. Sometimes, you will need the help of someone who is stronger and wiser than you. God has offered this kind of help to you. God is your bridge over troubled water. Sin caused a separation between God and mankind and you needed a way back to God. He provided that way through the gift of His Son, Jesus. He laid down His life to be that bridge to carry you back home. It is clear that God knew what man would do before he actually did and made provisions in light of that knowledge. Jesus freely laid down His life so you would never have to know what it feels like to try to live without the comfort, care and protection of God. He became your bridge. Because of what Christ did, God calls you His friend. Take time today to consider being a bridge for someone else as Jesus has been for you.

Affirmation Prayer: Heavenly Father, I'm crossing the bridge accepting forgiveness. I must admit, sometimes I row in circles. I haven't attached my boat to Your tow line. I haven't trusted You enough. Help me! Protect me from the enemy within, in the name of Jesus, Amen.

Daily Bread: Numbers 32; Luke 8:40-56; Luke 9:1-9; Psalm 40:1-8

MONTHLY REFLECTIONS

April: Sanctuary (Attendance and Altar Call)

Strength for the Journey

Heavenly Father,

You have commanded those who worship You and who desire to do Your will to assemble in Your sanctuary. I desire Your Word and I will hide it in my heart. Please let Your Holy Ghost fire burn more and more in me each time I attend the sanctuary and respond to the altar call. Empower me to obey Your command to assemble in public worship to hear Your Word. Please assure me that my current place of worship is where You have preordained me to be. Make me willing to share my gifts and talents, and work with other like-minded believers. Don't allow me to be consumed by anything that would attempt to pull my focus from Your Word. My desire is to assemble in a place where I can laugh, cry, confess, repent, praise and worship in spirit and in truth. Let it be so, in the name of Jesus, Amen.

April

Sanctuary (Attendance and Altar Call)

During the month of April, you will go on a journey, learning about the importance of church attendance and altar call. God has extended an invitation for you to come into His sanctuary. A sanctuary is defined as a place of refuge or safety. In the sanctuary, you are protected and you are safe. One of the benefits in the sanctuary is the altar call experience. Altar call is a time set aside for you to disconnect from the world and present yourself to God in prayer and thanksgiving. During this time, you will be given the chance to pray for yourself, expressing to God the deepest longings of your soul, with your own mouth, from your own heart. Even if you think you don't have adequate words to express your innermost needs, you don't have to worry; God is a reader of the heart. Altar call is a very personal experience, a time for you and God alone. The glory of His Presence will be felt as you offer Him the very essence of who you are. There is nothing hidden or withheld. It is my prayer that you will use this month's devotionals to gain a greater understanding of the need for you to accept God's invitation into His house and to the altar. So now, let's get ready to go into the sanctuary.

Quote: "Church attendance is as vital to a disciple as a transfusion of rich, healthy blood to a sick man." --- Dwight L. Moody

> "And I also say to you that you are Peter, and on this rock I will build my church, and the gates of Hades shall not prevail against it."
> ~ Matthew 16:18

A Joy To Have Your Love
April 1

Scripture: "May the God of hope fill you with all joy and peace in believing, that you may abound in hope by the power of the Holy Spirit."
~ Romans 15:13

Spiritual Vitamin

April Fool's Day – SMILE! *Does it give you joy to have the love of God?* If so, then you look forward to gathering with other believers each week for a time of fellowship and worship. During this experience, you look forward to being energized by their presence as they are energized by yours. You freely share your spiritual gifts with them and they do the same. People who are not a part of your fellowship should feel warmed, welcomed and drawn into the atmosphere of love. This is especially important for those who have been hurt from past church experiences. As you learn more of God's Word, you can follow the prescription given in the book of James, where it says "count it all joy my brothers, when you meet trials of various kinds". Feelings of loneliness and low self-esteem become a thing of the past because you have joined yourself to a body of like-minded believers who assist in keeping you grounded in the things of God. You have a deeply rooted sense of joy and peace that cannot be tampered with because of your strong faith and loving connection to God and those whom He has placed in your life. If you haven't already, take time today to link up with a strong, Bible-based Christian family who can aid you in your walk with God.

Affirmation Prayer: Heavenly Father, Your Word says I am fearfully and wonderfully made. My happiness, peace and joy come from You. The joy of the Lord is my strength. Help me to celebrate Your love for me, in the name of Jesus, Amen.

Daily Bread: Numbers 33 – 34; Luke 9:10-27; Proverbs 8:22-31

All of Me
April 2

Scripture: "And you shall love the Lord your God with all your heart, with all your soul, with all your mind, and with all your strength. This is the first commandment."
~ Mark 12:30

Spiritual Vitamin

Has your intimacy, desire and affection for something or someone surprisingly crept up and overtaken the place of God? Perhaps you didn't see it coming. It could be the love for your automobile, your home, your darling child or grandchild or your spouse or significant other. *In honest reflection, who has all of you?* Today's devotional speaks of the ideal relationship between a man and a woman and confesses an undying love between the two, imperfections and all. A perfect relationship with God requires total surrender on your part. God sent His one and only Son, Jesus to die for the sins of the world, so that He could bridge us back to God. Because of the sin in the Garden of Eden, man's perfect fellowship with God was broken. But, because of the Blood of Jesus, the relationship has been restored and our imperfections forgiven. Be willing to take advantage of all that God is offering you, through the gift of His Son. Once you do this, you will be able to extend this God-kind of love to your fellow man. Give your all to God; after all, He gave His all for you! If you are not an active member of a local church, make a commitment to become one. If you already attend church on a regular basis, find a way to increase your level of service. Take time today to surrender all to your heavenly Father and be willing to meet him regularly in the sanctuary.

Affirmation Prayer: Father God, I surrender everything I am to Your complete control and Lordship. Take my imperfect will and replace it with Your perfect will for my life. Thank You for Your forgiveness. Help me to continue to live in it, in the name of Jesus, Amen.

Daily Bread: Numbers 35; Numbers 36:1-13; Luke 9:28-56; Psalm 40:9-17

Somebody Told Me To Deliver This Message
April 3

Scripture: "For since, in the wisdom of God, the world through wisdom did not know God it pleased God through the foolishness of the message preached to save those who believe."
~ 1 Corinthians 1:21

Spiritual Vitamin

Have you read the "good news" lately? If so, do you believe what you've read? God's Word is His message to you. Everything He wants you to know about Him, as well as yourself, is written in His Word. Romans 10:14 says "How then shall they call on Him in whom they have not believed? And how shall they believe in Him of whom they have not heard? And how shall they hear without a preacher?"

When God's Word is preached, it becomes clearer to you that God has a message for you. The preacher is the one to whom God has delivered the message and it is his or her responsibility to share that message with you. Once the message has been shared, you are responsible for what you have heard. Not only are you responsible for hearing it, you become responsible for doing what it says and for sharing it with others. The Word is not just for you alone, but for everyone around you. When you hear good news, you should be willing to share it with someone else. Take time today to go into the sanctuary to hear the message of God. There is something life-changing in it, just for you.

Affirmation Prayer: Heavenly Father, give me the desire to regularly go into the sanctuary to hear Your Word and give me the strength to do what it says, in the name of Jesus, Amen.

Daily Bread: Deuteronomy 1; Deuteronomy 2:1-23; Luke 9:57-62; Luke 10:1-24; Psalm 41:1-6

At Midnight (My Love Will Lift You Up)
April 4

Scripture: "But at midnight Paul and Silas were praying and singing hymns to God, and the prisoners were listening to them."
~ Acts 16:25

Spiritual Vitamin

Been to the altar lately? Altar call doesn't have to be at church only. You can have your own personal altar call whenever and wherever you choose. Paul and Silas held an altar call in jail. As they sang and prayed to God, those around them heard. As they listened, their hearts were touched and this act of worship and praise prompted a change within them. *Have you allowed the Spirit of God to do the same within you?* In your darkest hour, God is closest to you. You will not be able to see Him with the natural eye. You must use your faith. Faith will allow your spiritual eyes to view the situation from a better perspective. If you do this, you will be able to see the hand of God moving on your behalf. God does not leave you when you are in trouble. It is in these times that He draws nearer and is waiting for you to cry out to Him. Take time today to pray and sing praises to God. The results will be nothing short of amazing!

Affirmation Prayer: Heavenly Father, You are my Alpha and Omega. Let me not be ashamed to give You glory; let praise be what I do, anytime, anywhere and any place, in the name of Jesus, Amen.

Daily Bread: Deuteronomy 2:24-37; Deuteronomy 3; Deuteronomy 4:1-14; Luke 10:25-42; Luke 11:1-4; Psalm 41:7-13

Easy Like Sunday Morning
April 5

Scripture: "And let us consider one another in order to stir up love and good works, not forsaking the assembling of ourselves together, as is the manner of some, but exhorting one another, and so much the more as you see the Day approaching."
~ Hebrews 10:24-25

Spiritual Vitamin

What is preventing you from committing to regular church attendance? God issues an invitation each Sunday. *Have you responded to it?* It seems easy to commit to everything else; things like family, friends, jobs, significant others, etc. Yet for some reason, we find it hard to commit to the One who makes it possible for us to enjoy all these things. Going to church should be easy, "Easy Like Sunday Morning." Once there, you can cast your cares on Jesus and leave them at the altar. God has a ministry for you to do for the up-building of His kingdom on earth. He has dealt with every blockage that could hinder your attendance. God allows you to have six days a week to do whatever you want to do. He desires that you come to His house at least one day a week to hear His Word, to worship with like-minded believers and to be an example for your family, your neighbors and the world to see. A man will go to the place where what he loves is housed. If he loves drugs, he will go to the crack house. If he loves liquor, he will go to the liquor store. If he loves pool, he will go to the pool hall. Similarly, if he loves God, he will go to God's house. Take time today to accept God's invitation, go into His house and demonstrate your love for Him.

Affirmation Prayer: Heavenly Father, I heard Your voice, inviting me to come and lay down my cares. I accept the invitation. Help me release every worry to You, in the name of Jesus, Amen.

Daily Bread: Deuteronomy 4:15-49; Deuteronomy 5; Luke 11:5-32; Proverbs 3:32-35

Come and Talk to Me
    April 6

Scripture: My heart has heard you say, "Come and talk with me." And my heart responds, "Lord, I am coming."
~ Psalm 27:8 NLT

Spiritual Vitamin

God is calling all mankind. *Have you heard the call? If so, did you answer?* God longs to spend time talking with you. He delights in you and the personal moments that the two of you share. He craves intimate fellowship with you, His "amazing miracle" and desires for you to familiarize yourself with His Word on a daily basis. He wants you to become a doer, not just a hearer only. You are God's creation. *Have you developed an appreciation for how He made and fashioned you? Who do you talk to the most?* God wants an even deeper connection with you than the one to whom you are the closest. Your connection and relationship with God is meant to transcend the walls of the church building. You can take God everywhere you go. There is no limit to the access you have been granted to Him. You will never have to walk alone. Take time today to carve out specific opportunities to be alone with God and to allow Him to speak to your soul.

Affirmation Prayer: Heavenly Father, in this world of advanced technology, I am often busy listening and responding to messages. Today, help me to be still and hear Your voice and respond to You, in the name of Jesus, Amen.

Daily Bread: Deuteronomy 6 – 8; Luke 11:33-54; Psalm 42:1-6

I Believe
> April 7

Scripture: As soon as Jesus heard the word that was spoken, He said to the ruler of the synagogue, "Do not be afraid; only believe."
~ Mark 5:36

Spiritual Vitamin

Are you having problems believing what God has said? When you pray, you must believe that God will answer. You need to apply some faith to the situation. God is not like man and He doesn't lie. What He says, He means. *Has God ever let you down before?* Belief and faith go hand in hand. *Where is your faith in God?* Fear is the enemy of faith, and you must give no place to fear. God has the power to work out every situation you are facing. But in order for Him to do so, you must activate your faith and believe in what He has said; only then can He do what He's promised. It doesn't matter what a situation looks like. If you only believe, God will cause things to work out in your favor. Take time today to replace doubt with faith and become determined that you won't stop believing in the will of God for your life.

Affirmation Prayer: Heavenly Father, I know that faith requires work. It is an action word. Give me the faith to believe in You without fear, in the name of Jesus, Amen.

Daily Bread: Deuteronomy 9 – 10; Luke 12:1-34; Psalm 42:7-11

Endless Love
April 8

Scripture: "Within your temple, O God, we meditate on your unfailing love."
~ Psalm 48:9 NIV

Spiritual Vitamin

Do you know that God's love is endless? Yes, God's love will last forever. You mean more than the world to God and once you begin a relationship with Him, His love will carry you from this world into eternity. There is no limit to the depth of His love; it will never wear out and He will never contemplate leaving you. When you are unfaithful (because at some point in time, you will be), His love is endless. When your behavior is less than lovely, His love is endless. When you harbor grudges and bitter feelings of unforgiveness, His love is endless. When you are just being you, His love is endless. Even when you make decisions that are outside of His will for your life, still His love is endless. There is nothing you have done to earn His love and nothing you can do to deserve it. In Isaiah 49:16, God says, "I have inscribed you on the palms of My hands...." His love is a direct result of His own decision. In order to experience God's endless love at its best, you must connect with a local body of believers. When you join in worship with them, you can learn your purpose and utilize your God-given gifts. Take time today to celebrate that love, God's endless love.

Affirmation Prayer: Heavenly Father, when I think about Your love, I think about a river so long, I can't see the end. I think about the sky that is everywhere I go. I think about the stars I cannot count. Make me grateful that Your love for me is endless, in the name of Jesus, Amen.

Daily Bread: Deuteronomy 11 – 12; Luke 12:35-59; Psalm 43:1-5

Signed, Sealed, Delivered
April 9

Scripture: "It's in Christ that you, once you heard the truth and believed it (this message of your salvation), found yourself home free — signed, sealed, and delivered by the Holy Spirit."
~ Ephesians 1:13 MSG

Spiritual Vitamin

Palm Sunday commemorates the joyful and exuberant entry of Christ into Jerusalem. The crowd was in a celebratory mood that day and it was clear that Jesus had many people who were in support of Him. During His triumphal entry, Jesus was accepted, exalted and honored. The atmosphere on this particular day was no indication of what was about to take place. Just a few days later, Jesus would be crucified. Those celebrating Him had no idea how drastically things would turn for the worse, but Christ knew. Jesus knew He would be celebrated then crucified; yet He still came. He fulfilled the terms of His contract on your behalf. Jesus signed, sealed and delivered you out of the hands of the enemy. You will have moments like this in your life. There will be days when you will be accepted, exalted and honored. There will also be days when you will feel like you're being crucified. Take heart and keep trusting God. He will never allow anything to overtake or defeat you. Take time today to welcome Jesus into your life and celebrate all He's done to secure your future with God.

Affirmation Prayer: Heavenly Father, thank You for sending Jesus into my life. Teach me how to live in a way that brings You glory, not shame, in the name of Jesus, Amen.

Daily Bread: Deuteronomy 13 — 14; Luke 13:1-30; Proverbs 9:1-12

I Can't Live, If Living Is Without You
April 10

Scripture: But He answered and said, "It is written, Man shall not live by bread alone, but by every word that proceeds from the mouth of God."
~ Matthew 4:4

Spiritual Vitamin

Today is National Siblings Day. Remember to honor your brothers and sisters with a call or kind gesture to celebrate the occasion.

Have you been trying to live without God? If so, then you know that this is a very difficult task. As a matter of fact, trying to live without God is not living at all; it's merely existing. There is a marked difference between the two. Living means taking full advantage of all that this life has to offer. Without God, it's not possible to take full advantage of all the possibilities. If God's Word is not a part of your daily existence, then you are not filled to capacity. Physical food only feeds the body. You also need nourishment for your soul. Imagine a life without God; no hope, no peace. Check your spiritual pulse. *Are you actively involved in the life of the modern-day church?* In John 14:6, Jesus said, "I am the way, the truth and the life. No man comes to the Father except through me." As described by Jesus, now that's living! Take time today to feast upon the Word of God and begin to live as He intended.

Affirmation Prayer: Heavenly Father, I can live without a lot of things and carry on without much but I can't live without You at the center of my life. I realize that there is no me without You. I ask that You continue to hold me in Your loving arms that I might have hope with every breath I take, in the name of Jesus, Amen.

Daily Bread: Deuteronomy 15; Deuteronomy 16:1-22; Luke 13:31-35; Luke 14:1-14; Psalm 44:1-12

I Just Had to Hear Your Voice
April 11

Scripture: "My sheep hear My voice, and I know them, and they follow Me."
~ John 10:27

Spiritual Vitamin

Can you hear the voice of God? If you have taken the time to nurture a relationship with your Heavenly Father, then you know His voice. His voice is very distinctive and doesn't sound like anyone else's voice you know. *Can you last a long time without hearing the voice of God?* The lyrics of the song say "one night without you is too much for my heart". *Do you feel that way too?* You should crave and desire to hear God speaking to you; leading and guiding you along life's path. You don't have to promise not to call God; in the end, you really don't have a choice. In Romans 14:11, it says "every knee shall bow and every tongue shall confess that Jesus Christ is Lord." God loves it when you have a longing to hear His voice. Take time today to attune your ears to the voice of God and allow Him to speak to your soul and spirit.

Affirmation Prayer: Heavenly Father, I long to feel Your touch and to hear Your voice. Speak Lord, for Your servant is listening, in the name of Jesus, Amen.

Daily Bread: Deuteronomy 17 – 18; Luke 14:15-35; Psalm 44:13-26

If I Didn't Have You
April 12

Scripture: "I am the vine, you are the branches. He who abides in Me, and I in him, bears much fruit; for without Me you can do nothing."
~ John 15:5

Spiritual Vitamin

How would you describe your relationship with God? Are you as close to Him as He desires for you to be? Only you can answer this question and if you're honest with yourself, you can admit there is always room for improvement. God alone is the key to your very existence. Everything you are, everything you have, everything you will become is because of Him. Every accomplishment you have ever or will ever achieve is because of the enabling power of God. The truth is, you can't even breathe without Him! *Is God in your life in a meaningful and fulfilling way? If not, do you want Him to be?* If your answer is yes, simply take advantage of the altar call that has been extended and accept Jesus Christ into your life. His Presence will make all the difference in the world. Sometime this world will seem to give more than you can take. It is then that you must realize the miraculous power of God. He can handle what you cannot. Take time today to express your heart to God. He's waiting to hear from you.

Affirmation Prayer: Heavenly Father, I will not keep You waiting to hear from me. I realize that if I didn't have you, I would be nothing. Make me willing to give You the praise that is due You each and every day, in the name of Jesus, Amen.

Daily Bread: Deuteronomy 19 – 20; Luke 15:1-32; Psalm 45:1-9

I Don't Deserve Your Love
April 13

Scripture: Then He came to Simon Peter. And Peter said to him, "Lord, are You washing my feet?" Jesus answered and said to him, "What I am doing you do not understand now, but you will know after this."
~ John 13:6-7

Spiritual Vitamin

Maundy Thursday is a commemoration of the Last Supper when Jesus shared the Passover meal with His disciples and washed their feet on the night before He was crucified. Despite the fact that Jesus was about to be betrayed, He was still able to keep His mind on the mission. At the supper, Peter felt as though Jesus should not wash his feet. He told Jesus that he would not permit it. But Jesus said that if He did not wash Peter's feet, that Peter would have no part with Him. Peter felt unworthy, as if he didn't deserve Christ's love. Sometimes we feel the same way. Yet Jesus exercised mercy. Mercy is defined as compassion or forgiveness shown toward someone whom it is within one's power to punish or harm. Jesus knew what awaited Him and He also knew the role that each person in His life would play. Armed with this reality, He still provided for and ministered to His disciples. This is a clear example of how we are to treat those with whom there is adversity. God calls us to love and pray for our enemies. There is never justification for vengeance. Take time today to show mercy to someone who may be guilty of treating you unkindly, thus following the example of Christ.

Affirmation Prayer: Heavenly Father, thank You for the love of Your Son, Jesus. Thank You for enabling Him to think of me when He could have chosen to save Himself. Help me to never forget His sacrifice for me, in the name of Jesus, Amen.

Daily Bread: Deuteronomy 21 – 22; Luke 16:1-18; Proverbs 9:13-18

The Adventure
April 14

Scripture: "You will show me the path of life; in Your presence is fullness of joy; at Your right hand are pleasures forevermore."
~ Psalm 16:11

Spiritual Vitamin

Good Friday, also known as "Holy Friday" is the Friday immediately preceding Easter Sunday. It is celebrated traditionally as the day on which Jesus was crucified. What happened to Jesus on this day was anything but good. This is the day He was crucified for proclaiming equality with God. What He said was the truth but because those to whom He said it were spiritually blind, they could not recognize what He said as truth. This act by Christ paved the way for you to receive salvation from God. Now, you can live a saved and promise-filled life.

Living a saved life is an adventure. There are surprises at every turn. You will experience good days and bad days but in the end, it will all work out in your favor. When you think in terms of an adventure, it can make you think of going on a journey. Your relationship with God can be just that; a journey. A journey from the known into the unknown. A journey from the uncomfortable into the comfortable. You belong to God and He longs to be the captain of your ship. God causes us to triumph. According to 2 Corinthians 2:14, "Now thanks be to God who always leads us in triumph in Christ, and through us diffuses the fragrance of His knowledge in every place." Adventure is exciting and fun. Living a saved and holy life can be the same. A relationship with God doesn't have to be a solemn, sullen and serious situation that drains all the life out of you. It can be exactly the opposite -- an exciting, exhilarating and uplifting experience that gives you great joy. Take time today to prepare for the adventure and settle in for the ride of your life!

Affirmation Prayer: Heavenly Father, show me the path of life You have designed for me. You are my only help and hope. Please help me find joy in Your presence, in the name of Jesus, Amen.

Daily Bread: Deuteronomy 23 – 25; Luke 16:19-31; Luke 17:1-10; Psalm 45:10-17

It's My House
April 15

Scripture: "And He said to them, "It is written, My house shall be called a house of prayer.""
~ Matthew 21:13a

Spiritual Vitamin

When was the last time you visited the house of God? The church, also known as God's house, is the place where He rules, Jesus reigns and the Holy Spirit resides. When you are in close fellowship with someone, at some point in time, you will visit their house. While there, you will experience fellowship and a refreshing and often a meal will be served. God's house is no different. When visiting, He will fellowship with you and allow you to experience times of refreshing. If you come at the right time, you may even get to partake of the Lord's Supper. The sanctuary is a holy place. A place designed for you to experience the Presence of God and the infilling of His Holy Spirit. The church is a place of beauty, peace and serenity, where you can lay everything at the feet of Jesus. Entering into the sanctuary should be viewed as a privilege not an obligation and should be treated with reverence and respect. The church is God's house and you are invited to come as often as you can. The doors of every church stand on welcome hinges. It's God's house and He is always home. He wants you to come over. Take time today to plan your next visit. God is waiting with open arms. Like Joshua (24:15) determine to declare, as for me and my house, we will serve the Lord.

Affirmation Prayer: Heavenly Father, I have anointed my house with oil, established my prayer room and the enemy is not welcome. Help me to always honor You as the head of my house, in the name of Jesus, Amen.

Daily Bread: Deuteronomy 26 – 27; Luke 17:11-37; Psalm 46:1-11

Rise Up
April 16

Scripture: "Arise, shine; For your light has come! And the glory of the Lord is risen upon you."
~ Isaiah 60:1

Spiritual Vitamin

Easter, also known by Christians as Resurrection Sunday, is the most important and oldest festival of the Christian Church. Easter is the celebration of the resurrection of Jesus Christ. What Jesus did for you on this day makes it possible for you to live a victorious, joyful and peace-filled life. Jesus faced what initially looked like the ultimate defeat, which was death. But because of the power of Almighty God, He rose from the dead. The ignorance of man killed Jesus. The omnipotence and omniscience of God brought Him back to life. Because Jesus rose, you too can rise out of the situations of life. Rise up, out of hurt and pain. Rise up, out of guilt and shame. Rise up, out of depression and despair. The enemy's plan for your life does not have to succeed, but you play a role in securing your victory. Even the bad times have been accounted for within the plan of God. There is nothing that can happen to you of which God is not already aware. Even the greatest misfortune is covered by the blood of Jesus. Jesus could not be defeated by death; neither can you, because death is simply the doorway to eternal life. While you are yet alive in your physical body, decide that you will not be hindered by the enemy. Rise up and declare that your victory is on the way! Take time today to honor God for sending Jesus Christ to pay the ultimate price for you. Let your life be a display of gratitude and a witness that will draw others to Christ.

Affirmation Prayer: Heavenly Father, thank You for Your resurrection power. With You as my guide. I am destined to reach my heavenly goals. Thank You for sending Jesus to die for my sins and to rise again, to provide eternal life for me, in the name of Jesus, Amen.

Daily Bread: Deuteronomy 28; Luke 18:1-30; Psalm 47:1-9

Lean On Me
April 17

Scripture: "Trust in the Lord with all your heart and lean not on your own understanding, in all your ways acknowledge Him and He shall direct your path."
~ Proverbs 3:5-6

Spiritual Vitamin

Who are you leaning on for help? God offers Himself to you to help you along life's journey. If you're not careful, it is easy to depend on your natural inclinations or begin to believe in your own wisdom and/or the wisdom of others rather than that of God. When situations and circumstances occur, it is tempting to try and figure out what you should do on your own, without the involvement of God. This is not wise and scripture warns against it. God has given you the option to lean on and to cast your cares on Him. Although it is the best thing for you to do, please understand that the choice is yours. *Why not take advantage of such an awesome privilege?* You no longer have to carry the heavy burden because in Matthew 11:30, Jesus said "for my yoke is easy and my burden is light". In times of uncertainty and doubt, lean on Jesus and He will carry you through. Take time today to lean on God and take Him up on His promise to care for you.

Affirmation Prayer: Heavenly Father, when I was experiencing crisis and hardship, I didn't always see You, but when I looked back, I saw Your footprints which carried me through. Help me to understand that the only way I made it over was by leaning and depending on You, in the name of Jesus, Amen.

Daily Bread: Deuteronomy 29 - 30; Luke 18:31-43; Luke 19:1-10; Proverbs 10:1-10

Run To You
April 18

Scripture: "The name of the Lord is a strong tower; the righteous run to it and are safe."
~ Proverbs 18:10

Spiritual Vitamin

Are you trying to do everything by yourself? God wants you to run to Him; for everything. He is interested in every intricate detail of your life and every decision you will ever have to make. He doesn't want you to leave Him out of anything. Nothing is too small or insignificant. You no longer have to fear coning into His Presence. This is not something you have to ask of Him. His earnest desire is to have you run to Him and when you do, be sure that He will never run away. He's waiting to have an "altar call experience" with you. Like David, you too can say "I run to you, God, I run for dear life. Don't let me down" (Psalm 31:1 MSG). You do not have to "get yourself together" first. God offers to do that for you. His outstretched arms are continuously available to you and He waits for you to come. You are safe in the arms of God and there is no better place to be. Take time today to run into the loving embrace of your Heavenly Father. Sit a while, meditate on His Word and rest in His Presence. You will be glad you did.

Affirmation Prayer: Heavenly Father, I am in the race of my life. You are my strong tower. Teach me to run to You for every need, in the name of Jesus, Amen.

Daily Bread: Deuteronomy 31; Luke 19:11-44; Psalm 48:1-8

Solid as a Rock
April 19

Scripture: "Truly my soul silently waits for God; From Him comes my salvation. He only is my rock and my salvation; He is my defense; I shall not be greatly moved."
~ Psalm 62:1-2

Spiritual Vitamin

The definition of solid is firm and stable in shape. God's love for you is like that, firm and stable; solid as a rock. It contains no emptiness; no spaces, no voids. For the sake of His love, God has given you forgiveness for every sin you have or will commit. Each mistake has been covered by the blood of Jesus. When you sinned, God, through Christ, forgave. By this point in your life, you should be learning how to trust God. You should no longer be trying to run away from His love. You have no time for games or indecision. For all that God has done for you, you should have a desire to begin building up your love for Him. He is waiting for you in the sanctuary. As previously stated, God's love for you is solid as a rock. *How is your love for Him?* You must develop a dependence on Him that keeps you going back into His Presence. Allow nothing to come between you and Him and stand on His Word, as in Matthew 7:24, which says "Therefore whoever hears these sayings of Mine, and does them, I will liken him to a wise man who built his house on the rock." Take time today to measure your love for God. Work on it, so that it becomes solid as a rock.

Affirmation Prayer: Heavenly Father, Your love for me is solid as a rock. Help me to place my trust, faith and hope in You, so that I shall not be moved, in the name of Jesus, Amen.

Daily Bread: Deuteronomy 32; Luke 19:45-48; Luke 20:1-26; Psalm 48:9-14

Sure Thing
April 20

Scripture: "God affirms us, makes us a sure thing in Christ Jesus. Putting His yes within us."
~ 2 Corinthians 1:21 MSG

Spiritual Vitamin

What are you sure of? In life, things regularly change but your relationship with God is a sure thing. It is not something to be taken lightly or toyed with. It is not dependent on any circumstance or condition outside of yourself. The validity and value of it has been sealed by God Himself. All you have to do is actively participate and remain willing to hold up your end of the bargain. One of the ways you do that is to participate in church activities and with regular church attendance. God created you for an exact purpose at this particular place in time. He made an investment in you, trusting that His investment will produce a return. All humanity will stray away from God. When you return to Him, He is able to change your course and set you on the path that was originally intended. Things in your life begin to line up with His will and you begin to mature in the ways of God. Take time today to evaluate where you are in this process. Surrendering your life to Christ is not a gamble, it's a sure thing. Something you'll never regret.

Affirmation Prayer: Heavenly Father, Your Word tells me of Your displeasure in my being lukewarm. I must make the decision to be hot or cold. Help me be confident that my relationship with You is a sure thing, in the name of Jesus, Amen.

Daily Bread: Deuteronomy 33 – 34; Luke 20:27-47; Luke 21:1-4; Psalm 49:1-20

That's the Way My Love Is
April 21

Scripture: "No man shall be able to stand before you all the days of your life; as I was with Moses, so I will be with you. I will not leave you or forsake you."
~ Joshua 1:5

Spiritual Vitamin

Are you in a relationship that makes you feel safe and protected? In the words of Saint Augustine, God sees each of us as if there were only one of us. Included within the love of God is His protection. He takes great care to see after the details of your life, leaving nothing out — that's the way His love is. Nothing will come into your life that has not passed through the filter of God's watchful eye. Anything that makes it into your life has been pre-screened by God. He knows what you're made of and what you are able to withstand. He will never give you a weight you cannot bear. When adversity comes into your life, seek the face of God so that He can tell you what to do. He's already planned a way of escape for your good. 1 Corinthians 10:13 says, "No temptation has overtaken you except such as is common to man; but God *is* faithful, who will not allow you to be tempted beyond what you are able, but with the temptation will also make the way of escape, that you may be able to bear *it.*" You can call on God because He's always there for you. Take time today to consider the depth of God's love for you and worship and praise Him.

Affirmation Prayer: Heavenly Father, no matter what I have done, You have loved me in spite of myself. You are my true lover. Teach me to recognize the depth of Your love and give you praise, in the name of Jesus, Amen.

Daily Bread: Joshua 1 — 2; Luke 21:5-38; Proverbs 10:11-20

This Will Be
    April 22

Scripture: The Lord has appeared of old to me, saying: "Yes, I have loved you with an everlasting love; therefore with lovingkindness I have drawn you."
~ Jeremiah 31:3

Spiritual Vitamin

Who can love you forever? There is only one relationship that can take you from time into eternity. That is your relationship with God. Your earthly experience can only carry you so far and only God knows how much time you have to be here. Nothing from the earthly realm can pass into the eternal realm, except your soul. This is where the sanctuary comes into the picture. The sanctuary is where you learn how to make your connection to God your first priority. It begins at the altar, as you take your first step toward accepting God and making Jesus the Lord of your life; after which you regularly return to receive much-needed guidance from the Word of God. His love will be an everlasting love and nothing will ever be better or able to take its place. Allow God to wrap you in His love and assure you that you never have to walk alone. Take time today to bask in the light of God's love for you. For certainly, this will be an everlasting love.

Affirmation Prayer: Heavenly Father, I have moved from relationship to kinship with You. I know this is an everlasting love. Let Your love embrace me and warm my heart, in the name of Jesus, Amen.

Daily Bread: Joshua 3 – 4; Joshua 5:1-12; Luke 22:1-38; Psalm 50:1-15

Be Intentional
    April 23

Scripture: "Having made known to us the mystery of His will, according to His kind intention which He purposed in Him."
~ Ephesians 1:9 NASB

Spiritual Vitamin

As the end of the month draws near, I want to encourage you to be intentional about your presence in the sanctuary of God, through attendance and altar call. The word intentional means "done on purpose". This is how your relationship with God and His Word should be; done on purpose. Things should not be left to chance or haphazardly expected to occur. God is precise and deliberate concerning you and your life. For this reason, you should be precise and deliberate concerning your connection to Him and your obedience to His Word. It takes effort on your part to develop and maintain a committed and growing relationship with God. *Are you willing to put in the work?* Jesus really is the best thing that can ever happen to you but if you've never had an encounter with Him, then you don't know that yet. *Do you want Jesus enough to run after Him?* You have relentlessly pursued things that have far less value and benefit. *Why not decide to pursue something you know is worth far more?* Be intentional about your relationship with God and your salvation. Take time today to gauge where Kingdom business stands on your priority list and consider making it number one.

Affirmation Prayer: Heavenly Father, thank You for being intentional in the way You care for me. No matter where I go, You are with me, even till the end of the world. Teach me to be intentional about my service to You, in the name of Jesus, Amen.

Daily Bread: Joshua 5:13-15; Joshua 6 – 7; Luke 22:39-62; Psalm 50:16-23

Up Where We Belong
April 24

Scripture: "The Spirit lifted me up and brought me into the inner court; and behold, the glory of the Lord filled the Temple."
~ Ezekiel 43:5

Spiritual Vitamin

Do you know where you belong? You belong *to* God and you belong *with* God. The sanctuary is your home base and you need to stay close to home. As you grow in your knowledge of God, you are promoted and God takes you higher in Him. During this process, you learn more and more about God and become more like Jesus. He gives you opportunities to exercise your faith and trust in Him. As you do, you are entrusted with more and more spiritual responsibility. God is taking care of everything for you but you must believe that in order for it to benefit you. Don't spend your life in the valley of despair and discouragement.

Allow God's love to lift you; to lift you up where you belong. Take a step in the right direction and decide that you are through with low living, doubt and despair. Decide to live a life of hope and faith. Take time today to allow the Spirit of God to speak peace into every area of your life, so you can reach new heights in Him.

Affirmation Prayer: Heavenly Father, you have lifted me up, where I belong. Help me to remember that I will never walk alone, in the name of Jesus, Amen.

Daily Bread: Joshua 8; Joshua 9:1-15; Luke 22:63-71; Luke 23:1-25; Psalm 51:1-9

When I Found You (I Found Love)
April 25

Scripture: "And you will seek Me and find Me, when you search for me with all your heart."
~ Jeremiah 29:13

Spiritual Vitamin

Is God real to you? God promises to allow Himself to be found by you. By no means is God lost. When speaking of finding Him, I refer more to the discovery of your need for His Presence in your life. Because of sin, man was separated from God. Now, he must search for God with all his heart. You must be purposeful and deliberate about discovering your connection to and your relationship with God. Be determined to carve out time to spend with Him. Read and meditate on His Word. It is necessary to immerse yourself in His wisdom and take full advantage of the knowledge that He shares with you. God will equip you to serve Him by helping others. You will possess a spirit so kind and loving, that it will attract others and allow you to witness to them of His goodness to you. When you discover God, you will find love. Take time today to chase after God. Run into His Presence and let Him fill you with Himself through the power of His Holy Spirit.

Affirmation Prayer: Heavenly Father, I have come to realize that You were never lost, I was. You allowed me to discover You and You saved my soul. Teach me to celebrate Your Presence in my life, in the name of Jesus, Amen.

Daily Bread: Joshua 9:16-27; Joshua 10; Luke 23:26-56; Proverbs 10

You Are My Friend
April 26

Scripture: "No longer do I call you servants, for a servant does not know what his master is doing; but I have called you friend, for all things that I have heard from My Father, I have made known to you."
~ John 15:15

Spiritual Vitamin

Do you have a lot of friends? As the songwriter, Joseph M. Scriven, wrote "what a friend we have in Jesus. All our sins and griefs to bear, what a privilege it is to carry, everything to God in prayer". Jesus is the best friend you will ever have. In order to benefit from this fact, you must develop a personal relationship with Him. Often, we spend more time developing relationships with human beings rather than seeking God in a meaningful way. *Humanly speaking, who is your best friend?* Sadly, some people don't discover the power of having Jesus as their best friend until something happens to sever or damage the relationship they have with their earthly best friend. Then, they go to Jesus and suddenly realize that He was there all the time. Don't let this be your story. Go to Jesus now. Don't waste precious time without the realization and benefit of having Him as your friend. Take time today to rearrange your priorities and make Jesus your closest and dearest friend.

Affirmation Prayer: Heavenly Father, thank You for being, not just my friend, but my best friend. Help me to remember that no one else can love me like You, in the name of Jesus, Amen.

Daily Bread: Joshua 11 – 12; Luke 24:1-35; Psalm 51:10-19

You Are On My Mind
April 27

Scripture: "You will keep him in perfect peace, whose mind is stayed on you, because he trusts in You."
~ Isaiah 26:3

Spiritual Vitamin

What's on your mind? You are on God's mind. *What consumes your thoughts? Is your mind pure or does it constantly entertain thoughts of vengeance and evil?* The Bible says that you can think like Christ. *Do you want this kind of mind?* Jesus maintained a pure thought life. He kept His mind on what God wanted at all times. You can do this as well, but you need the supernatural help of God's Holy Spirit to help keep your mind. As a human being, your natural inclination is toward evil and you need the Holy Spirit to help keep your mind focused and trained on Godly things. Don't leave your thought life to chance. Don't entertain impure thoughts or anything ungodly that tries to enter your mind. Take control of your thoughts and keep them pure. Take time today to focus on God, the importance of the sanctuary and your participation in the altar call. Let God guide your thoughts toward Him and what He has in store for you.

Affirmation Prayer: Heavenly Father, I am Yours; all that I am and all I am not. Teach me to always think of You and to be mindful of my attitudes and behavior at all times, in the name of Jesus, Amen.

Daily Bread: Joshua 13 – 14; Luke 24:36-53; Psalm 52:1-9

You Bring Me Joy
April 28

Scripture: "You will show me the path of life; In Your presence is fullness of joy; at Your right hand are pleasures forevermore."
~ Psalm 16:11

Spiritual Vitamin

What brings you joy? Is it a person or perhaps a possession? Is it an accomplishment? Joy is defined as a feeling of great pleasure and happiness. Temporal things are only able to produce a temporary sense of satisfaction, which should never be confused with joy. When you have the type of joy that God gives, you have strength. Nehemiah 8:10 says in part "Do not sorrow, for the joy of the Lord is your strength". I would venture to say that if you have little joy then you also have little strength. *Would you agree? Do you need to have an external circumstance to take place in order for you to have joy or do you have it within you?* There is an old devotional song that says "this joy I have, the world didn't give it and the world can't take it away". *Can you identify?* Some people confuse joy with happiness, when in fact the two are quite different. Happiness requires an event or circumstance to produce its benefits. Joy needs nothing external to take place in order for it to exist. It comes from an understanding and assurance of the surety of the Word of God. Take time today to ponder on the blessings of God in your life and allow them to bring you joy, then give joy to others.

Affirmation Prayer: Heavenly Father, no matter what I am going through, when I think of Your goodness, You bring me joy. Teach me to appreciate Your blessings, in the name of Jesus, Amen.

Daily Bread: Joshua 15 – 16; John 1:1-28; Psalm 53

You Give Good Love
April 29

Scripture: "If you sinful people know how to give good gifts to your children, how much more will your Heavenly Father give to those who ask of Him."
~ Matthew 7:11

Spiritual Vitamin

What criteria are you using to determine whether someone's love is good or bad? Love is a gift from God and originates in the heart. God is the source of love. People sometimes equate love with the material things they receive from others. This should not be the case. Love is often taken for granted and misunderstood. The relationship that best brings love out of human beings is that between a parent and their child. This is the best example of love that the human mind can comprehend. Yet, still God's love is GREATER. God's love is the only love that will never hurt you. Human beings are flawed and not capable of perfect love. This is why forgiveness is needed. God will never require your forgiveness but you will always require His. The good news is He will always give it, no matter what you have done; and that, my dear friend is "good love". Take time today to express your gratitude to God for His good love.

Affirmation Prayer: Heavenly Father, I have been in some bad relationships but since I have given my heart to You, You have given me good love. Teach me how to love You more, in the name of Jesus, Amen.

Daily Bread: Joshua 17 – 18; John 1:29-51; Proverbs 11:1-8

Your Love Keeps Lifting Me Higher
April 30

Scripture: "And I, when I am lifted up from the earth, I will draw all people to myself."
~ John 12:32

Spiritual Vitamin

Who are you lifting — your husband, your wife, your Pastor? God is faithful and full of love and mercy. He deserves to be exalted and lifted up by His creation. It is Jesus who is exalted and God who should be praised. *Are you fulfilling your privilege of praising God for how He is blessing your life?* Jesus says that if you will lift him up, He will draw all men unto Himself. *Will anybody lift up Christ?* It is not too much to ask. There is someone in all of our lives we like to brag on. Most often, this is someone we believe has the power to do things for us. Sometimes, our motives may be selfish in doing this and it could be just so that we can get something from the person upon whom we brag. But God does not need you to brag on Him for Him to bless you. Now, don't get me wrong, He loves praise but that is not His motive for blessing your life. He blesses you because He chooses to do so; because He loves you just that much. Blessings fall down like rain on the just and the unjust. But if you are willing to surrender your life to Christ, then His love will lift you higher. Take time today to allow the love of God to take you to a higher place; one where you have never been lifted before.

Affirmation Prayer: Heavenly Father, Your love lifts me higher. Help me to be faithful in lifting You higher because You are worthy of my praise, in the name of Jesus, Amen.

Daily Bread: Joshua 19 — 20; John 2:1-25; Psalm 54:1-7

Selwyn B. Cox

MONTHLY REFLECTIONS

May: Support (Creating Stable Relationships Among Family and Friends)

Strength for the Journey

Heavenly Father,

How excellent is Your name in all the earth. You have made each one of us individually and no one else can fit my mold. I did not choose the family of which I am a part, but was strategically placed by You, according to Your purposes. Help me to provide support to my loved ones, thereby creating stable relationships among my family and friends. You created each of us for a purpose --- to worship and praise You as well as to love and support one another. I will let my light shine among my family and friends. Please let the work I do bring glory to Your name. Guide me into true forgiveness for myself and others. Allow me to pull down every demonic stronghold, such as jealousy, envy, strife, gossiping, lying and anything else that is not pleasing in Your sight. I will spread the love You have given me to everyone I encounter. The power of Your love will be a cure for those who believe no one cares about them, a comfort for those who are lonely and healing for those who are hurting. As I follow You, please help me to create and maintain healthy, fulfilling relationships, in the name of Jesus, Amen.

May

Support (Creating Stable Relationships Among Family and Friends)

Up to this point, the monthly themes have been geared toward your growth as an individual person and your own relationship with God. Now, it's time to include others. During the month of May, you will learn about support and creating stable relationships among your family and friends. We will examine how to receive support from God and then discuss the process of sharing support with our loved ones. Support is defined as "giving assistance to; enabling to function or act." If we are honest, we can admit that the family relationship is generally the one that is the most challenged in today's society. Within the family unit, there can be dysfunction on many levels, but with the help of a loving God, there is always hope. Christ said He has overcome the world, and with Him in our lives, we have power to do the same.

Within the family structure, you must learn to take your rightful place. If you are a husband and father, then you are the priest of your home. If you are a wife and mother, then you are the rib and helpmeet of your husband. If you are single, then Christ should be the Priest of your home.

Your family should be your support unit. They should provide you with a sense of comfort and peace. Your circle of family and friends provides a safety net wherein you can find the celebratory hug and pat on the back when you achieve something you've been working toward or the shoulder you need to cry on when things don't go quite the way you planned. The proper kind of support gives you that extra layer of confidence that it is okay to step out and try new things. This is something we all need.

Not only should you receive support from family and friends, you should be prepared to lend it to them as well. Just as you want your family and friends to be there for you, commit and follow through in being there for them. Some of you may not feel that you have the support you need within your family unit, so you are challenged in this area. There may be many voids in your life that you don't know how to fill. No matter what people have failed to do for you, know that God is able to fill every empty space within your being with the power of His Presence. Before you can give or receive support in the proper way, you must be emotionally healthy and whole. Seek the help of God first and if needed, those who have been medically trained in the field of mental health and wellness for assistance in this regard. I must stress that if this is something you need, it is perfectly fine to do so.

In the end, when dealing with family members and friends, forgiveness is the order of the day. Everyone, allow me to repeat, "EVERYONE" has been hurt by someone during the course of their lives. We all have depended on other human beings to fill voids when we should have been depending on God. Truth be told, the people we depended on were most likely not even capable of meeting that particular need. It is my prayer that you will use this month's devotionals to celebrate healthy and spiritually nourishing relationships that contribute to your natural and emotional well-being.

"This is My commandment, that you love one another as I have loved you. Greater love has no one than this, than to lay down one's life for his friends."
~ John 15:12-13

What About the Children
May 1

Scripture: "Fathers, do not provoke your children to anger, but bring them up in the discipline and instruction of the Lord."
~ Ephesians 6:4 ESV

Spiritual Vitamin

Are you active in the lives of your children? Do you know where your children are and what they are doing? God wants you to pour into your children. He wants you to mentor them, even if you did not have anyone to pour into and mentor you. Teach your children what you know. Tell them right from wrong and show them how to live a Godly life. Your children are your future. You begin by taking care of them but in the end, they will be responsible for taking care of you. If you have been good to them, if you have loved and nurtured them and done your very best to provide for their needs, they should have no problem returning the favor. They will be willing to support you in whatever way they can. Even if you don't have children of your own, you can decide to take a child under your wing through mentoring programs, volunteer efforts or maybe even adoption. Take time today to invest in the lives of God's gift to mankind – the gift of children.

Affirmation Prayer: Heavenly Father, help me to sow into a child's life that he/she may become an adult disciple for you. Teach me that this is part of my reasonable service, in the name of Jesus, Amen.

Daily Bread: Joshua 21 – 22; John 3:1-21; Psalm 55:1-11

Ain't Nothin' Like the Real Thing
May 2

Scripture: "And they were astonished at His teaching, for He taught them as one having authority, and not as the scribes."
~ Mark 1:22

Spiritual Vitamin

Jesus is the real thing. There is no one who qualifies as His equal or who can be used as a substitute. There are many things in our world that can be used in place of other things. For instance, people who cannot eat salt can use a salt substitute. For people who cannot eat sugar, there are sugar substitutes. But in terms of His personhood, identity and authority, there is no substitute for Jesus. He is the real thing and there "ain't nothin' like the real thing!" Jesus has never had an identity crisis. He has always been confident in who He was created to be, which is why He is able to guide you through these types of crisis moments. But you must go to Him in order to receive His help. Jesus wants to teach you how to love. His very essence is love. 1 John 4:7-9 says "Beloved, let us love one another, for love is of God; and everyone who loves is born of God and knows God. He who does not love does not know God, for God is love. In this, the love of God was manifested toward us, that God has sent His only begotten Son into the world that we might live through Him." Take time today to get connected to the real thing -- God's only Son, the Lord Jesus Christ!

Affirmation Prayer: Heavenly Father, You have proven to me that Your Son is the real thing. He has fulfilled every promise in Your Word. Teach me how to be a shining example of Your goodness and faithfulness to me, in the name of Jesus, Amen.

Daily Bread: Joshua 23 – 24; John 3:22-36; Psalm 55:12-23

As Days Go By
	May 3

Scripture: "Be kindly affectionate to one another with brotherly love, in honor giving preference to one another."
~ Romans 12:10

Spiritual Vitamin

Your Bible, which is God's Word, contains a tremendous amount of good news. *Have you read it lately?* The best way to receive the support you need is to go first to your Heavenly Father. He will feed your spirit, which will then aid in the feeding of your body and soul. Once you do this, you will be equipped to help others. As days go by, allow God to fill your spiritual house as well as your physical house with peace and joy. This will not only benefit you, but the rest of your family too. According to Romans 12, you are to be "kindly affectionate in brotherly love". *After all God has done for you, is this too much to ask?* God will help you and when He does, He expects you to help someone else. *Will you rise to the challenge?* You are blessed to become a blessing and it really is more blessed to give than to receive. Take time today to seek ways in which you can honor and bless the life of someone else.

Affirmation Prayer: Heavenly Father, thank You for feeding my spirit and filling my spiritual house with joy. As days go by, empower me to become a continuous blessing to others, in the name of Jesus, Amen.

Daily Bread: Judges 1; John 4:1-26; Proverbs 11:9-18

Say A Little Prayer
May 4

Scripture: "Call upon Me in the day of trouble; I will deliver you, and you shall glorify Me."
~ Psalm 50:15

Spiritual Vitamin

The National Day of Prayer is defined as a solemn request for help or expression of thanks addressed to God. It is an honor and a privilege to be able to be heard by God. God has power beyond human comprehension and He made everything that exists. Yet, He takes the time to listen to your voice when you call out to Him. Every morning, when you awaken, you should say a prayer. Several times throughout the day, you should say a prayer. Prayer is not just for bad times; it is also necessary when things are going well. Prayer is also a great way to provide support to your family members and friends. Prayer is not to be taken lightly because it accomplishes great and mighty things. It is a priceless gift that can be shared by everyone. Take time today to exercise the privilege of prayer. Pray for yourself and others. God is listening and He still answers prayer.

Affirmation Prayer: Heavenly Father, thank You for the privilege of talking to You directly, one on one. I am grateful that I don't have to go to anyone else to pass messages between us. Thank You for the opportunity You have provided to me through prayer. Help me to always appreciate the fact that You are delighted to hear my voice when I cry out to You, in the name of Jesus, Amen.

Daily Bread: Judges 2 – 3; John 4:27-42; Psalm 56

Come Together (Right Now)
May 5

Scripture: "Two are better than one, because they have a good reward for their labor."
~ Ecclesiastes 4: 9-12

Spiritual Vitamin

Why is it so hard for humans to stick together? God desires for us to come together and put aside our differences. *Why do we find it so difficult to help one another?* God has enough blessings to go around and there is never a need for you to be jealous or envious of your fellow man. It has been said that what you make happen for others, God makes happen for you. *Can you use this as inspiration to become determined to help someone else reach their goals?* In the words of a quote from Dr. Martin Luther King Jr., "Life's most persistent and urgent question is, 'what are you doing for others?'" You can only feel good about helping others achieve their goals if you are confident and secure in your own relationship with God. Being confident and secure in who God created you to be will free you. Freedom is a must. You need it in every aspect of your life. You need emotional freedom, spiritual freedom, physical freedom and mental freedom. You must have all four, because if not, there will be an imbalance in some area of your life. *Is there someone you can link up with and accomplish something for the Kingdom of God?* God will always send you someone to help. Take time today to come together with fellow ministry partners for the purpose of Kingdom building.

Affirmation Prayer: Heavenly Father, I am my brother's keeper. Teach me how to let brotherly love continue, inside and outside my immediate family circle, in the name of Jesus, Amen.

Daily Bread: Judges 4 – 5; John 4: 43-54; John 5:1-15; Psalm 57:1-6

Ordinary People
May 6

Scripture: "When they saw the courage of Peter and John and realized that they were unschooled, ordinary men, they were astonished and they took note that these men had been with Jesus."
~ Acts 4:13 NIV

Spiritual Vitamin

God can use you right now, just as you are. *Isn't this exciting news?* There are no specific qualifications needed to be used by God. All you need is a willingness to surrender to His will for your life. As you yield to God more and more, you will ultimately become the person He created you to be. Then you will be more eager to provide help and support to others. Once you surrender to the Lordship of Jesus Christ, you will be conformed into His image and you will not remain the same as you were when you came to Him. Everything you will ever do wrong was taken to the cross with Christ and has been covered by His blood. You are no longer under the penalty of sin, so there is no excuse not to surrender to God. Once you repent for your sins and turn away from them, you are free to be used for His purposes. You may still have doubts, but please believe me when I tell you that God can use you; little old ordinary you! He just needs you to be a willing vessel. *Will you accept His offer for Kingdom service?* Take time today to step out of ordinary service into extraordinary service for the Kingdom of God.

Affirmation Prayer: Heavenly Father, thank You for loving ordinary people. The world's systems often isolate those who are not of privilege and means. Yet, You accept me, just as I am. Use me for Your glory, in the name of Jesus, Amen.

Daily Bread: Judges 6 – 7; John 5:16-30; Psalm 57:7-11

Everywhere You Look
May 7

Scripture: "Behold, I am with you and will keep you wherever you go, and will bring you back to this land; for I will not leave you until I have done what I have spoken to you."
~ Genesis 28:15

Spiritual Vitamin

Do you sometimes feel alone or abandoned? This title is taken from the theme song of a television show that chronicled the everyday lives of a certain family. No matter what happened, they were always there to help one another. Each family member knew they were never without the love and support they needed. Look around you; God has put people in place to help you. He's created other individuals to become a support system for you. That means you never have to walk alone. *Isn't that a comforting thought?* Sharing the life experiences of others is God's design. He loves fellowship. This is why it's important to attend church on a regular basis. Even if you are feeling isolated and alone, know that this could never be completely true because God is "Everywhere You Look!" Don't let the enemy fool you. You are not alone. Make yourself available to connect with others. When someone experiences a joyous occasion, you should celebrate with them and share their joy. Likewise, when someone experiences a sad occasion, you should bring comfort to them and share their sadness. Do what you can to lighten the load of others. Take time today to walk with someone who may be in need of your support and commit to helping them meet their need.

Affirmation Prayer: Heavenly Father, thank You for providing help for me when I need it. Thank You for being my joy in sadness and my hope for tomorrow. Please send someone today whose spirits I may uplift as You do for me each day, in the name of Jesus, Amen.

Daily Bread: Judges 8; John 5:31-47; Proverbs 11:19-28

I'll Be There
May 8

Scripture: "God is not a man, that He should lie, nor a son of man, that He should repent. Has He said, and will He not do? Or has He spoken, and will He not make it good?"
~ Number 23:19

Spiritual Vitamin

Have you been let down? Someone told you that you could count on them for help and support. You were convinced this was true. You believed it, until the day came when you needed their help. You called on them, but they did not answer. You left a message and never heard back from them. Now, you're not sure what to do or where to turn. It's time to rely on God. He has told you before that He would be there for you and that His love would never fail. *Have you made your pact with God? Have you become a member of His team?* Through the death of His Son on the cross, salvation was brought to mankind. Because of that, you have the right to live eternally with God. Now, it is up to you to share that news with everyone you know, so that they can also make the decision to choose Jesus as their Lord. Take time today to celebrate the fact that God has always been there for you, so that you can be there for someone else.

Affirmation Prayer: Heavenly Father, I've made a conscious decision to make You Lord of my life. When You need a witness, I'll be there. You can count on me to be available to be used by You in whatever way You see fit. Strengthen me to fulfill this commitment, in the name of Jesus, Amen.

Daily Bread: Judges 9; John 6:1-21; Psalm 58

A Family Affair
May 9

Scripture: "Then God blessed them, And God said to them, "Be fruitful and multiply; fill the earth and subdue it; have dominion over the fish of the sea, over the birds of the air, and over every living thing that moves on the earth."
~ Genesis 1:28

Spiritual Vitamin

The Israelites were God's chosen people. Through them, God established order for those who were alive during biblical times, as well as for generations to come. God expected them to pass down the spiritual traditions that were learned from one generation to the next. *What spiritual traditions have you learned?* Those of us alive today are descendants of God's chosen people and we are expected to govern ourselves by the same spiritual disciplines of biblical times. God wants us to pass our spiritual experiences down to our children so that they can repeat the cycle with their children. When we do this, we can ensure that the rich heritage of our Heavenly Father remains alive in the hearts and minds of His people. If we will do this, the blessings and favor we are receiving right now will also be experienced by God's people for years to come. Yes, it is a family affair because God made us family. He longs for us to come together peacefully because this honors Him. Take time today to fulfill your part in establishing a spirit of oneness within your family and passing down the spiritual principles, traditions and lessons that you have learned.

Affirmation Prayer: Heavenly Father, help me to be bold and courageous enough to live before my family, friends and future generations in such a way that they develop a hunger and thirst for You, in the name of Jesus, Amen.

Daily Bread: Judges 10 – 11; John 6:22-59; Psalm 59:1-8

Family Reunion
May 10

Scripture: "Also your descendants shall be as the dust of the earth; you shall spread abroad to the west and the east, to the north and the south; and in you and in your seed all the families of the earth shall be blessed."
~ Genesis 28:14

Spiritual Vitamin

Have you gotten together with your family lately? Some people do not look forward to getting together with their relatives, because of the family dynamic. Sometimes trying to get everyone together is stressful because of unresolved issues associated with anger and unforgiveness. There can also be hard feelings due to family secrets such as issues of rape, incest or abuse. Even in extreme cases like this, God can bring restoration and wholeness through prayer and spiritual counseling. God created our families to live peacefully together. *Do you get along with your family members? When was the last time your family had a reunion?* It is best to get together by choice rather than by force. *What do I mean?* I'm glad you asked! At some point, there will be a gathering; whether it's a reunion or a home-going. For purposes of fellowship, the reunion is a better way to connect. That way, the occasion is joyous because everyone is still alive. God wants to be included in what's going on in your family. He wants to be invited to spend time with you as you spend time with one another. Who knows, maybe it's time for you to plan your own family reunion! If you put God at the center of the family, things will go well when you come together. Take time today to invite God into your family circle and allow Him to help you love everyone despite their shortcomings and faults.

Affirmation Prayer: Heavenly Father, You placed me in the family of Your choosing. Help me to love them as You have loved me, in spite of how I sometimes feel, in the name of Jesus, Amen.

Daily Bread: Judges 12 – 13; John 6:60-71; John 7:1-13; Psalm 59:9-17

Grandma's Hands
May 11

Scripture: "when I call to remembrance the genuine faith that is in you, which dwelt first in your grandmother Lois and your mother Eunice, and I am persuaded is in you also."
~ 2 Timothy 1:5

Spiritual Vitamin

Do you have pleasant memories of your grandma? Did the two of you make memories that you still fondly recall to this very day? Grandparents are a gift from God and the backbone of every family. To have many living generations within a family is something that should be honored and celebrated. As your parents age, it is important to continue to share life's circumstances with them, giving them an opportunity to speak into and positively influence the decisions and choices you will make. This will benefit both sides, in that they continue to feel wanted and needed by you and it gives them a feeling of being connected to what's going on in your life. Back in the day, Grandma was known as "Big Mama". She ruled with an iron fist, but also managed to sprinkle her correction and discipline with love. If you are fortunate enough to still have the joy of your loved one, take some time to visit and hold grandma's hands. If not, take time today to celebrate the memory and contributions of former generations.

Affirmation Prayer: Heavenly Father, thank You for grandparents. I celebrate the blessing of generations within my family and the things I have learned from those who are older and wiser. Help me to always remember to celebrate my heritage, in the name of Jesus, Amen.

Daily Bread: Judges 14 – 15; John 7:14-44; Proverbs 11:29-31; Proverbs 12:1-7

Have I Told You Lately That I Love You?
May 12

Scripture: "I have told you this so that my joy may be in you and that your joy may be complete."
~ John 15:11 NIV

Spiritual Vitamin

Father God, have I told You lately that I love You? This is a good description of a conversation someone might have with God. The words sound somewhat like a prayer. God has done more than we will ever deserve in order to prove His love to us. His power and His great love eases troubles, disappointments and pain. You need to know that God loves you so much that He gave His only Son to die for your sins. That should bring you great joy. His love will never diminish as a result of what you do or don't do. It stems from His own decision to remain with you forever. *Do you tell your family and friends that you love them?* The freedom to speak your love to others will be determined by how well you verbalized these feelings while you were growing up. If you easily told your family and friends that you loved them as a young person, then that habit grew up in you. If not, you may struggle in this area. You may be thinking to yourself that those close to you already know you love them. Although that may be true, it never hurts to tell them. Take time today to express your love for those in your life who have demonstrated their love and concern for you.

Affirmation Prayer: Heavenly Father, thank You for assuring me of Your love. Please let Your joy be in me and let it be complete, in the name of Jesus, Amen.

Daily Bread: Judges 16 – 17; John 7:45-53; John 8:1-12; Psalm 60:1-4

I Believe In You and Me
May 13

Scripture: "I in them and you in me — so that they may be brought to complete unity. Then the world will know that you sent me and have loved them even as you have loved me."
~ John 17:23 NIV

Spiritual Vitamin

Do you believe in God? He wants you to believe in Him. Relationship is exactly what God wants concerning mankind. He wholeheartedly believes in you and loves you more than you will ever understand. *Can you recall instances when you felt cared for and supported by God?* In Him, you have the ultimate support. You never have to worry about being left alone. *How has God shown you that He's there for you?* Your challenges are not yours alone. Jesus says His yoke is easy and believing that will make your burden light. God is waiting for you to cast your burden upon His Son and allow Him to lighten your load. *Will you cast your cares on the Lord?* He is never too far away. Take time today to develop or deepen your connection to God, so that you too may remain eternally in love with Him as He is eternally in love with you.

Affirmation Prayer: Heavenly Father, I believe in You. Show me how to deepen my connection to You, so that our love remains forever, in the name of Jesus, Amen.

Daily Bread: Judges 18 — 19; John 8:13-30; Psalm 60:5-12

I'll Always Love My Mama
May 14

Scripture: "Her children will rise up and call her blessed."
~ Proverbs 31:28a

Spiritual Vitamin

Every day should be Mother's Day! The mother-child relationship is the one that teaches us how to love. The closest example of the love of God is the love of a mother, which is unconditional. A mother loves you when you are right and a mother loves you when you are wrong. God loves the same way, except on a deeper level. There is nothing a mother would not do for her child. There is nothing God would not do for His. God tells us to honor our father and mother, that we may have long life. If there has been a breach in your relationship with your parents, determine what is necessary to bring healing and restoration. In learning how to honor our parents, we also learn how to honor the requests and wishes of God. God rewards our obedience. His promises can flow freely into our lives when we obey His Word.

If your mother is deceased, perhaps your memory of her is not a happy one. Maybe your relationship wasn't as loving and close-knit as the one described in this song. Maybe you feel that your mother did not take good care of you. If this is your story, there is good news. No matter what the relationship was between you and your mother, you have a loving and caring Father who is waiting to meet you at your point of need. He's been guiding you from the beginning of your life until this very moment. *Have you acknowledged His Presence?* You don't have to stumble through life with regrets or longings from the past. Embrace the love God is so willing to give you right now. He created you and knows your innermost desires. Go to Him and talk about any deficiencies or voids in your life. Take time today to ensure that you are obeying God's command to honor your mother so that you may receive blessings from the Lord. If your mother has passed on, remember Mama, honoring her memory in a way that will bring peace and comfort to yourself and those she left behind.

Affirmation Prayer: Heavenly Father, thank You for my mother. She is the vessel You chose to bring me into this world. Teach me how to honor, love and cherish her (or the memory of her) in the name of Jesus, Amen.

Daily Bread: Judges 20 – 21; John 8:31-59; Psalm 61:1-8

I'll Stand By You
May 15

Scripture: "You will not need to fight in this battle. Take up your positions; stand firm and see the deliverance the Lord will give you, Judah and Jerusalem. Do not be afraid; do not be discouraged. Go out and face them tomorrow, and the Lord will be with you."
~ 2 Chronicles 20:17 NIV

Spiritual Vitamin

When times are hard, God will stand by you and even fight your battles. Especially when it's hard to find someone to stand with you, it won't be hard for God to do so. The wonderful truth is that God is well equipped and able to do battle on your behalf. Often times, you may have a desire to fight the battle for yourself. You may have been tempted to take matters into your own hands. It wasn't until you fought and lost that you saw the importance of allowing God to fight for you. If you listen to Him, you will always receive His best for you. Leaning on your own understanding will lead you down a destructive path. Take time today to allow God to stand at the crossroads of life with you and allow Him to fight your battles for you, as you stand firm and await His deliverance.

Affirmation Prayer: Heavenly Father, I realize that the battle is not mine. I am healed, set free and delivered. While I have put on the whole armor, remind me that You are the One who fights my battle, in the name of Jesus, Amen.

Daily Bread: Ruth 1 – 2; John 9:1-34; Proverbs 12:8-17

I Apologize
May 16

Scripture: "Confess your trespasses to one another, and pray for one another, that you may be healed. The effective fervent prayer of a righteous man avails much."
~ James 5:16

Spiritual Vitamin

Do you owe someone an apology? A good way to provide support to family members and friends is to be ready to extend apologies and forgiveness when needed. No one is perfect and every person alive will need to apologize and ask for forgiveness at different stages during the course of their lives. Some offenses are done on purpose, while others are completely by accident or mistake. Two of the most healing words you can say to another person are "I apologize". A heartfelt apology can bring more healing and restoration to a relationship than any words of excuse or explanation ever could. We can learn to forgive through the actions and example of Jesus Christ. He is the perfect One to teach us about this principle because He paid for our sins with His life. When He Himself was sinless, He made the decision to die on the cross to pay the penalty that we owed. This is a demonstration of love beyond comprehension. Take time today to apologize to someone you have offended and watch these healing words do miraculous work in the heart of someone close to you.

Affirmation Prayer: Heavenly Father, thank You for giving me the courage and desire to apologize when I am wrong. Please keep me humble and always ready to extend forgiveness to those who need it from me, in the name of Jesus, Amen.

Daily Bread: Ruth 3 – 4: John 9:35-41; Psalm 62

I Wanna Be Down
May 17

Scripture: Peter spoke up and said to Jesus, "I will never leave you, even though all the rest do!"
~ Matthew 26:33 (GNT)

Spiritual Vitamin

Please be careful about the promises you make to other people. According to Matthew 5:37 (ESV), "let what you say be simply yes or no; anything more than this comes from evil." A man (woman) is only as good as his (her) word. Depending on the circumstances, you may very well end up breaking your promise. Never speak arrogantly about what you will do for someone else, especially in comparison to what another is or is not doing. Jesus predicted that His disciples would fall away. Peter emphatically denied this to Jesus, telling Him that even though the others would, he would not. In the end, Peter could not deliver on what he said. Decide to be there for someone in a tangible way. Show up when that person needs you the most. If everyone else walks away, you stay and provide support and encouragement for them. You never know when you will have to walk in their shoes. Take time today to reflect on a time when someone was there for you.

Affirmation Prayer: Heavenly Father, I have disappointed and denied You; I am sorry. In certain situations, I have not kept my word. Please forgive me and empower me to keep my promises, to You and others, in the name of Jesus, Amen.

Daily Bread: 1 Samuel 1 – 2; John 10:1-42; Psalm 63:1-11

Let's Stay Together
May 18

Scripture: "How good and pleasant it is when God's people live together in unity!"
~ Psalm 133:1 NIV

Spiritual Vitamin

Some people have been called to your life. Their presence is God-ordained. But in other cases, there are those who were only meant to be there for a season, or who were never meant to be there in the first place. Because of this, break-ups have occurred. We all have this in common. There are people who were once in your life, whom you thought would be there forever, but unforeseen circumstances caused the relationship to end. It is important to seek God to find out which relationships should be restored and which ones should not. God will direct you concerning who is a part of His plan for your life. He will provide the information you need concerning each person and tell you what their purpose is concerning you. There should never be a question about God's place in your life. He wants to be in a permanent relationship with you. He wants the two of you to "stay together". God's commitment is to love you; in good times and bad. God's Presence will prevail -- through the highs and lows, the ups and downs. Take time today to make a commitment to stay with God. Your life will never be the same.

Affirmation Prayer: Heavenly Father, in You I have found everything I need. Keep me rooted and grounded in Your Word, in the name of Jesus, Amen.

Daily Bread: 1 Samuel 3 – 4; John 11:1-44; Psalm 64

Stand By Me
May 19

Scripture: "The Lord Almighty is with us"
~ Psalm 46:11a

Spiritual Vitamin

Have you experienced dark days in your life? Circumstances will come that you were not expecting and they will catch you off guard. During these times, you don't have to panic. All you need to do is remember that God is still in control. Pray to Him for the support and help you need. Jesus is always waiting to help His amazing miracles, and He looks forward to any chance to do just that. Call on Him anytime of the day or night and no matter what you're facing, He will stand by you. His power is not dependent on anything in the human realm. God is the Creator of the universe and everything is at His disposal. He has all power and authority, naturally and supernaturally. Take time today to give God a chance to do what He promised in your life.

Affirmation Prayer: Heavenly Father, thank You for standing by me. Sometimes, I have been wrong and undeserving of Your love. Keep me honest in my dealings and willing to stand for others when they need my support, in the name of Jesus, Amen.

Daily Bread: 1 Samuel 5 – 7; John 11:45-57: John 12:1-11; Proverbs 12:18-28

Time After Time
May 20

Scripture: "Ask, and it will be given to you; seek, and you will find; knock, and it will be opened to you."
~ Matthew 7:7

Spiritual Vitamin

If you're lost, just stop what you've been doing and decide to make a different choice. In a moment like this one, you will find God if you search for Him with your heart. This is one of God's promises to you. When you were born into this world, you were born into sin. It is because of the saving work of Jesus Christ that you can find your way back into the grace of a loving God. He will be there for you, time after time. No matter how much you call for God's assistance, He will be there to help you, no matter what. As mentioned in Matthew 7:7, all you have to do is ask God for his help. He has also assigned family members and friends to support you as well. God will never tire of hearing you call. He loves to come to the aid of His children. Take time today to allow God's love and care for you to prompt you to perform deeds and/or random acts of kindness for others. Express your appreciation to God for the way He lovingly provides for you.

Affirmation Prayer: Heavenly Father, I may stumble from time to time, but because of You, I will not fall. Help me to perform unexpected kindnesses for others, in a time when they are most needed, in the name of Jesus.

Daily Bread: 1 Samuel 8 – 9; 1 Samuel 10:1-8; John 12:12-26; Psalm 65

Walk with You
May 21

Scripture: "I will walk among you and be your God, and you shall be My people."
~ Leviticus 26:12

Spiritual Vitamin

Do you recognize that God is with you? God walks with you every day. Whether you acknowledge His Presence or not, He is there, waiting to hear from you. God has a plan for your life, one that He specifically designed just for you. He wants you to help Him build His kingdom. He has gifted you with special abilities that will help you accomplish this task. *Can you feel the Presence of God, walking with you through your days and nights?* Just like in the poem entitled "Footprints in the Sand", God is carrying you during the most troublesome times in your life. Once He restores strength to you, God is standing behind the scenes cheering you on and making sure that you are safe, cared for and loved. Take time today to consider ways in which you can serve the people of God and accomplish the purpose He has for you.

Affirmation Prayer: Heavenly Father, I have a desire to walk with You. Thank You for the angels You have assigned to walk with me. Keep me inspired to continue walking in my purpose, in the name of Jesus, Amen.

Daily Bread: 1 Samuel 10:9-27; 1 Samuel 11 – 12; John 12:37-50; John 13:1-17; Psalm 66:1-12

Selwyn B. Cox

What Would We Do Without Us?
May 22

Scripture: "For as we have many members in one body, but all the members do not have the same function, so we, being many, are one body in Christ, and individually members of one another."
~ Romans 12:4-5

Spiritual Vitamin

What would you do without the person you love? People need other people. 1 Corinthians 13 speaks to the power of love and God has shared with us that love has the power to cover many sins. The enemy knows this and tries to keep you at odds with others. You have the power to control how you respond as well as how you react to others. You are at your best when you are encouraging someone else to be their best. Everyone is spiritually gifted and when we work together, something beautiful is produced. Single instruments make beautiful music alone but when played together with other instruments, the sound can take your breath away. Humanity was meant to be an orchestra, everyone working together to accomplish the purposes of God. Take time today to find your place in life's orchestra and to make your contribution to the building of God's Kingdom on earth.

Affirmation Prayer: Heavenly Father, Your will and work for my life exist outside of the four walls of a building. Guide me to those with whom I am destined to help and to form relationships. You desire for us to fellowship with and to help other believers. Keep us connected to one another, in the name of Jesus, Amen.

Daily Bread: 1 Samuel 13; 1 Samuel 14:1-23; John 13:18-38; Psalm 66:13-20

We Are Family
May 23

Scripture: "But to all who did receive him, who believed in his name, he gave the right to become children of God."
~ John 1:12 ESV

Spiritual Vitamin

Do you wish you could have picked your family? If so, chances are you would not have chosen the same one you currently have. It has been said that you can pick your friends, but you can't pick your family. Very true. You can't choose your natural family, but you can choose your spiritual family. You get to decide which body of believers and which house of God you will join. Your spiritual family is critically important to your spiritual growth. God is your Father and He desires that you fellowship with like-minded believers. If you do not attend fellowship on a regular basis, a vital component of your life is missing. Take time today to listen for God's direction on which spiritual family to choose. Then, go all in, sharing the gifts, talents and abilities that God has given you.

Affirmation Prayer: Heavenly Father, I have associated myself with the family of God to which You have led me. Help me to freely share my gifts and talents in this branch of Zion, in the name of Jesus, Amen.

Daily Bread: 1 Samuel 14:24-52; 1 Samuel 15; John 14:1-31; Proverbs 13:1-9

Just To Be Close To You
May 24

Scripture: "The Lord is near to all who call on Him, to all who call on Him in truth."
~ Psalm 145:18 ESV

Spiritual Vitamin

When was the last time you spent some time alone with God? Getting away is something you can actually do; and it doesn't involve packing or airplanes or any of the things normally involved in taking a trip. Going into the Presence of God can give you wonderful feelings of refreshment and rejuvenation and there's no hassle or complicated issues attached. Enjoying quiet solitude with Him can be more rewarding than a visit to the most exotic location. God's Presence can fill you on the inside with joy, peace and serenity. There are no requirements that must be met or preparations that need to be made. Take time today to block out all of the worldly distractions and focus on the nearness of God. Then you will be in the Presence of the One who longs to be close to you!

Affirmation Prayer: Heavenly Father, I will not be blindsided by satan. I will keep my eyes on You for in You lies my strength and help. Never let me forget this truth, in the name of Jesus, Amen.

Daily Bread: 1 Samuel 16 – 17; John 15; John 16:1-4; Psalm 67

Why Do We Hurt Each Other?
May 25

Scripture: "Let all bitterness, wrath, anger, clamor, and evil speaking be put away from you, with all malice. And be kind to one another, tenderhearted, forgiving one another, even as God in Christ forgave you."
~ Ephesians 4:31-32

Spiritual Vitamin

Why do we hurt each other? In some cases within the human spirit, there is the need for revenge. When a person is hurt, their first response is to devise a way to hurt the person who hurt them. This is where the statement "hurt people hurt people" originates. There is a high occurrence of this type of behavior among family and friends but it doesn't have to be the case. You can take the advice of Ephesians 4 and let anger and bitterness go, along with all the other negative emotions that it brings. You can decide to be kind, forgiving and loving toward everyone, especially those who have hurt you. The real truth is that somewhere along the way, you have hurt someone else and needed their forgiveness. If you received that forgiveness, you know how good it feels. If not, you know the pain of trying to move on without it. Don't delight in holding people hostage. Open the prison doors and let them go free. After all, this is what God has done for you. Take time today to give someone the gifts of love and forgiveness. It's a decision you will never regret.

Affirmation Prayer: Heavenly Father, I have hurt You and others. I have not always been able to forgive but because of Your forgiveness toward me, I am willing to change. Teach me to extend love and forgiveness to my enemies, in the name of Jesus, Amen.

Daily Bread: 1 Samuel 18; John 16:5-33; John 17:1-5; Psalm 68:1-6

You and I
May 26

Scripture: "Fear not, for I am with you; Be not dismayed, for I am your God. I will strengthen you, yes, I will help you; I will uphold you with My righteous right hand."
~ Isaiah 41:10

Spiritual Vitamin

Do you want to join Team Jesus? You have a chance to join a winning team. Your partner is highly qualified in every aspect and is completely self-sufficient. Together, the two of you can accomplish great things. He is the One whom you absolutely cannot live without. When family members or friends let you down, you can rely on God for the support you need. In fact, sometimes in life, human companionship will be unavailable and it will be just you and the Lord. Jesus said He has overcome the world and through the power of His blood, you can do the same. No situation can overtake or overpower you, as long as you are walking in the will of God for your life. There is nothing in this world that can destroy you if you walk in His will and do as He commands. There is nothing that can defeat you if you allow God's Word to rule your thoughts, actions, behavior and decisions. God is waiting for you to say yes to Him. *Are you still making plans for yourself or have you surrendered to the plan He already made?* Take time today to work on achieving your God-given purpose and discover how much better your life can be.

Affirmation Prayer: Heavenly Father, thank You for being with me at all times. Together, You and I can overcome every obstacle that comes my way. Help me to accept and receive Your strength, in the name of Jesus, Amen.

Daily Bread: 1 Samuel 19 – 20; John 17:6-26; Psalm 68:7-14

Just the Two of Us
May 27

Scripture: "Again I say to you that if two of you agree on earth concerning anything that they ask, it will be done for them by my Father in heaven."
~ Matthew 18:19

Spiritual Vitamin

Do you believe that relationships are important? It was the whole reason God created man; because He wanted someone with whom to share relationship. When we think of this word in human terms, our minds immediately go to our spouses or significant others. *But what if you don't have a significant other? Can you ever use the phrase "just the two of us?"* You may not think so but the answer is yes. Just because you don't have a spouse or significant other doesn't mean you are all alone. You belong to God. Paired up with Him, you can be referred to as "us". If you are single, God is willing to be your significant other. It can be you and God! The two of you make a majority. You never have to feel as if you have no one to support you in your time of need. God has promised to always make Himself available to you and whether it's become clear to you or not, He always has. Not one promise He's ever made has gone unfulfilled. Take time today to celebrate with the One who makes you whole. Together, you and God are a winning team!

Affirmation Prayer: Heavenly Father, thank You for wanting to be with me and for making me emotionally healthy and whole. Whether I'm in an earthly relationship or not, I know that I am cared for and loved. Help me to share Your love with others, in the name of Jesus, Amen.

Daily Bread: 1 Samuel 21 – 23; John 18:1-24; Proverbs 13:10-19

You'll Never Find
May 28

Scripture: "No one is holy like the Lord, for there is none besides You, nor is there any rock like our God."
~ 1 Samuel 2:2

Spiritual Vitamin

You'll never find a greater love than the love of God. *Have you accepted this great love?* If you have, then it has changed your life in ways you never thought possible. God's love has changed your perspective on a number of things. Things you once thought were of the utmost importance have become things that almost don't matter at all, while things of lesser importance that used to mean a great deal, no longer carry as much weight. You have been empowered to do what you once thought you could not. You have found the courage and strength to confront obstacles that once stood in your way. Your family and friends are your earthly support system and you also have a heavenly support system to help you do what is needed each day. God's love has so filled your being that now, you are able to freely share it with others without restraint. This was God's original intent when He created you. He wants the love He gives you to pour out onto and into the lives of others. God's love will never be in short supply. Take time today to cherish God's love. Stop searching for a greater love because that is something "You'll Never Find."

Affirmation Prayer: Heavenly Father, thank You for Your great and immeasurable love. Help me to understand that I'll never find it anywhere but in You, in the name of Jesus, Amen.

Daily Bread: 1 Samuel 24 – 25; John 18:25-40; Psalm 68:15-20

One Sweet Day
May 29

Scripture: "Truly the light is sweet, and it is pleasant for the eyes to behold the sun."
~ Ecclesiastes 11:7

Spiritual Vitamin

Memorial Day is observed on the last Monday of May and is the day we remember those who died while serving our country as well as celebrate the memories of our family members and friends. When a loved one transitions, your heart is broken because you will not be able to see or talk to that individual as you once did. The Bible instructs us not to sorrow over the loss of someone we love as those who have no hope. There is hope in Christ Jesus! God is asking that you entrust the care of your departed loved one into His hands. If your loved one has accepted Jesus Christ as their Savior and if you have faith and trust that God is true to His Word, then you will know that your loved one is in good hands. The Bible teaches that when someone is absent from the body, they are present with the Lord. As much as you loved that individual, you must realize that God loves them more. Your loved one has not been taken away to some unknown destination and is not somewhere out there lost in space. When Jesus is your Savior, your destination is sure and your future is secure. Take time today to thank God for the time you had with those who have gone from time into eternity, knowing that there will be a great reunion, one sweet day!

Affirmation Prayer: Heavenly Father, some of my loved ones are now with You. Sometimes, I miss them terribly. I want to see my loved ones who have gone on, but most of all, I want to see Jesus. Keep me filled with hope until the day when we are all together again, in the name of Jesus, Amen.

Daily Bread: 1 Samuel 26 – 28; John 19:1-27; Psalm 68:21-27

You Needed Me
May 30

Scripture: "You, Lord, are all I have, and you give me all I need; my future is in your hands."
~ Psalm 16:5 (GNT)

Spiritual Vitamin

God doesn't need man, man needs God. We need Him to dry the tears we cry. We need Him to teach us how to obey His Word, so that when troubled times arise, we'll know what to do and how to handle them. When we are confused, we need Him to clear our minds. When our souls were lost in sin, He bought them with the precious blood of Jesus. God doesn't need us, but the glorious truth is that He wants us; each and every one. What a mind-blowing thought! He wants you to tell of His goodness to everyone you know. Witnessing to one's family and friends is of the utmost importance; God wants it and they need it. *When you hear good news, don't you want to share it?* The Word of God is the best news ever. *Have you shared it lately?* God is a strong deliverer and He has kept you from wandering in the wilderness of life and created a wonderful plan for you to have an abundant and prosperous existence. Take time today to respond to the need of your witness to those whom God wants as a part of His family.

Affirmation Prayer: Heavenly Father, I know I need You in my life. There were times when I didn't always recognize that. Thank You for supplying all my needs. Keep me reliant upon You as my source, in the name of Jesus, Amen.

Daily Bread: 1 Samuel 29 – 31; John 19:28-42; John 20:1-10; Psalm 68:28-35

You Remind Me
May 31

Scripture: "Remind me each morning of your constant love, for I put my trust in you. My prayers go up to you; show me the way I should go."
~ Psalm 143:8 GNT

Spiritual Vitamin

As this month comes to a close, I want to encourage you in regards to the necessity of giving and receiving the support that is needed to create stable relationships among your family and friends. People need each other and it is not wise to attempt to navigate your way through life alone. After all, people who *have* people, are the most blessed people in the world. Think of a time when you were able to make pleasant memories with family and friends. *Doesn't that make you smile?* Certain things can happen and serve as triggers that will remind you of something or someone that made you happy. God reminds us every day of His tender mercies that are new every morning. He watches over you and allows you to rest your body from all the activities and stresses of the day. While sleeping you are in an unconscious state, one that could be likened to death. If the thought of death causes you to be afraid, consider the fact that death is the doorway to eternal life. As you sleep each night, God prepares you for death because being unconscious is the closest thing to death. It is important to be reminded that death is nothing to fear because to be absent from the body is to be present with the Lord. If God wakes you up to a brand new day, you owe Him praise for blessing you with new promises and possibilities. When unfortunate circumstances arise, God reminds you that His power has brought you through before and that He is able to do it again. God requires your trust and faith and when you give Him that, miracles occur. God's favor will follow you through the course of your entire life. There is no expiration date attached to His goodness. Take time today to be reminded of God's constant love and put your trust in Him.

Affirmation Prayer: Heavenly Father, there is a sweet, sweet Spirit in my heart. I know it is Your Presence. Please remind me of your constant love, in the name of Jesus, Amen.

Daily Bread: 2 Samuel 1; 2 Samuel 2:1-7; John 20:11-31; Proverbs 13:20-25; Proverbs 14:1-4

MONTHLY REFLECTIONS

Selwyn B. Cox

June: Self-*Esteem (Learning Self-*Love, God's Way)

Strength for the Journey

Heavenly Father,

You are great and I praise and adore You. I come asking Your forgiveness because at times, I have not recognized the wonder of Your works or lived up to Your expectations for me. I have not always loved myself the way You instructed and I need Your help. You have washed away all my sins and shown me who I am, according to Your Word. Because of the sacrifice of Your Son, Jesus, I will not be condemned for my past. Help me to walk in Your will for my life and to stop believing the lies the enemy has told me about myself. Make me willing to follow You as You guide me into all truth concerning my life and purpose. I will no longer be moved by what others say about me; instead, I will seek only Your face. Fill me with love and self-esteem by the power of Your Holy Spirit. Only then, can I become confident about who I am in You. Teach me how to love myself the way You originally intended. I am the child of a King! Thank You for setting me free, in the name of Jesus, Amen.

June

Self-Esteem (Learning Self-Love, God's Way)

During the month of June, you will go on a journey, learning about self-esteem; how to love yourself the way God intended when He created you. Self-esteem is defined as confidence in one's own worth and abilities. Learning self-love is essential because without knowing how to properly love yourself, you will never master the art of loving God and others. Mastering the art of love begins with the ability to be able to receive God's love for yourself. As a basic principle, you will only love others as much as you know how to love yourself. As you grow in your mastery of this principle, the Holy Spirit will begin to show you how to move to new levels of understanding, love and appreciation for yourself and those whom God has placed in your life. The more love you accept from God, the more love you'll extend to others. Let God fill you up with His love and then, like an overflowing fountain, be willing to pour it out on those around you. It is my prayer that you will use this month's devotionals to learn self-love, God's way.

Quote: "Our deepest fear is not that we are inadequate. Our deepest fear is that we are powerful beyond measure. It is our light, not our darkness that most frightens us. We ask ourselves who am I to be brilliant, gorgeous, talented, fabulous? Actually, who are you not to be? You are a child of God. Your playing small does not serve the world. There is something enlightening about shrinking so that other people won't feel insecure around you. We are all meant to shine, as children do. We are born to make manifest the glory of God that is within us."
~ Marianne Williamson

> "You are all fair, my love; there is no spot in you."
> ~ Song of Solomon 4:7

Be Yourself
June 1

Scripture: "For we are His workmanship, created in Christ Jesus for good works, which God prepared beforehand that we should walk in them."
~ Ephesians 2:10

Spiritual Vitamin

Have you ever tried to be like someone else? God created each person as a unique individual. Each one of us has different fingerprints and looks different. As you grow and develop physically, mentally and emotionally, it is important that you explore the details of what makes you different and unique. Don't allow the differences of those whom you are close with or admire to discourage you from being your authentic self. You are not nor should you be in competition with anyone else. Once you discover what your authentic characteristics are, you can work to sharpen them to their fullest potential. You only have to please God. He has a specific purpose for you and a certain way you were designed to bless the Body of Christ. Before you can be a blessing to anyone else, you must develop a love and appreciation for yourself. Don't attempt to hide the distinct attributes that make you who you are; celebrate them! Discover them and allow others to see them in operation. Take time today to identify the qualities that make you the unique person you are; "Be Yourself" and shine!

Affirmation Prayer: Heavenly Father, thank You for creating me as You have. Protect me from the desire to imitate others or to be like anyone but You. Teach me how to love myself as I am and to commit to becoming better, in the name of Jesus, Amen.

Daily Bread: 2 Samuel 2:8-32; 2 Samuel 3:1-21; John 21:1-25; Psalm 69:1-12

I Will Survive
June 2

Scripture: "He who finds his life will lose it, and he who loses his life for My sake will find it."
~ Matthew 10:39

Spiritual Vitamin

What is your method of survival when it comes to dealing with truth? Can you handle the truth? You must speak the truth to others and you must be prepared to receive truth when it is spoken to you. God gave you a voice and you have His permission to use it but you must season your speech with love. The guidelines are that you speak the truth in love. You should never feel pressured to "go along" just to get along with others. God holds you responsible for the truth YOU know. No matter what the situation, you will survive if you let God control the outcome. If those around you cannot see your point of view, it is alright to agree to disagree. Don't compromise your morals and integrity for the sake of someone else. You alone must answer to God for the choices and decisions you make during the course of your life. Listen to your inner voice, which is how God's Holy Spirit communicates with you. Never allow someone to talk you out of something you feel strongly about within your spirit. Likewise, never allow someone to talk you into something that you know is wrong. Take time today to consider your own feelings and make a commitment to yourself that you will survive any and all attacks with the help of your heavenly Father.

Affirmation Prayer: Heavenly Father, I ask that You guard and guide my tongue to speak only as You lead me. Help me to be strong and courageous in the face of adversity, realizing that You are with me wherever I go, in the name of Jesus, Amen.

Daily Bread: 2 Samuel 3:22-39; 2 Samuel 4; 2 Samuel 5:1-5; Acts 1:1-22; Psalm 69:13-28

Come As You Are
June 3

Scripture: "And the Spirit and the Bride say "Come!" And let him who hears say, "Come!" And let him who thirsts come. Whoever desires, let him take the water of life freely."
~ Revelation 22:17

Spiritual Vitamin

Have you been trying to "fix yourself" before you take a step toward God? God issues an invitation to mankind. He invites you to come to Him, just as you are. He doesn't expect you to be able to fix yourself before you come. He will accept you as you are, flaws and all. While He will accept you in a flawed state, He does not expect you to remain that way. If you let Him work in your heart, you will not be able to remain that way. He will wash you in the blood of Jesus and sanctify you for His purposes. God has been speaking to you. *When you take the time to sit and ponder the things that He has said, and what He has offered you, how can you not respond?* There is nothing better than the love of God. Every need you will ever have has been taken into account and provided for by a faithful and caring Heavenly Father. If you come to Him, God will teach you how to love yourself. He loves you with a perfect love, one that cannot be matched on human terms. God's love is deep and everlasting; far beyond anything the human mind can comprehend. Because He loves you so much, He is more than qualified to teach you how to love yourself. Take time today to receive God's love for you. If you have not yet done this, then accept God's invitation to come, just as you are.

Affirmation Prayer: Heavenly Father, today I am responding to Your invitation to come to You. I come before You, praying for your knowledge. I am open to Your will for my life. Teach me how to continually respond to Your voice when You call to me, in the name of Jesus, Amen.

Daily Bread: 2 Samuel 5:6-25; 2 Samuel 6; Acts 1:23-26; Acts 2:1-21; Psalm 69:29-36

Make Me Over Again
June 4

Scripture: "Therefore, if anyone is in Christ, he is a new creation; old things have passed away; behold, all things have become new."
~ 2 Corinthians 5:17

Spiritual Vitamin

Pentecost Sunday is the commemoration and celebration of the receiving of the Holy Spirit by the early church. Pentecost always falls 50 days after Easter.

Are you willing to be reborn? Will you give God permission to perform a spiritual makeover in and through you? God's Word says that we are born in sin and shaped in iniquity. At the point when you realize you need Jesus Christ as your personal Lord and Savior, you will also realize that you need to be "born again". The process of salvation and baptism involve a rebirth; a remaking of sorts. I am not referring to a physical rebirth but a rebirth in your spirit man or woman. There will be some things you must allow to leave your life. There will be some people you must allow to leave your life. You must waive your rights to your "likeness" and take on the likeness of Christ. This involves a drastic change and those who are closest to you should be able to see a difference between the person you used to be and the person you are becoming. This process is called conversion and within the process, if your likeness becomes unrecognizable to those closest to you, then you have succeeded in your efforts to become more like Christ. Once you say yes to God, don't put limits on Him or hold back certain areas of your life from Him. Allow Him free reign to change all that needs to be changed. Take time today to give God permission to make you over.

Affirmation Prayer: Heavenly Father, today I consent to becoming a new creation in You. Give me a desire to always say yes to Your will and Your way, in the name of Jesus, Amen.

Daily Bread: 2 Samuel 7 – 8; Acts 2:22-47; Proverbs 14:4-14

Got 2 Find Love
 June 5

Scripture: "Delight yourself also in the Lord, and He shall give you the desires of your heart."
~ Psalm 37:4

Spiritual Vitamin

Have you been searching for someone to love you? With God in your life, you don't have to go searching for love. There's no need to find love because you already have love. Unfortunately, before we have a full and deep understanding of God's love, humans value the love from other humans more than the love of God. This should never be the case. God loves on a totally different level. God's love is not based on the performance of the one being loved. It is not contingent on any behavior or favor or attitude, it just is. As a result of His own decision, God loves you and there's nothing you can do about it. Don't waste your valuable time searching for something that may not be true and real. God's love has been tested and proven so there is no need to question or doubt it. If you would only accept the eternal and everlasting love of God, your spirit will be filled to capacity and He will supply the longings of your soul. You will value who He created you to be and love yourself from within. You will never enter into a relationship with another human being based on desperation and emptiness. If you let it, God's love will fill every void within you. Take time today to tap into the love that God has for you and allow Him to fill you up. There's no need to look anywhere else.

Affirmation Prayer: Heavenly Father, please give me a clean heart, so that I may delight myself in You. Fill my mouth with praise and keep my mind stayed on You so that I can receive the love You have for me, in the name of Jesus, Amen.

Daily Bread: 2 Samuel 9 – 10; Acts 3; Psalm 70:1-5

Fix You
June 6

Scripture: "fixing our eyes on Jesus, the pioneer and perfecter of faith. For the joy set before him he endured the cross, scorning its shame, and sat down at the right hand of the throne of God."
~ Hebrews 12:2 NIV

Spiritual Vitamin

Do you believe you are the only one experiencing brokenness? Every person will experience some type of brokenness in their lives. If they are honest, every adult human being and some younger persons as well have already been at this point. The reason for this is that people are flawed. No one is perfect but there is hope! Jesus can fix us, flaws and all. If you keep your eyes on Him, He will perfect your faith. He endured the cross on your behalf, to pay the price for your sins. He bought you back from the enemy and paid your ransom with His precious blood. You do not need to struggle to get yourself together. All you have to do is surrender and repent. With repentance, you have already been forgiven. All you need to do is give control of your life to God and allow Jesus to take over. He knows how to safely lead and guide you through this thing called life. It should be comforting to know that there is someone who loves you so much that He is willing to handle every detail of your life and is waiting to lead you and direct you so that you know which way to go. He will not force His directions upon you; you must ask for them. The moment you ask, He stands ready to answer. Take time today to let God fix you, making every necessary repair for your good and His glory!

Affirmation Prayer: Heavenly Father, I fix my eyes on You. I know there are areas in my life that need fixing. Help me to be willing to allow You to do what is necessary for me to live within Your perfect will, in the name of Jesus, Amen.

Daily Bread: 2 Samuel 11 – 12; Acts 4:1-22; Psalm 71:1-8

Be Optimistic
June 7

Scripture: "You have allowed me to suffer much hardship, but you will restore me to life again and lift me up from the depths of the earth."
~ Psalm 71:20 NLT

Spiritual Vitamin

Are you optimistic about your future? Being optimistic is defined as being hopeful and confident about the future. Having a relationship with God brings hope. If you are confident about your relationship with and connection to God, then you know there is no need to fear what will happen in your life. You can rest on the promises of God. There are so many good things in store for you if you are willing to live a life of faith. With God on your side, you can choose to have a positive attitude and outlook on life. You don't have to be weighed down with the cares and concerns of the world. Jesus agrees to take your cares and deal with them on your behalf, so that your burden can be light. You can be free to enjoy the peace and blessings of God. You can feel good about who God made you to be and share the reasons for your hope with the people in your life. Take time today to adopt an optimistic attitude of faith and experience the restoration of your joy and peace.

Affirmation Prayer: Heavenly Father, thank You for bringing me through the hardships and trials in my life. You are restoring hope and life to me again. At times, I struggle and worry, when there is no need because You are on my side. Help me to be optimistic and confident about my future, in the name of Jesus, Amen.

Daily Bread: 2 Samuel 13; Acts 4:23-37; Acts 5:1-11; Psalm 71:9-18

I Believe I Can Fly
June 8

Scripture: "But those who wait on the Lord shall renew their strength; they shall mount up on wings like eagles; they shall run and not be weary, they shall walk and not faint."
~ Isaiah 40:31

Spiritual Vitamin

What is holding you together? God's arms are the everlasting arms. In this life, you will experience times of weakness and struggle. Perhaps you have struggled all your life. You have the opportunity to make a change. Aside and apart from God, your life will be difficult. But once you meet and fall in love with Jesus, you begin to understand the meaning of true love. Then you can stop struggling and just lean on the everlasting arms of God and allow Him to take care of you, the way He planned to all along. God believes in you. *Can you believe in yourself?* God knew what He was doing when He made you and He knows the purpose for which you were created. *Have you taken the time to let Him share that information with you?* If not, you're missing out on some very important facts, details and possibilities. Everything and everyone has a purpose. *Do you know your purpose?* Once you discover it, you will be unstoppable. Take time today to let God "cover you with His feathers and under His wings you will find refuge" (Psalm 91:4a).

Affirmation Prayer: Heavenly Father, thank You for renewing my strength. I can always count on You because You protect me and keep me safe. Help me to always be willing to run into and lean on Your everlasting arms, for You are my refuge, in the name of Jesus, Amen.

Daily Bread: 2 Samuel 14; 2 Samuel 15:1-12; Acts 5:12-42; Proverbs 14:15-24

I'm Coming Out
June 9

Scripture: "And they shall know that I am the Lord their God, who brought them up out of the land of Egypt, that I may dwell among them. I am the Lord their God."
~ Exodus 29:46

Spiritual Vitamin

Are you hiding who you really are and the things you are capable of doing? Don't hide your true identity or your gifts. God made you who you are for a reason. He gave you the special set of skills you possess for a purpose. Use them to the glory and honor of God. You don't have to be like anyone else. God made you individually wonderful. He did not make any mistakes in the way He fashioned you. You are fully equipped to accomplish His purpose. You have been packed with everything you will need to do the work you were assigned and designed to do. *Can you accept and believe this fact?* If so, it will change what you do next. You will no longer remain in a shell, afraid to speak up and out on your own behalf. You will not allow anyone to take away your voice because you will possess the assurance that what you have to offer truly matters. God made you unique and powerful. Embrace it and let it take you higher. Take time today to come out of whatever has held you back or prevented you from becoming the best you that you can be!

Affirmation Prayer: Heavenly Father, the sins of my past had me bound and ashamed, but I called on You from the depths of my heart. Now, I'm coming out of bondage, more confident and secure than before. Keep me free, in the name of Jesus, Amen.

Daily Bread: 2 Samuel 15:13-37; 2 Samuel 16:1-14; Acts 6: Acts 7:1-19; Psalm 71:19-24

I'm Here
June 10

Scripture: "in everything give thanks; for this is the will of God in Christ Jesus for you."
~ 1 Thessalonians 5:18

Spiritual Vitamin

Are you living a bountiful life? You have everything inside of you that is needed to do so. If you are not, it is time to examine why not. You are here and you are worthy of good things. It is time for you to learn to love your true self; not the person you present to the world but the person you are in private. *Do you love who you really are?* It is one thing to love someone based on who you think they are. It's something totally different to continue to love them once you <u>know</u> who they really are. The only way you can accomplish this awesome feat is to learn how to love who you really are first, then you can pass that same love on to the other people in your life. You can stand tall in the face of adversity because, through Jesus Christ, you have already won. As 1 Thessalonians 5:18 suggests, be thankful, no matter what. Live one day at a time. You must love yourself, give to yourself and value yourself. Learning to appreciate yourself rids you of the need to receive appreciation from others. You are beautiful, inside and out. Take time today to celebrate being here and give thanks to God in all circumstances, for this is His will in Christ Jesus for you.

Affirmation Prayer: Heavenly Father, thank You for teaching me how to love myself. I am no longer bound by falsehood and lies concerning who I am. Help me to live according to the power principles that are laid out for me in Your Word, in the name of Jesus, Amen.

Daily Bread: 2 Samuel 16:15-23; 2 Samuel 17; 2 Samuel 18:1-18; Acts 7:20-43; Psalm 72:1-20

Invisible (For the Last Time)
June 11

Scripture: "For by Him all things were created that are in heaven and that are on earth, visible and invisible, whether thrones or dominions or principalities or powers. All things were created through Him and for Him."
~ Colossians 1:16

Spiritual Vitamin

Do you feel like no one "sees" you? Jesus carries real hope for people who feel marginalized, ignored and passed over. Nobody goes unnoticed by Jesus. For Jesus, there are no invisible people. *How could there be?* The scripture today reminds us that each and every one of us was "created through Him and for Him". You are not just some random person wandering around. You are one of Jesus' amazing miracles (JAMS) and the Designer's original, the Designer being God Himself. You were created for a loving relationship with Him through His Son Jesus Christ. You matter. What you think matters; how you feel matters. You are not invisible. God made you to be seen and to show forth His glory. Once you are able to do this for yourself, you will be equipped to help others. Take time today to find someone who feels overlooked or left out and do what you can to make them feel valued, loved and appreciated.

Prayer: Heavenly Father, because of You, I am not invisible. You see me and You know me. Help me to regard myself as worthy, just as You do, in the name of Jesus, Amen.

Daily Bread: 2 Samuel 18:19-33; 2 Samuel 19; Acts 7:44-60; Acts 8:1-3; Psalm 73:1-14

Looking For Love
    June 12

Scripture: "But from there you will seek the Lord your God, and you will find Him if you seek Him with all your heart and with all your soul."
~ Deuteronomy 4:29

Spiritual Vitamin

Are you looking for love? There are different kinds of love and different degrees to each kind. Until you find something you believe to be true and genuine, you will continue looking for love. If it comes from any source other than God Himself, it will eventually disappoint you. There is only One who can fully meet your need and desire to be loved. He is Jesus Christ and until you really grasp that, you will continue to look for love in all the wrong places. *Where do you look for love? Could it be at the bank (where you keep your money); or with your boo (who supplies your honey); or even from your flesh (all wrapped up in mess)?* Until we grasp the full measure of God's love for us, we can't possibly understand what "true" love is. We can't love unless we have first been loved. *Who better to love you than the Lord?* Once you embrace the love of God, you will find that you don't expect as much from other people. You are now empowered to allow others to be who they are, without all the added pressure of meeting your expectations. Give God an opportunity to meet your needs, forgive your faults, cleanse your heart and change your thoughts. Take time today to accept the love of God and explore the many possibilities it brings.

Affirmation Prayer: Heavenly Father, my search for true love is over. I have found all I need in You. Make me satisfied in You alone, in the name of Jesus, Amen.

Daily Bread: 2 Samuel 20 – 21; Acts 8:4-40; Proverbs 14:25-35

Love Has Finally Come At Last
June 13

Scripture: "For God so loved the world that He gave His only begotten Son, that whoever believes in Him should not perish but have everlasting life." ~ John 3:16

Spiritual Vitamin

Have you been waiting for a certain someone to love you? Have you overlooked the love of someone who <u>wants</u> to love you for someone who seems to need convincing that you are worth their love? Accept the love of God and it will fill the void that is lingering deep on the inside. God has been waiting for you to accept His love. He has so many wonderful things to give you, none of which have strings attached. God's love contract is different from what we know a contract to be. There is no fine print and no hidden rules or obligations. There is no expiration date and no cancellation clause. God's decision to love you cannot be altered by anything you do or don't do. It is a decision from within Him and He never changes His mind. He already knows everything about you and decided to love you anyway. There are no secrets to contend with and nothing that can disqualify you or make Him turn away. The bottom line: God loves you — period, end of story. Take time, at last, to accept the love that God has always intended for you to have.

Affirmation Prayer: Heavenly Father, I've wasted a lot of time searching for something that I had all the time. You have loved me from the beginning and now I finally recognize that. Help me to teach others to do the same, in the name of Jesus, Amen.

Daily Bread: 2 Samuel 22; 2 Samuel 23:1-7; Acts 9:1-31; Psalm 73:15-28

Man In the Mirror
June 14

Scripture: "Anyone who listens to the word but does not do what it says is like someone who looks at his face in a mirror and, after looking at himself, goes away and immediately forgets what he looks like."
~ James 1:23 NIV

Spiritual Vitamin

Do you examine yourself? Change begins with you. In order to obey God's Word, you must change. Flesh and spirit will never agree. It is easy to examine other people in an effort to tell them what's wrong with them. But examining other people to discover their flaws is not a good way to spend your time. It is your responsibility to examine yourself because you are the only one you can change; but you can't change by yourself. You need God to help you do that. God can make the change in you through the power of His Holy Spirit. Before you can allow God to help you change, you first must decide to surrender your will for His. Then, His plans for you can come forth. His plan far supersedes any plans you could create for yourself. Begin with yourself. Allow those close to you to see the evidence of the work of the Lord in your life. Take a critical look in the mirror. You have the power to make the world a better place. Take time today to make that change!

Affirmation Prayer: Heavenly Father, I can now look at the man (woman) in the mirror. That person is me. Thank You for enabling me to face myself in truth and love. Empower me to continue to grow in you and to accept Your will for my life, in the name of Jesus, Amen.

Daily Bread: 2 Samuel 23:8-39; 2 Samuel 24:1-25; Acts 9:32-43; Acts 10:1-23; Psalm 74:1-9

Me Time
June 15

Scripture: "You are altogether beautiful, my love; there is no flaw in you."
~ Song of Solomon 4:7

Spiritual Vitamin

Do you constantly put others before yourself? If so, it's time to choose you. At some point, you must stop taking better care of others than you do of self. You must begin to pay attention to your own wants and needs and stop being so eager to meet the wants and needs of others. I am not suggesting that you become so self-absorbed that you exclude everyone else. But you must include yourself as you create a plan to serve others. You must allow God to fill you with His Spirit so that you will have something to pour out onto others. If you are empty on the inside, you have nothing to offer anyone else. Reward yourself by paying attention to the cries of your thirsty soul. Don't allow your spirit to slowly dry up and wither away, while you feed and water the spirits of those around you. Take time today to realize that you are altogether beautiful and according to God, there is no flaw in you.

Affirmation Prayer: Heavenly Father, thank You for creating me. I see what You have made and I agree that "it is good". Help me to love myself as You love me, in the name of Jesus, Amen.

Daily Bread: 1 Kings 1; 1 Kings 2:1-12; Acts 10:24-48; Acts 11:1-18; Psalm 74:10-17

Hot-N-Cold
June 16

Scripture: "I know your works, that you are neither cold nor hot. I could wish you were cold or hot."
~ Revelation 3:15

Spiritual Vitamin

Are you serving God with a divided heart? When it comes to our connection to God, He prefers that we be hot or cold. He tells us that if we are lukewarm, He will spit us out of His mouth. Nothing is worth missing God. He deserves your absolute best and a firm commitment to serve Him. Obedience must be the order of the day. Being lukewarm can be compared to being average. There is nothing average about God. He is perfect and excellent in every way. As you grow to become more like Him, your attitudes and behaviors will display more of a reflection of God's character and things such as gentleness, kindness, patience and compassion will be more evident in you. As you surrender your will for His, you become moldable clay in the hands of the Master Potter. You will learn that you do not have to settle for less in your life because God offers you His best. You also learn that you must do your best for God. He deserves nothing less. God desires that you make a decision because indecision is dangerous. Take time today to consider your temperature toward God — hot or cold?

Affirmation Prayer: Heavenly Father, You are deserving of my absolute best, yet You have loved me even when I have given You less. Please help me to be hot rather than lukewarm, in the name of Jesus, Amen.

Daily Bread: 1 Kings 2:13-46; 1 Kings 3:1-15; Acts 11:19-30; Acts 12:1-19; Proverbs 15:1-10

One In a Million
June 17

Scripture: "For where your treasure is, there your heart will be also."
~ Matthew 6:21

Spiritual Vitamin

When something is categorized as "one in a million", it's considered priceless and rare. I believe this is how God feels about you. God created every human being with distinct traits and characteristics. No two people are exactly alike. Even identical twins have specific differences. God took the time to create you and you are the only one of you there is. *How awesome is that?* This is why it's so important that you make your mark on this world because no one can do it but you. God has given you certain talents and the ability to influence others for good. You will have to give an account of how you used your talents to God. If they are wasted, God will not be pleased. You will pay a price for wasting your talents and performing beneath the level that He knows you are capable of performing. Take time today to treasure your relationship with God, for where your treasure is, there your heart will be also.

Affirmation Prayer: Heavenly Father, You are more than one in a million. You are more precious than silver and gold and nothing I desire compares to You. Teach me how to treasure our relationship as my most priceless gift, in the name of Jesus, Amen.

Daily Bread: 1 Kings 3:16-28; 1 Kings 4 – 5; Acts 12:19-25; Acts 13:1-12; Psalm 74:18-23

Dance with My Father
June 18

Scripture: "Honor your father and your mother, that your days may be long upon the land which the Lord your God is giving you."
~ Exodus 20:12

"And you, fathers, do not provoke your children to wrath, but bring them up in the training and admonition of the Lord."
~ Ephesians 6:4

Spiritual Vitamin

Fathers are irreplaceable. To some, this is a day to celebrate the accomplishments and support of the wonderful man who raised you and helped you become the person you are today. To others, it is a day filled with bad memories of neglect and absence and is no real cause for celebration. God's Word is clear on what we are to do concerning our parents. We have a mandate to honor them. There is no criteria that says they have to be good; just that we must show honor. *Are you honoring your father? Is there harmony in your relationship with him?* If so, you know how beautiful this relationship can be. If not, consider taking the necessary steps to restore and forgive the offenses that have caused the separation.

In case your relationship is not good with your earthly father, there is hope. Your Heavenly Father is waiting with outstretched arms to embrace you. David accepted God's invitation and developed a meaningful relationship with Him. God so blessed David's life that he danced before the Lord with all his might. God has extended the invitation and is waiting for you to come and dance with Him. Dancing with a partner requires that one leads and one follows. The leader shows you what steps to take and you take them. God wants to lead and to have you eagerly follow. In your walk with God, you need to learn the skill of following His lead, much like in the art of dancing. He has some great things in store for you, but you cannot find His path on your own. You must allow Him to lead you to the path, so that you are sure to travel in the right direction; one that leads you to an eternity with Him. Take time today to communicate with and celebrate your earthly father while getting in sync with the steps of your Heavenly Father. If your earthly father has passed on, honor his memory in a meaningful way.

Affirmation Prayer: Heavenly Father, help me to celebrate and honor my earthly father. Whether he has measured up to my expectations or not, he is still my father. Help me to do what is necessary to maintain a good relationship with my father. If our relationship is strained, enable me to be willing to make it right, in the name of Jesus, Amen.

Daily Bread: 1 Kings 6; 1 Kings 7:1-22; Acts 13:13-41; Psalm 75:1-10

One Moment in Time
June 19

Scripture: "So teach us to number our days that we may gain a heart of wisdom."
~ Psalm 90:12

Spiritual Vitamin

Do you believe in yourself? Most people do not give themselves enough credit for the things they have already achieved. Hopefully, you have not allowed the situations and circumstances of life to steal your hopes and dreams for a bright future. When you were young, you probably had all sorts of aspirations and goals you wanted to achieve. *How are you doing with that?* No matter what stage you are currently in at this time in your life, you can still dream. You still have time to realize those dreams. Sometimes, you just can't take no for an answer. Keep trying until you achieve your highest goal. Don't waste time worrying about things that are outside of your control. Learn to appreciate life's moments as they unfold, each and every day. Take the necessary steps that will yield you a fulfilled and happy life. Take time today to enjoy your life, one moment at a time.

Affirmation Prayer: Heavenly Father, I realize that worrying does nothing for me. Help me let go of the need to be in control and to rest in surrendering control to You, in the name of Jesus, Amen.

Daily Bread: 1 Kings 7:23-51; 1 Kings 8:1-21; Acts 13:42-52; Acts 14:1-7; Psalm 76:1-12

Pocketful of Sunshine
June 20

Scripture: "Truly the light is sweet and it is pleasant for the eyes to behold the sun; But if a man lives many years and rejoices in them all, yet let him remember the days of darkness, for they will be many. All that is coming is vanity."
~ Ecclesiastes 11:7-8

Spiritual Vitamin

Have you ever experienced a broken heart? If so, you know how devastating it can be. To have a special love in your life, one that you know is a guarantee; one that will never mistreat you in any way, is a miraculous and valuable treasure. Human love is not capable of reaching the level of God's love. Human love is flawed but God's love is perfect. If your heart has been broken, place it in the hands of God. He is a heart specialist and is extremely skilled in restoring and repairing what has been broken. Once you experience the love of God for yourself in a personal and intimate way, you will feel like you've got a "Pocketful of Sunshine!" God's love belongs to you; it's all yours. There is no shortage in any capacity. There is nothing you need to do to earn it. It is freely given to you. All you need to do is be willing to accept it. Take time today to enjoy the benefit of God's sunshine as well as His rain.

Affirmation Prayer: Heavenly Father, You continue to demonstrate Your love for me in every phase of my life. Thank You for letting the sun rise and shine on me. Help me to enjoy the benefits of your love each day, in the name of Jesus, Amen.

Daily Bread: 1 Kings 8:22-66; 1 Kings 9:1-9; Acts 14:8-28; Proverbs 15:11-20

Respect
June 21

Scripture: "Show yourself in all respects to be a model of good works, and in your teaching show integrity, dignity ...."
~ Titus 2:7 ESV

Spiritual Vitamin

Are you giving God respect or neglect? God has what you want and everything you need. Most often than not, you only have a desire to receive your wants from God, not your needs. God knows what you need. He sometimes withholds what you want, because if He were to always give you what you wanted instead of what you needed, you could end up hurt. God uses His infinite wisdom in the way He takes care of you. He does not freely give you things that He knows will cause you pain and disappointment. But, within His permissive will, He sometimes allows things to come into your life to grow and mature you. *Have you ever begged and pleaded with God to give you something and later found out that the thing you wanted would have caused you harm? Can you remember how grateful you were for God's protection and the fact that He did not allow that particular thing into your life?* Give God your respect because He took the time to become so acquainted with who you are that He knows what to give you and what not to. Take time today to show yourself, in all respects, to be a model of good works, and in your teaching show integrity.

Affirmation Prayer: Heavenly Father, thank You for providing for me. Help me to be willing to pray as earnestly for my needs as I do for my wants, in the name of Jesus, Amen.

Daily Bread: 1 Kings 9:10-28; 1 Kings 10; 1 Kings 11:1-13; Acts 15:1-21; Psalm 77:1-9

Somebody Loves You
June 22

Scripture: "In this is love, not that we have loved God but that He loved us and sent His Son to be the propitiation for our sins."
~ 1 John 4:10

Spiritual Vitamin

Do you sometimes wonder if anyone loves you? Deep down inside, you know that God loves you. You have heard it somewhere before. Different people have told you at different stages of your life. *The question is, do you really believe it?* God's foundational message is love. God Himself is love. According to 1 John 4:19 (ESV), the reason we love God is because He first loved us. This is love at its best. Before you were even born, the plan for your salvation was already put in place. The natural, human love you are seeking will never fill the space within you intended for God's love. There is a vast difference between the two. You never have to feel alone because somebody loves you and you know who it is. You don't have to go on a wild goose chase and possibly end up with counterfeit love. You can chase after God and end up with authentic, life-changing love. Take time today to accept and receive God's love that you might be able to repeat the lyrics of the song to someone else; somebody loves you and you know who it is!

Affirmation Prayer: Heavenly Father, You thought I was worth salvation and You sent Jesus to give His life for me. This proves the depth of Your love. Empower me to tell others about Your grace and mercy, in the name of Jesus, Amen.

Daily Bread: 1 Kings 11:14-43; 1 Kings 12:1-24; Acts 15:22-41; Psalm 77:10-20

The Best of Me
June 23

Scripture: "For the Lord God is our sun and our shield. He gives us grace and glory. The Lord will withhold no good thing from those who do what is right."
~ Psalm 84:11(NLT)

Spiritual Vitamin

Are you willing to give God first place in your life? God did this for you; He gave you the best of Himself and that is amazing. He manifested Himself in human form through His Son, Jesus Christ. The process through which Jesus came to earth is amazing. As a matter of fact, the way you were created is amazing. There are so many things in the process of conception and birth that man has absolutely nothing to do with. The fact that two human beings can come together in an intimate way and create life is amazing. *In light of what God did for you, can you give your best to Him?* God knows what you are capable of because He created you; He made you one of His amazing miracles. He expects you to perform at your highest level. Take time today to give the best of yourself to God because He gave His best to you.

Affirmation Prayer: Heavenly Father, You died for me so I will live for You. Make me a bold witness, in the name of Jesus, Amen.

Daily Bread: 1 Kings 12:25-33; 1 Kings 13; 1 Kings 14:1-20; Acts 16:1-15; Psalm 78:1-8

The Great Pretender
June 24

Scripture: "You can't hide behind a religious mask forever; sooner or later the mask will slip and your true face will be known."
~ Luke 12:3a MSG

Spiritual Vitamin

Do you pretend to be someone you're not? You may feel you have to pretend with the people in your life but you don't have to pretend with God. Keeping up appearances is stressful and sometimes causes you to lie in order to make people think things are better than they really are. God knows you better than you know yourself. When you do things to attempt to fool Him, it will never work because He already knows the truth about you. You don't have to impress God because He already loves you. Before you could even try to do anything to deserve it, He already loved you. There's nothing you can do to change His mind. People may pressure you to earn their love but God never will. You don't have to be the great pretender. Be who you really are and give those close to you the chance to get to know that person. Take time today to consider removing your mask, revealing your authentic self, to the glory of God.

Affirmation Prayer: Heavenly Father, I looked in the mirror and did not like what I saw. I was pretending in certain areas of my life rather than facing the truth. Thank You for changing my ways. Help me to be unafraid and free to remove the mask, in the name of Jesus, Amen.

Daily Bread: 1 Kings 14:21-31; 1 Kings 15; 1 Kings 16:1-7; Acts 16:16-40; Proverbs 15:21-33

To Be Real
June 25

Scripture: "For the word of the Lord is right, and all his work is done in truth."
~ Psalm 33:4

Spiritual Vitamin

What do you know to be real? If you have experienced the wisdom of God, you know that you should never rely on what you think or feel when it comes to things of the spirit. Flesh and spirit will never agree and most of what God's Word is telling you to do are things your flesh doesn't feel like doing. God is real. You must have a strong personal relationship with Him in order to experience His power. What you think is real may not be. What you feel is real may not be. But if you consult God and tap into His wisdom, what He will tell you and show you will be real. There are two forces in the world, good and evil. Evil also has a voice. You must learn the difference between the two. If you are a born-again believer, what evil speaks to you will not feel good to your soul and spirit. That will help you distinguish between the voices. As you grow closer to God, the sound of His voice will be unmistakable. He will help you decipher between the counterfeit and the authentic and anyone who comes into your life from that point on has got "To Be Real!" Take time today to acknowledge the true Word of God and His righteousness.

Affirmation Prayer: Heavenly Father, thank You for being real to me. Because of You, I can see clearly now and I have a keen ear to hear Your voice. Teach me to obey Your Word, in the name of Jesus, Amen.

Daily Bread: 1 Kings 16:8-34; 1 Kings 17; 1 Kings 18:1-15; Acts 17:1-21; Psalm 78:9-16

Let's Talk About Love
June 26

Scripture: "Beloved, let us love one another, for love is of God."
~ 1 John 4:7a

Spiritual Vitamin

How can one have a conversation about love and not include God? His Word teaches us that God is love. His very essence is love. *How does one go through life without love?* The only way to truly have love in your life is to have God in your life. The things of God are the only things that will last forever. You will experience many temporal things while you have this earthly experience but spiritual things will follow you from the natural, earthly realm into the eternal realm. When you talk about love, you should be talking about God. When you think about love, you should be thinking about God. The amazing thing about God's love is that it must be shared. If His love is inside of you, it can't help but spill out onto everyone around you. God's love is meant to be shared. It's not to be selfishly held onto and kept to oneself. The love of God is for everyone. Take time today to talk about and share the love of God with everyone you meet.

Affirmation Prayer: Heavenly Father, I realize that Your love has everything to do with my life. When I talk about love, I will always speak of You. Teach me how to spread the Good News of Your love, in the name of Jesus, Amen.

Daily Bread: 1 Kings 18:16-46; 1 Kings 19; Acts 17:22-34; Acts 18:1-8; Psalm 78:17-31

Where Do Broken Hearts Go?
June 27

Scripture: "The Lord is near to those who have a broken heart, and saves such as have a contrite spirit."
~ Psalm 34:18

Spiritual Vitamin

Where do broken hearts go? Heartbreak is common to humanity. Every person has or will experience it during their lifetime. Broken hearts must go to God for healing. God never meant for you to put your heart into human hands. He knows that human hands are weak and frail. His Word tells you to keep vigilant watch over your heart, that's where life starts (Proverbs 4:23 MSG). It is best to follow the Word of God. *Where do broken hearts go?* They go to Jesus. *Can they find their way back to wholeness?* Following the leading and the example of Christ, they absolutely can. This has everything to do with your ability to trust God. Broken hearts can go back to the open arms of His love; the love that patiently waits for them. Jesus loves you now and will always love you. Take time today to experience the nearness of God and allow Him to mend your broken heart.

Affirmation Prayer: Heavenly Father, when I've been hurt and bruised, I sometimes tried to work things out alone. That never helped. You are the only One who can mend a broken heart and I thank You for mending mine. Teach me to always come to You, in the name of Jesus, Amen.

Daily Bread: 1 Kings 20 – 21; Acts 18:9-28; Acts 19:1-13; Psalm 78:32-39

Winner In You
June 28

Scripture: "Yet in all these things we are more than conquerors through him who loved us."
~ Romans 8:37

Spiritual Vitamin

As the end of the month draws near, I want you to continue learning self-love, God's way. I believe there is a winner in you. Everyone needs a friend like that. Someone who will not allow you to sink into the depths of despair but to reach into the darkness and pull you out. In the absence of a human being, you still have someone who has gone to great lengths to secure your sense of self-worth and joy. That someone is God. He created you and made you special and He loves what He created. God will always go above and beyond to rescue you. This is the level of love He has for you. *What does it say to God when He loves you unconditionally but for whatever reason, you can't love yourself?* God is always right and He never makes mistakes. He made you to be a conqueror. He made you to win. There is nothing in this life that can defeat you. Take time today to believe about yourself what God knows about you — that there is a winner in you — then encourage others that there is a winner in them too.

Affirmation Prayer: Heavenly Father, in my weakness, You show me my own strength. Because of You, I have come out a winner at the finish line. Help me to share the details of my victory with others, in the name of Jesus, Amen.

Daily Bread: 1 Kings 22:1-53; Acts 19:14-41; Proverbs 15:31-33; Proverbs 16:1-7

You Are So Beautiful
June 29

Scripture: "He has made everything beautiful in its time. Also He has put eternity in their hearts, except that no one can find out the work that God does from beginning to end."
~ Ecclesiastes 3:11

Spiritual Vitamin

Can you see the beauty of God in your life? This song title is a great summation of the thoughts and feelings one may have toward God. The way in which God takes care of and provides for you is a beautiful illustration of His great love for His creation. Once you accept Him and offer yourself to Him, there is nothing He will not do for you. There are no words to adequately describe the depth of God's love for you and for that, you owe Him your highest adoration and your best praise. He truly is everything you could hope for and everything you need. As a matter of fact, He far exceeds any human expectations that you can have. When God created you, He did so in His own image. By looking at yourself and others, you get a glimpse of the image of your Heavenly Father. It should give you a sense of appreciation and love for yourself to know that you were created in the image of God. Take time today to acknowledge the fact that God has made everything beautiful in its time and to realize the beauty that resides with you.

Affirmation Prayer: Heavenly Father, You are so beautiful to me. You have taught me that my outward appearance does not define my inner beauty. It is my resemblance of You which makes me beautiful. Help me share this knowledge with others, in the name of Jesus, Amen.

Daily Bread: 2 Kings 1; 2 Kings 2:1-25; Acts 20:1-38; Psalm 78:40-55

You've Got the Love
June 30

Scripture: "And we have known and believed the love that God has for us. God is love, and he who abides in love abides in God, and God in him."
~ 1 John 4:16

Spiritual Vitamin

Isn't it encouraging to know that you can count on God and that His love will see you through? Everyone goes through rough times. The question is not whether there will be challenges in your life, the question is *how will you handle the challenges when they come?* You must be willing to stand on the promises of God. He has made a commitment to see you through. *Will you give in to the desire to throw your hands in the air and give up out of frustration or will you allow God's love to see you through?* The truth of the matter is that you do care what happens in your life but sometimes the frustration of it all makes you say that you don't care. Sometimes the way gets hard and the sun is hidden behind the clouds. During those times, you must remember one very important thing — God is still in control. Take time today to realize that "You've Got the Love" of God; and that should be enough to carry you through whatever's going on in your life.

Affirmation Prayer: Heavenly Father, You have turned all of my baggage into blessings. I love living this new life in You. Make me willing to live in Your love each and every day of my life, in the name of Jesus, Amen.

Daily Bread: 2 Kings 3; 2 Kings 4:1-37; Acts 21:1-26; Psalm 78:56-72

MONTHLY REFLECTIONS

July: Satisfaction (Living Within God's Plan For Your Life)

Strength for the Journey

Heavenly Father,

Your awesome Presence fills this room and I bow down in total adoration and praise to You. Please hear my prayer and allow Your Holy Spirit to fall fresh upon me. There was a time when I was consumed by the cares of the world and was unable to find a sense of peace, no matter what I tried. I could not find satisfaction in various areas of my life because I was not living within Your plan for me. Please forgive me. Since becoming a born again believer, my life has changed in countless ways. Thank You for filling every void within me and for becoming everything I need to be fulfilled and satisfied. Thank You for waiting for me during my moments of disobedience. Please keep me near You and always able to feel Your Presence and to hear Your voice. Empower me to continuously submit to Your leading, so I will continue to walk the path of righteousness, in the name of Jesus, Amen.

July

Satisfaction (Living Within God's Plan For Your Life)

During the month of July, you will go on a journey, learning how to experience satisfaction while living within God's plan for your life. You will also learn how to become content with God's purpose for you. Satisfaction is defined as the fulfillment of one's wishes, expectations, or needs, or the pleasure derived from this. When you decide to let God be the pilot of your life, you willingly climb into the seat next to Him. Buckle your seatbelt and simply enjoy the ride, with every expectation of safely arriving at your divine destination. You understand that while there may be turbulence along the way, you have an experienced pilot whose flight record is without blemish or error. He is more than capable of handling any and all technical difficulties that attempt to hinder the success of the journey. It is my prayer that you will use this month's devotionals to learn how to enjoy the satisfaction of living within the will of God.

Quote: "If you live gladly to make others glad in God, your life will be hard, your risks will be high, and your joy will be full." --- John Piper

"The Lord will guide you continually, And satisfy your soul in drought, And strengthen your bones; you shall be like a watered garden, And like a spring of water, whose waters do not fail."
~ Isaiah 58:11

All My Life
July 1

Scripture: "I will praise the Lord all my life; I will sing praise to my God as long as I live."
~ Psalm 146:2 NIV

Spiritual Vitamin

Can you feel God's presence near you? Every day, every second, every minute, every hour, God is closer to you than you can imagine. He wants to be included in your life in a meaningful and satisfying way. According to Isaiah 58:11, "the Lord will guide you continually, and satisfy your soul in drought. And strengthen your bones; you shall be like a watered garden, and like a spring of water, whose waters do not fail." *Can you receive that into your spirit?* If you have already done so, seeking God and living passionately for Him can start at this very moment. All your joy and satisfaction can be found in living for Jesus. He is often overlooked because He can no longer be seen in the physical realm. Because He now sits at the right hand of your Heavenly Father, He is Spirit and no longer flesh. However, this does not diminish His power. As a matter of fact, it further validates the strength of it. Perhaps you have been looking for someone to love you all your life. Now, you have discovered Him and He is available. For this, you owe God praise. Take time today to afford God the opportunity to demonstrate His strength and power on your behalf.

Affirmation Prayer: Heavenly Father, I humble myself before Your presence for Your majesty is too great for me to behold. You have blessed me all my life. Help me to do what honors You, in the name of Jesus, Amen.

Daily Bread: 2 Kings 4:38-44; 2 Kings 5; 2 Kings 6:1-23; Acts 21:27-40; Acts 22:1-22; Psalm 79:1-13

All Right Now
July 2

Scripture: "The Lord is on my side; I will not fear. What can man do to me? The Lord is for me among those who help me; therefore I shall see my desire on those who hate me. It is better to trust in the Lord than to put confidence in man. It is better to trust in the Lord than to put confidence in princes."
~ Psalm 118:6-9

Spiritual Vitamin

Is this a season of hardship for you? Every person alive has experienced hurt and pain. Sometimes things happen in your life that catch you completely off guard and take you by surprise. You may feel like you are all alone and have nowhere to turn. But take courage because the Lord is on your side. Man has no power over you if Jesus Christ is your Savior. Allow the Lord to help you through your moments of crisis and confusion. He is eager to take away your hurt and pain. Jesus knows exactly how you are feeling about what has happened. Every pain you will ever feel in your physical experience was felt by Christ in His physical experience on earth. He has felt your pain. Take refuge in His Presence and allow Him to replace your sorrow with joy. If you entrust yourself into the loving arms of Almighty God, no matter what has happened in your life in the past, you can declare that it's all right now. Take time today to trust God and to show your appreciation for how He has made everything alright.

Affirmation Prayer: Heavenly Father, thank You for being on my side; because You are with me, everything is alright now. You protect me when I am right and correct me when I am wrong. Keep me grateful and willing to show You my appreciation for everything You do, in the name of Jesus, Amen.

Daily Bread: 2 Kings 6:24-33; 2 Kings 7; 2 Kings 8:1-15; Acts 22:22-30; Acts 23:1-10; Proverbs 16:8-17

At the Cross
July 3

Scripture: Then He said to them all "If anyone desires to come after Me, let him deny himself, and take up his cross daily, and follow Me."
~ Luke 9:23

Spiritual Vitamin

Are you trying to live your life without God? Living life without God is like living in darkness. You cannot accomplish very much in darkness because when it's dark, it's difficult to see. God provided a way out of that darkness through His Son, Jesus Christ, who is the Light of the world. *Have you received the light of Christ in your life?* If you have, then you already know that salvation from a life of sin produces a deep sense of satisfaction. Especially when you finally embrace the full meaning of the fact that Jesus paid the penalty for your sins when He died on the cross. He Himself did nothing worthy of punishment or death, yet He decided to take your place and He carried your sins to the cross. According to Galatians 2, your old nature has been crucified with Christ. It is no longer you who live, but Christ who lives in you. The life you now live in the flesh, you live by faith in the Son of God, who loved you and gave Himself for you. Now, He asks you to take up your cross daily by denying your selfish desires and following after Him. Take time today to give some thought to the depth of the meaning of what Jesus Christ did when He gave His life for you.

Affirmation Prayer: Heavenly Father, thank You for the finished work of Christ on the cross. Help me to walk in light and not in darkness, in the name of Jesus, Amen.

Daily Bread: 2 Kings 8:16-29; 2 Kings 9; Acts 23:11-35; Psalm 80:1-7

Beautiful Life
July 4

Scripture: "He has made everything beautiful in its time."
~ Ecclesiastes 3:11

Spiritual Vitamin

Happy Independence Day! While the country is celebrating its freedom, I thought it might be a good time to also celebrate the spiritual freedom you have received from your Savior, Jesus Christ! *Can you think of a time you couldn't see the beauty in your life that you now see?* If you do not have God in your life, you will not be able to see the beauty that you were created to see. Your vision will be distorted and the sun will not be as bright as it should. As you develop a relationship with God, He removes the blinders from your eyes and allows you to see things from a higher perspective. You are able to recognize progress and welcome change. According to Ecclesiastes 3:11, God made everything beautiful in its time. You may not always see the beauty in every situation and circumstance, but if you allow God to work things out for your good, then beauty will soon emerge. During difficult times, you must take courage in the fact that your Heavenly Father has the ability to turn things around in your favor, changing your darkness into light. Trials and obstacles come to make you stronger and as they pass, you are able to once again see and appreciate the beauty in your life. You must learn to take the bitter with the sweet, knowing that God ultimately has your best interest at heart. As you learn to rely upon and trust in Him, you can enjoy the beautiful life that He intended when He created you. Take time today to celebrate, not only the freedom of your country but the freedom of your soul!

Affirmation Prayer: Heavenly Father, teach me how to completely rely on You to make everything beautiful in Your time. Help me to avoid becoming impatient and cause me to wait on You, knowing that You are my light and salvation, in the name of Jesus, Amen.

Daily Bread: 2 Kings 10 – 11; Acts 24:1-27; Psalm 80:8-19

Better Life
July 5

Scripture: "You will show me the path of life; In Your presence is fullness of joy; At Your right hand are pleasures forevermore."
~ Psalm 16:11

Spiritual Vitamin

Do you ever think about heaven? Eternity is waiting for you after this earthly experience. Yes, paradise is coming. Your earthly experience will contain a mixture of things: joy and sorrow, laughter and tears, ups and downs. Just know that at the end of it all, God promises a better life. For now, there are some harsh facts you must face. As you journey through life, you will experience broken promises and disappointments. You will have scars and bruises from the trials and tribulations that come into your life. There will be times of joy and bliss but there will also be times of hurt and pain. There will be times of sorrow and tears that you must endure. There will be moments when you will wonder what tomorrow is going to bring and you will hope for a better life than the one you are currently living. Take heart in knowing that trouble won't last always. Through the shed blood and the finished work of Jesus Christ, you can find peace, joy and hope for a brighter tomorrow. Lose yourself in His love and He will guide you through the most difficult of times. If you would be willing to place your hope in God, there will be no surprise ending to your life. C.H. Spurgeon wrote "the truest lengthening of life is to live while we live, wasting no time but using every hour for the highest ends. So be it this day." Jesus promised you a place in paradise. God has plans for you. Take time today to surrender to the plan of God and experience abundant life.

Affirmation Prayer: Heavenly Father, You are the Great Shepherd, I am one of Your sheep. You have great plans for me. Teach me how to follow Your lead as You lead me into a better life, in the name of Jesus, Amen.

Daily Bread: 2 Kings 12 – 13; 2 Kings 14:1-22; Acts 25:1-22; Psalm 81:1-7

Cloud Nine
July 6

Scripture: "For He draws up drops of water, which distill as rain from the mist, which the clouds drop down and pour abundantly on man."
~ Job 36:27-28

Spiritual Vitamin

Do things always go as you expect? Of course there will be times in your life when things will not go as planned. When that happens, you might decide to look for an easy way out. But you do not have to do that. You can simply rely on the promises of God, to be with you in times of trouble. You do not have to look for a magical escape when things go wrong. Just put your mind on Christ and rest in the magnitude of His power. You can love the life you live and within the perfect will of God, you can live the life you love. There is nothing that can stop you from doing just that. It's simply a decision and it's time for you to make that decision and commit to it. You don't have to look for the Rapture each day, hoping that today is the day that Christ will come and instantly whisk you out of your trouble. It's okay to look forward to being with Jesus but not at the expense of rushing through your earthly experience altogether. Christ is with you now, dwelling on the inside of you. Learn to enjoy the indwelling of His Presence now. Take time today to experience a little bit of heaven, here on earth. Relax in the Presence of God. He'll show you things you have never seen.

Affirmation Prayer: Heavenly Father, thank You for Your promises. Even when things don't look like I want them to, I can still rest in You for You have promised me abundant life. Please keep me certain that You have it all under control, in the name of Jesus, Amen.

Daily Bread: 2 Kings 14:23-29; 2 Kings 15; Acts 25:23-27; Acts 26:1-23; Proverbs 16:18-27

Do It Til You're Satisfied
July 7

Scripture: "The Lord will guide you continually, and satisfy your soul in drought, and strengthen your bones; You shall be like a watered garden, and like a spring of water, whose waters do not fail."
~ Isaiah 58:11

Spiritual Vitamin

Today is recognized as Global Forgiveness Day. Let's all take advantage of this chance to extend love and grace to our fellow man.

Have you surrendered your life to Christ? Once you surrender your life to Christ and allow Him to become the Lord of your life, you also come to the realization that it is not wise to continue along life's path, doing what pleases you. It is better and far more beneficial to do what pleases God. Find out what it is that He wants you to do and delight in doing it. Do not view your assignment as an obligation or a burden. First, find your place in God and then find joy in whatever God wants you to do. In other words, take the time to discover your purpose. Whatever it is that God created you to do, go on and do it. Whatever your calling is, do it until you're satisfied that you are pleasing Him and fulfilling His will for your life. Serving God is a privilege. It is an honor that we as humans take all too lightly. God doesn't need us but He wants us. He created us for His pleasure. *Is what you're currently doing with the miracle of life honoring and blessing God?* If not, it's time for a change. Take time today to earnestly pray and seek the face of God so that He can share with you the purpose for which you were created.

Affirmation Prayer: Heavenly Father, thank You for your continued guidance. Without You, I cannot survive. Keep me in a surrendered state so that I am continually blessed and satisfied, in the name of Jesus, Amen.

Daily Bread: 2 Kings 16 – 17; Acts 26:24-32; Acts 27:1-12; Psalm 81:8-16

Do You Love What You Feel?
July 8

Scripture: "Though you have not seen him, you love him. Though you do not now see him, you believe in him and rejoice with joy that is inexpressible and filled with glory."
~ 1 Peter 1:8 ESV

Spiritual Vitamin

How is your life going right now? When you decide to fully surrender to God, He will change your life and you will begin to take on the attributes of Christ. God's Holy Spirit will direct and guide you into making better choices and decisions for your life. You will start to love what you feel, because you will love what God's Holy Spirit is doing in your life. You will no longer entertain feelings of low self-esteem, depression, loneliness or any other self-defeating emotion. God will replace low self-esteem with a healthy self-image, depression with a sense of joy and loneliness with fulfillment and satisfaction. You will begin to see yourself the way God sees you and you will love what you see, which will in turn allow you to love what you feel. Your sense of dependence on God will grow and you will be transformed from the inside out. Enjoy your newfound freedom in the Spirit. This is the way God intended your life to be. Take time today to enjoy the special moments God is making possible for you.

Affirmation Prayer: Heavenly Father, with You as my source, I love what I feel! I feel free. You have set me free to do Your will. Help me to stay on the path that leads to You, in the name of Jesus, Amen.

Daily Bread: 2 Kings 18; 2 Kings 19:1-13; Acts 27:13-44; Psalm 82:1-8

Good Times
July 9

Scripture: "When times are good, be happy; but when times are bad, consider this: God has made the one as well as the other. Therefore, no one can discover anything about their future."
~ Ecclesiastes 7:14 NIV

Spiritual Vitamin

Have you placed your life in the hands of God? When you put your life in God's hands, you will no longer view things the way you did before. You begin to experience the truth of Romans 8 — which simply says that all things work together for good. While all things right now may not seem to be good, with the help of God, they can be made to work out for your good. God will take the details of it all and work them out in your favor in the end. The pressure to try to solve your own problems is removed from you. You realize that God is always with you, even when things go wrong. It is during hard times when He is holding you closer to Himself, hoping that you will recognize His Presence. You don't have to fight and struggle. You can simply rest in Him and allow Him to work it all out on your behalf. Luck has nothing to do with having good times. That my friend, is all God's doing and it truly is marvelous in our eyes. Take time today to be satisfied in your current condition and celebrate the fact that you have a God who will fight for you --- and win!

Affirmation Prayer: Heavenly Father, thank You for good times. In those times, I will rejoice. Even when times are not so good, I will continue to give You praise. Help me to remain in a posture of worship and praise, in the name of Jesus, Amen.

Daily Bread: 2 Kings 19:14-37; 2 Kings 20; Acts 28:1-16; Psalm 83:1-18

Happy Days
July 10

Scripture: "The Lord is my strength and my shield; My heart trusted in Him, and I am helped; Therefore my heart greatly rejoices, And with my song I will praise Him."
~ Psalm 28:7

Spiritual Vitamin

Are you experiencing happy days? God has made provisions for you to do so. You have that right as well as many others as a Kingdom citizen. God's Word tells us that we are to rejoice in the days that He has made. You have so much for which to be grateful. Each day that you are blessed to still be counted among the living, you should rejoice. No one knows when their time on earth will be through, so every day is its own miracle. God has given you a certain number of days in which to fulfill His call on your life. *Are you working for the Lord and living a life that appeals to those who do not know Christ in the pardoning of their sins?* The opportunity to be an ambassador for Christ is an honor. God could have chosen anyone to represent Him and He chose you. Take time today to express your gratitude to God through praise to Him and service to mankind.

Affirmation Prayer: Heavenly Father, You have already seen each day of my life. Thank You for the happy days. You have created each one. Thank You for the joy that spills forth into my soul. Help me to always be willing to praise You, in the name of Jesus, Amen.

Daily Bread: 2 Kings 21 – 22; Acts 28:17-31; Proverbs 16:28-33; Proverbs 17:1-4

I Can't Get No Satisfaction
July 11

Scripture: "There is an evil to which I have seen under the sun, and it is common among men; a man to whom God has given riches and wealth and honor, so that he lacks nothing for himself of all he desires; yet God does not give him power to eat of it, but a foreigner consumes it. This is vanity, and it is an evil affliction."
~ Ecclesiastes 6:1-2

Spiritual Vitamin

Are you tired of temporary satisfaction? A life lived apart from the saving grace of Jesus Christ will be a life filled with just that; you deserve more. Without God in your life, there will be no consistency. You will experience days when things are going very well and you will experience days when things are going terribly wrong. Your mood and attitude will depend upon what's going on. There will be no lasting joy or peace. *What satisfies you? Is your happiness connected to material possessions or desires?* The only way to achieve true satisfaction is to know your purpose. Everything has a specific purpose. Without knowing yours, you will stumble through life haphazardly experiencing one catastrophe after another; you will never be able to find a lasting joy. But in Christ Jesus, you will find joy everlasting. In Christ, not only will you find satisfaction but you will find contentment as well. There is such joy and freedom in a right relationship with God. Take time today to gain satisfaction from a lasting connection with Jesus Christ, the Savior of the world.

Affirmation Prayer: Heavenly Father, forgive me for seeking satisfaction in anything outside of You. Help me to cultivate a deep and lasting connection with Jesus, my Savior so that temporary satisfaction will become a thing of the past, in the name of Jesus, Amen.

Daily Bread: 2 Kings 23; 2 Kings 24:1-7; Romans 1:1-17; Psalm 84:1-7

In Your Eyes
July 12

Scripture: "I will instruct you and teach you in the way you should go; I will guide you with My eye."
~ Psalm 32:8

Spiritual Vitamin

Did you know that God's eyes are always upon you? The eyes are fascinating organs. With the eyes, one can communicate the thoughts and feelings of the heart. Look deeply into the eyes of another human being and you will begin to see their level of comfort within themselves. You must be relatively close to someone to be able to look into their eyes. A songwriter wrote that God would guide you with His eye. *Can you feel the warmth and acceptance of God's love?* It is important to learn to walk by faith because when you walk by faith, you are not controlled by what you see with your eyes. When situations and circumstances don't look right through your natural eyes, you can use your spiritual eyes to take a closer look. Your spiritual sight will allow you to see things that your natural sight never could – you were once blind, but now you see. Spiritual sight gives you the opportunity to see things from a Godly point of view. When you see things the way God sees them, it completely changes your perspective. Take time today to look at the situations in your life through your spiritual eyes. You will be able to see what you could never see before.

Affirmation Prayer: Heavenly Father, I once was blind, but now I see. You saw me in my sin, and You delivered me from it all. Help me filter all that I see through my spiritual eyes not my natural eyes, in the name of Jesus, Amen.

Daily Bread: 2 Kings 24:8-20; 2 Kings 25; Romans 1:18-32; Psalm 84:8-12

Is It the Way You Love Me?
July 13

Scripture: "Behold what manner of love the Father has bestowed on us, that we should be called children of God! Therefore the world does not know us, because it did not know Him."
~ 1 John 3:1

Spiritual Vitamin

Do you feel loved? When you are in a relationship in which you feel loved, valued, cared for and appreciated, you are happy and fulfilled. Your mood is light and very little frustration can take control of you. You have a positive outlook and it seems as if you can take on the world. You feel empowered, strong and capable of reaching your desired goals. Having the support of someone who is good to you and who demonstrates their love for you in tangible ways makes you feel larger than life. If a relationship with another human being can do this, just imagine what a relationship with a true and living God can do. God has always been and will always be on your side. He desires the ultimate best for you. His love propels you forward and the power of it can bring out the greatness within you. *So the next time you find yourself smiling for no apparent reason, ask yourself a question -- could it be because God loves you?* Take time today to give God thanks and praise for His unconditional love toward you.

Affirmation Prayer: Heavenly Father, I am happy and full of joy. Is it because of the way You love me? I celebrate our love today and every day. Show me how to be more like You and how to give unconditional love, in the name of Jesus, Amen.

Daily Bread: Jonah 1 – 4; Romans 2:1-16; Psalm 85:1-7

I Still Haven't Found What I'm Looking For
July 14

Scripture: He asked her, "Woman, why are you crying? Who is it you are looking for?" Thinking He was the gardener, she said, "Sir, if you have carried Him away, tell me where you have put him and I will get him."
~ John 20:15 (NIV)

Spiritual Vitamin

Is there a void within you? There's a space inside all of us that only God can fill. Without God, we will experience a void that nothing else can satisfy. *What are you looking for? What is the deepest longing of your soul?* If you seek God first, His Holy Spirit will guide you each day into the blessings that have been prepared just for you. You will learn how to forge ahead through trying circumstances to a place of perfect peace. You won't waste time on things that were never meant for you. You will enjoy an abundance of God's best and realize that there is no time to waste in moving toward your God-given destiny. You will be able to experience God's love for you in a way that fulfills your soul. Then, His love will begin to spill out of you onto those around you. Love will become the deciding factor in all of your decisions. Seek God first and the thing that you're looking for will become easier to find. Take time today to search your heart and seek the face of God. He loves to hear you call and delights in answering the petitions of your heart.

Affirmation Prayer: Heavenly Father, thank You for filling the voids within me. Your Word is true. My sincere desire is to habitually practice the example of love that You have mapped out in Your Word. Help me to realize that in You, I already have more than I'll ever need, in the name of Jesus, Amen.

Daily Bread: Amos 1 — 2; Romans 2:17-29; Romans 3:1-8; Proverbs 17:5-14

Selwyn B. Cox

I've Been to Paradise but I've Never Been To Me
July 15

Scripture: "He who has an ear, let him hear what the Spirit says to the churches. To him who overcomes I will give to eat from the tree of life, which is in the midst of the Paradise of God."
~ Revelation 2:7

Spiritual Vitamin

How would you define paradise? Is it someplace where the sky is clear, the water is blue and the sand is white? Paradise could be defined as a place of perfect peace. When one thinks of being in paradise, they might consider a place where there is no stress, worry, fear or anxiety. One might also think of paradise as a specific destination. But paradise can also be a state of mind. *How can this be?* If you know God and if you have an honest, committed relationship with Him, you can go to paradise anytime you want. God made you and He knows you inside and out. His desire is for you to get to know yourself. There is one way to do that; spend time in His Presence so that He can teach you who you are. In the process of learning who you are, you will also learn who He is. The best destination to visit is the land of self. This is a trip you can take as often as you'd like and it's free of charge. Get to know you. Get to love you. No destination is more exotic or beautiful. Take time today to discover who God created you to be. You may even learn something about yourself that you never knew.

Affirmation Prayer: Heavenly Father, thank You for an ear to hear what You are saying to me. Thank You that true paradise awaits me at the end of my earthly experience. Grant me the ability to live each day in joyful anticipation of the place you have prepared for me, in the name of Jesus, Amen.

Daily Bread: Amos 3 – 4; Romans 3:9-31; Psalm 85:8-13

Take Time Out
July 16

Scripture: "Nothing is better for a man than that he should eat and drink, and that his soul should enjoy good in his labor. This also, I saw, was from the hand of God."
~ Ecclesiastes 2:24

Spiritual Vitamin

When was the last time you stopped to smell the roses? Everything is not urgent. Stop rushing your way through life. Life is meant to be enjoyed. It takes special moments to create memories and those moments happen gradually, not all mixed up together. Sometimes, you just need to slow down and relax. Every now and then, you need to take some time out because God has already taken care of the details. *Can you take some time to enjoy what He's done?* Stop trying to reinvent the wheel and take a ride on the wheel that has already been invented! Plan some down time into your schedule. Time where you simply clear your head and take in the beauty of nature. *When was the last time you played a game from your childhood?* The one thing adults seem to forget to do is play. As children, we loved to play. As adults, we take life too seriously. In reality, there is very little that is within our control. We must learn to rely on God. Taking care of you is something He wants to do. Take time today to relax and enjoy God's beauty, wherever you are. You have His permission to do so and you will be glad you did.

Affirmation Prayer: Heavenly Father, it is my season for fulfillment. I am resting in You. Thank You for some "down time", where I can relax in Your Presence. Help me to enjoy sweet communion with You, in the name of Jesus, Amen.

Daily Bread: Amos 5; Romans 4:1-15; Psalm 86:1-10

Let's Chill
July 17

Scripture: "The Lord is good to those who wait for Him, To the soul who seeks Him. It is good that one should hope and wait quietly for the salvation of the Lord."
~ Lamentations 3:25-26

Spiritual Vitamin

When was the last time you "hung out" with God? Have you ever taken a day to rest, pray, worship, study and meditate on God's Word? It is very important that you learn how to spend quality time with God. There are several ways you can do this. Relaxing in the Presence of God will ease your mind from the cares of this world. Being alone in His Presence will bring you comfort and peace in a way you can't find otherwise. Once you step into the Presence of God, all negativity will melt away. Your spirit will be revived and renewed and any worry or fears you had will disappear. You can talk to God about everything or nothing at all. God has the ability to read your heart and He knows what you are in need of, even before you ask. God has so many wonderful things to tell you and even more to give you. His blessings are endless and abundant. Take time today to plan a "chill" day with God. You owe it to yourself and those you love.

Affirmation Prayer: Heavenly Father, You are kindly affectionate toward me and that makes me long to spend time with you. Thank You that I don't have to rush and hurry my way through life. Let me know when it is time to step away from the busyness of life and quiet myself in Your Presence, in the name of Jesus, Amen.

Daily Bread: Amos 6 – 7; Romans 4:16-25; Romans 5:1-11; Psalm 86:11-17

(God's) Masterpiece
July 18

Scripture: "For we are His workmanship, created in Christ Jesus for good works, which God prepared beforehand that we should walk in them."
~ Ephesians 2:10

Spiritual Vitamin

Have you ever been told that you are a piece of work? In actuality, you are a work of art. You were created by a master craftsman who is an expert in His line of work. He comes highly recommended and has a perfect record. Everything He has made has been declared as "good" and He has never made a mistake. Although physical construction on you has been completed, the inner you is still being developed and revealed. Your character is still being worked on and you are becoming the product of your thoughts and feelings. *Are they positive or negative?* God gave you a gift called free will. When He made you, He placed something in you called a conscience, which is connected to Him and His desires for you. When you are in line with His will, you can feel His approval. Likewise, when you are not in line with His will for you, you can sense His disapproval. You must learn to trust your inner self, which speaks to you and confirms what you already know to be right and true. You are God's masterpiece. Take time today to make sure that your choices are in line with what He desires for you and what you were created to do.

Affirmation Prayer: Heavenly Father, thank You for making me a one of a kind masterpiece. You have formed and fashioned me as You have seen fit. Help me to remain moldable in Your hands, in the name of Jesus, Amen.

Daily Bread: Amos 8 – 9; Romans 5:12-21; Proverbs 17:15-24

Movin' On Up
July 19

Scripture: "For it is written: 'He shall give His angels charge over you, To keep you,' and, 'In their hands, they shall bear you up, Lest you dash your foot against a stone.'"
~ Luke 4:10-11

Spiritual Vitamin

Have you ever been moved up or promoted unexpectedly? If so, this is because God sees more in you than you see in yourself. God is a God of progression. During His public ministry, Jesus encountered people with various problems, situations and concerns. But He never left anyone the way He found them. It does not matter what kind of problem you are having or even how long you have been having it. When God arrives, change occurs. God wants to take you to a higher place. When you praise God, it raises you out of the depths of despair. Praise changes the atmosphere around you. This is because light and darkness cannot exist together. One will chase away the other. You have the choice as to which one is allowed to remain. When you have the opportunity to change your circumstances for the better, you should never hesitate to do so. With God, you have this chance every day. *Will you take it?* Allow God to improve your current condition. Take time today to praise God and allow Him to move you out of the difficult places in your life to a higher place in Him.

Affirmation Prayer: Heavenly Father, You have moved me to higher places in You. I shower You with reverence, worship and humility for taking me to new levels in You, in the name of Jesus, Amen.

Daily Bread: Hosea 1 – 2; Romans 6:1-14; Psalm 87:1-7

New Attitude
July 20

Scripture: "and be renewed in the spirit of your mind, and that you put on the new man which was created according to God, in true righteousness and holiness".
~ Ephesians 4:23-24

Spiritual Vitamin

Do you want a new attitude? You can change your mindset and reinvent yourself at any stage of life. As you grow and mature, if you find that there are certain attitudes and behaviors that have not served you well, you can change them for something that works better for you. You are free to make the necessary adjustments in your life whenever you are ready to do so. You can begin a physical "home improvement" project at whatever point you decide. Your temple can go under spiritual renovation with God's Holy Spirit and you will come out of it a brand new person. As you grow older, you should also grow wiser. However this does not just happen. It requires intentional effort, planning and execution. Don't allow life to happen to you without your input. Be a good steward over everything God has given you. Protect your assets as if your life depends on it, because truthfully, it does. Just as God has a plan for you, the enemy has one too. *Who will win?* Only you can make the choice. Take time today to check and adjust your attitude to be certain that you are on the winning side; that of Jesus Christ.

Affirmation Prayer: Heavenly Father, Your Word is engrafted in me. It says if I keep my mind stayed on You, that You will keep me in perfect peace. Let it soak into every part of my spirit, mind, and soul, in the name of Jesus, Amen.

Daily Bread: Hosea 3 – 5; Romans 6:15-23; Romans 7:1-6; Psalm 88:1-9

Over the Rainbow
July 21

Scripture: "It shall be, when I bring a cloud over the earth, that the rainbow shall be seen in the cloud; and I will remember My covenant which is between Me and you and every living creature of all flesh."
~ Genesis 9:14-15a

Spiritual Vitamin

What do you wish for? Is there something you want or something you want to do that you have been told is impossible? Hopes and dreams are made possible by God but in order to see them realized, you need to exercise faith. You don't need a lucky star or a magic wand. You just need faith in the Lord Jesus Christ. *Instead of wishing upon a star, why not say a little prayer?* Answered prayer can do far more than wishing on a star. Answered prayer can turn your gray skies into blue and make your trouble melt away. Many times, what you view as trouble is nothing more than an opportunity waiting to be realized or a blessing wrapped in sandpaper. You don't need fairytales and lullabies, you need faith. God can do whatever you believe He can. When you exercise your faith, that is His signal to move ahead and to bring into your reality that which you are expecting. *What do you see by faith?* Believe your way into everything God has for you. Take time today to reverse the curse of relying on what you see with your natural eyes and begin to look at life through the eyes of faith.

Affirmation Prayer: Heavenly Father, thank You for the beauty of the rainbow and the promise that comes along with it. You will never let me be harmed. Hold me close to You and remind me constantly of Your great love, in the name of Jesus, Amen.

Daily Bread: Hosea 6 – 7; Romans 7:7-25; Psalm 88:10-18

Practice What You Preach
July 22

Scripture: "You, therefore, who teach another, do you not teach yourself? You who preach that a man should not steal, do you steal?"
~ Romans 2:21

Spiritual Vitamin

Do you live like you know the God you say you serve? It does no good to tell people what the Bible says and then go out and live a spiritually reckless and careless life. In many cases, people read the actions of other people more than they read their Bibles. They need to see the God you serve at work in your life before they can gain a genuine desire for Him to operate in their lives. *What does your life say about your relationship with God? Does what you do show Him to be a kind, loving and faithful God?* You may be the only God someone will ever see. You must represent Him well. *What do your words, actions and behaviors say about Him?* If you are self-absorbed and selfish, then that is what others will think of God. There comes a time in your spiritual walk when you must practice what you preach. Do what God tells you to do so that He can be seen operating through you. Take time today to ensure that your life lines up with the will of God, so others can see Him in you.

Affirmation Prayer: Heavenly Father, I want my yes to be yes and my no to be no; seeking Your face for every area of my life. Enable me to walk uprightly, to be a strong witness for You and to practice what I preach, in the name of Jesus, Amen.

Daily Bread: Hosea 8 – 9; Romans 8:1-17; Proverbs 17:25-28; Proverbs 18:1-6

Stir It Up
July 23

Scripture: "And let us consider one another in order to stir up love and good works."
~ Hebrews 10:24

Spiritual Vitamin

Do you stir up the gift in you? Love is meant to be given and received. God wants to teach you how to love without conditions or strings. This is the kind of love He shares with you. God's love for you is not based on your ability to earn it because He knows that is not something you are capable of doing. Human beings are flawed and do not possess the capacity to love as God loves, apart from His leading and guiding. There is something supernatural that is needed in order to attain this goal. But with God's help, it can be reached. The first lesson is to allow yourself to receive the love of God for yourself. Secondly, you must allow Him to stir up the love that is now on the inside of you. Then you will be equipped to share it with those around you. Your selfish desires will become a thing of the past. You will have a zeal for life and an earnest desire to do what is pleasing to God. Take time today to allow God to pour His love into you and then to stir it up to be poured out on others.

Affirmation Prayer: Heavenly Father, I am an empty pitcher and You are a full fountain. Fill me up. Stir up what is within me until it overflows. Please increase my zeal for You, in the name of Jesus, Amen.

Daily Bread: Hosea 10 – 11; Romans 8:18-39; Psalm 89:1-8

Tell Me Something Good
July 24

Scripture: "You intended to harm me, but God intended it for good to accomplish what is now being done, the saving of many lives."
~ Genesis 50:20 NIV

Spiritual Vitamin

When was the last time you heard good news? In the world in which we live, there is an abundance of troubling and disturbing events that occur each day. For this reason, it is important to pray for the protection and covering of our loving God. Because of Him, there is still good news. Despite all the negativity, there is still something good to share. The good news is the gospel of Jesus Christ. The Bible is ageless and timeless and is just as powerful today as when it was written. This collection of writings will never be outdated and its contents has no expiration date. What God did in Biblical times, He can still do today. No matter what's going on in your life, there is an answer contained in the Word of God. In His human experience, Jesus encountered everything we will encounter and dealt with the things we will have to deal with in order to be an example for us. Now, all we have to do is follow His lead. Take time today to study the Word of God. You will find many nuggets of wisdom and ultimately discover the plan, purpose, power and promises of Jesus.

Affirmation Prayer: Heavenly Father, Your Word tells me something good. Help me to willingly pick it up each day to receive the latest news and to quickly act according to what You say, in the name of Jesus, Amen.

Daily Bread: Hosea 12 – 14; Romans 9:1-21; Psalm 89:9-13

The Boss
July 25

Scripture: "Work willingly at whatever you do, as though you were working for the Lord rather than for people. Remember that the Lord will give you an inheritance as your reward, and that the Master you are serving is Christ."
~ Colossians 3:23-24 NLT

Spiritual Vitamin

Who is your boss? The word boss is used very lightly in our society. In most cases, it is used to refer to the person for whom you work, who exercises authority over your activities and to whom you report. The word supervisor is a better term to describe that individual because he or she is actually supervising the way you do your work and watching over how well you perform your duties. Even if you work for someone else, in the end, that person is really not your boss. You are your own boss because you are the only one who can make decisions regarding what you will or will not do. It is God's desire to become your boss. *Have you ever considered allowing Him to be?* If you do, you will never again have to worry about not being promoted. God wants to take you higher and if you let Him, He will exceed your expectations. You can surrender control of your life over to Him and allow Him to guide your decisions, which will put you in a position for a better life. *Will you trust God enough to allow Him to be the boss?* Take time today to make God your boss. Then, get ready to soar to new heights as He takes you to your preordained destiny.

Affirmation Prayer: Heavenly Father, You alone are in control of me. While I may work for another human being, You are my boss. Teach me to operate with integrity in all that I do and say, in the name of Jesus, Amen.

Daily Bread: 1 Chronicles 1; 1 Chronicles 2:1-17; Romans 9:22-33; Romans 10:1-4; Psalm 89:14-18

This Time I'll Be Sweeter
July 26

Scripture: "How sweet are Your words to my taste, sweeter than honey to my mouth!"

~ Psalm 119:103

Spiritual Vitamin

Is it time to make a commitment to yourself? In the past, you have treated yourself unkindly and unfairly. You have not taken full advantage of the rights and privileges afforded to you by God and at times that decision caused you to end up broken and hurt. It is time to be sweeter to yourself. It is time to make a different choice. Sometimes the person we abuse the most is ourselves. We promise to lose weight and then don't make good on the goal. Then our bodies start to breakdown as a result of our poor habits. We promise to make time for rest and relaxation and instead, push ourselves beyond our physical limits. Then, our minds start to breakdown as a result of overload and neglect. There comes a time when we need a recharging and there is only one thing that will do, the Word of God. The only way to recharge your spirit is to spend time in the Presence of God. As you nourish your spirit, God takes care of everything else. Allow His Spirit to revive, refresh and rejuvenate your spirit. Take time today to pay attention to the needs of self. Only then, can you begin to meet the needs of others.

Affirmation Prayer: Heavenly Father, the way I have handled some things in my past was not good. Now that You have changed me, I can handle things differently. When adversity comes into my life again, this time, I'll be sweeter. I will operate in Your love, in the name of Jesus, Amen.

Daily Bread: 1 Chronicles 2:18-55; 1 Chronicles 3; 1 Chronicles 4:1-8; Romans 10:5-21; Romans 11:1-10; Proverbs 18:7-16

Love Changes
July 27

Scripture: "Count it all joy, my brothers, when you meet trials of various kinds, for you know that the testing of your faith produces steadfastness. And let steadfastness have its full effect, that you may be perfect and complete, lacking nothing."
~ James 1:2-4 ESV

Spiritual Vitamin

What changes are you going through because of love? Just like the weather, love follows the pattern of seasons. There is spring, when things are growing and blossoming; summer when the sun is high and the sky is a beautiful shade of blue; there is fall, when the leaves are in hues of earthen splendor; and there is winter, when it's snowy and cold. Yes, love has its seasons. In the spring of love, things may be going well and according to your plans. In the summer of love, you may be taking a vacation with your family or just spending quiet time at home. In the fall of love, you may be experiencing change that you did not previously know was coming and in the winter of love, you may be dealing with a loss of something you dearly loved. Here is something to comfort you. God is aware and concerned about every detail of your life. He remains with you through each stage and season of love. Sometimes you will be able to see His hand moving on your behalf and other times, it will seem as if He is nowhere to be found. Take courage. He has promised never to leave you alone. Take time today to trust in the Word of God. Be willing to experience each season of love and all that comes along with each one, knowing that God will see you through.

Affirmation Prayer: Heavenly Father, thank You for guiding me through my seasons of love. Your promises are wonderful. I am having the time of my life. Help me celebrate the love I now feel and that which still awaits me, in the name of Jesus, Amen.

Daily Bread: 1 Chronicles 4:9-43; 1 Chronicles 5; Romans 11:11-32; Psalm 89:19-29

Walking On Sunshine
July 28

Scripture: "For the Lord God is a sun and shield; the Lord will give grace and glory, no good thing will He withhold from those who walk uprightly."
~ Psalm 84:11

Spiritual Vitamin

As the end of the month draws near, I want to encourage you to be satisfied, living within God's plan for your life. God loves you and wants to shower you with good things. Your ability to receive from Him requires your obedience to His Word. When you line up with God's will, doors open that would have once remained closed. God will place opportunity before you and there will be nothing too hard for you to accomplish or overcome. You will sense God's Presence and as a result of it, you will experience a great deal of satisfaction. You will not be worried about how everything is going to work out because you will be certain that God is in control. You begin to feel like your best days are ahead of you and you will look forward to the coming days, weeks and months with an excitement that you did not have before. You will enjoy the feeling that all things are possible for you with the help of God. You will indeed feel like you are walking on sunshine and like everything is right in your world; that is because when you have God on your side, it is. Take time today to walk in the sunshine and light of Christ and allow your light to draw others to Him.

Affirmation Prayer: Heavenly Father, You have showered me with blessings and it feels like I am walking on sunshine. Assure me that You will never leave me or forsake me, in the name of Jesus, Amen.

Daily Bread: 1 Chronicles 6; Romans 11:33-36; Romans 12:1-21; Psalm 89:30-37

When You've Been Blessed
July 29

Scripture: "Blessed is the man who walks not in the counsel of the ungodly, nor stands in the path of sinners, nor sits in the seat of the scornful."
~ Psalm 1:1

Spiritual Vitamin

Are you blessed? When you've been blessed, it should propel you into action. You should have the desire to tell someone else about the good things that have been done for you and to then go out and do something that will bless another person. God is the only One who has the power to bless you. I know you may think it is the others in your life that accomplish the things you count as blessings, but ultimately, it is God who places the desires on the hearts of man to perform acts of service and kindness for one another. This works perfectly into the plan of God. You are blessed to become a blessing. The more blessed your life becomes, the more of a desire you should have to live as God ordained. You will begin to seek out Godly, like-minded people who will encourage and inspire you in your walk with God. You will also develop the desire to perform random acts of kindness for others. This will bring you a great sense of satisfaction because that is what serving others was meant to do. *Have you done something for someone else lately? In what ways have you been a blessing to others?* Take time today to reflect on just how blessed you are; then do what you can to bless the life of someone else.

Affirmation Prayer: Heavenly Father, I have been blessed. Help me to continually reflect on how good You have been to me, so that I will have the desire to be good to others, in the name of Jesus, Amen.

Daily Bread: 1 Chronicles 7 – 8; Romans 13:1-14; Psalm 89:38-45

Never Knew Love Like This Before
July 30

Scripture: " to know the love of Christ which passes knowledge; that you may be filled with all the fullness of God."
~ Ephesians 3:19

Spiritual Vitamin

What is your definition of love? You have your own definition of love because it means different things to different people. Human love can heal but it can also hurt. Once you have been hurt by someone, it is easy to become guarded against loving again. This is not God's design. You never have to worry about hurt when it comes to God's love. The love of God is the best love you will ever have. God's very essence is love and it makes up who He is. *Do you know God's love this way?* Once you experience it, you will understand that it's something you have never known before. God's love will satisfy you in a way that nothing else can or will. You don't have to knock yourself out trying to earn or maintain it. Just receive it and enjoy all of the benefits. God has already decided to give it to you in endless measure. You can never lose it and nothing will replace it. Take time today to discover the amazing love of God for yourself. Afterwards, share it with everyone else you know.

Affirmation Prayer: Heavenly Father, thank You for Your amazing love. I never knew love like this before. Help me to accept and receive it, in the name of Jesus, Amen.

Daily Bread: 1 Chronicles 9; 1 Chronicles 10:1-14; Romans 14:1-18; Proverbs 18:17-24; Proverbs 19:1-2

Nothing Compares To You
July 31

Scripture: "Again, the kingdom of heaven is like a merchant seeking beautiful pearls, who, when he had found one pearl of great price, went and sold all that he had and bought it."
~ Matthew 13:45-46

Spiritual Vitamin

Human beings frequently make comparisons about many things. We compare things like physical attributes, titles and positions, material possessions, employment levels and financial status. In each case, we make decisions about each other according to the things we have attained. We make judgements about who is better than whom, based on these things as well. We embrace those we believe to be worthy of us and reject those whom we believe are not. When it comes to God, we never have to worry about this because with God, there is no comparison. Nothing compares to Him. There is no position, possession, employment level or financial status that can come close to the greatness of God. He does not consider what you have, He looks at who you are. His love for you is based more on Himself than on you. He loves you because He decided to do so. There is no interview or screening process to go through in order to be accepted by God. He wants you and loves you, in whatever state you are in at this very moment. He will accept you as you are, but will not leave you that way. Take time today to receive the incomparable love of God. Doing so will bring you a sense of satisfaction you never thought possible.

Affirmation Prayer: Heavenly Father, nothing compares to You. Help me to remember that there is no substitute for You in any area of my life, in the name of Jesus, Amen.

Daily Bread: 1 Chronicles 11; 1 Chronicles 12:1-22; Romans 14:19-23; Romans 15:1-13; Psalm 89:46-52

MONTHLY REFLECTIONS

August: Spirit (God's Holy Spirit Within)

Strength for Journey

Heavenly Father,

How excellent is Your name in all the earth! I am not worthy of all the blessings You have given me. I have sinned and come short of Your glory; please forgive me. In spite of myself, You have loved me. You died for me and best of all, You will return one day to take me home. While I await that glorious day, I can experience the power of Your Holy Spirit within me --- leading, guiding and directing me in the way that I should go. I am powerless without this precious gift and can do nothing on my own. Thank You for allowing Your Holy Spirit to guide and to guard me. Increase my desire to spend time in Your Presence and to follow Your lead, in the name of Jesus, Amen.

August

Spirit (God's Holy Spirit Within)

During the month of August, you will go on a journey, learning the importance of bonding with and being filled with God's Holy Spirit. The Holy Spirit is the third person of the Trinity and is very real (because the Holy Spirit is a "person", I will at times make reference as "Him" or "He"). When Jesus was preparing to leave the earthly realm, He spoke of sending a Comforter, who is the Holy Spirit. He has great significance and lives on the inside of every born-again believer in Jesus Christ. You are the temple of the Holy Spirit. He is your most valuable possession and a very precious gift from God. It is my prayer that you will use this month's devotionals to ignite the power and purpose of God's Holy Spirit within you.

Quote: "It is the Holy Spirit's job to convict you, God's job to judge you and my job to love you." --- Billy Graham

"But the Helper, the Holy Spirit, whom the Father will send in My name, He will teach you all things, and bring to your remembrance all things that I said to you."
~ John 14:26

Amazing Grace
August 1

Scripture: "For by grace you have been saved through faith, and that not of yourselves; it is the gift of God, not of works, lest anyone should boast."
~ Ephesians 2:8-9

Spiritual Vitamin

Are you grateful for the grace of God? God gives man His grace. It has been said that grace is favor that we don't deserve. Because of man's sin, he was separated from God and needed a redeemer. Jesus Christ volunteered to become that redeemer. Because of Him, man's relationship with God has been restored. Jesus promised a Comforter before His departure from the earthly realm. The Comforter is God's Holy Spirit. Now, the Holy Spirit lives on the inside of every born again believer. God freely gives His grace to all who seek Him. Grace is something that cannot be fully explained or understood on a human level. The only explanation one can readily come up with is that God loved His creation so much, that He could not abandon or release it into the hands of the enemy. In the book of Genesis, God gave mankind free will, hoping that we would choose Him. When we did not, He then gave His Son to die for our sins, so that we would never be eternally lost. Now that's grace and it truly is amazing. Take time today to thank God for His amazing grace that will follow you from now into eternity.

Affirmation Prayer: Heavenly Father, thank You for Your amazing grace. It is a precious and priceless gift. Teach me to never take it for granted, in the name of Jesus, Amen.

Daily Bread: 1 Chronicles 12:23-40; 1 Chronicles 13 – 14; Romans 15:14-33; Psalm 90:1-10

Ascension
August 2

Scripture: "But you shall receive power when the Holy Spirit has come upon you; and you shall be witnesses to Me in Jerusalem, and in all Judea and Samaria, and to the end of the earth."
~ Acts 1:8

Spiritual Vitamin

When something ascends, it is raised to a higher level. *Do you want to go higher in Him?* Jesus ascended from earth to be seated at the right hand of the Father. When He left, God knew you would need someone to help you navigate your way through life. So He sent His Holy Spirit. When you receive God's Holy Spirit, you receive power. This is not to be confused with strength. While strength may be used to cope with situations and circumstances as they are, power can change the dynamics of the situations themselves. God is not bound by the laws of nature. He can at any time, in any way, change the particulars in regards to how things operate and function. With God, there are no limits. Your faith and belief in the power of God can take you higher. With God on your side, you don't have to remain where you are. Set new goals for yourself and believe that you can reach them. God is your helper and He won't let you down. Take time today to allow the Holy Spirit to raise your level of faith in God. He wants to take you higher for His name's sake.

Affirmation Prayer: Heavenly Father, Jesus sealed my life with His finished work on the cross. Thank You for the power I have received through Your Holy Spirit. Help me to increase my faith in You, in the name of Jesus, Amen.

Daily Bread: 1 Chronicles 15; 1 Chronicles 16:1-36; Romans 16; Psalm 90:11-17

Black or White
August 3

Scripture: "There is neither Jew nor Greek, there is nether slave nor free, there is neither male nor female; for you are all one in Christ Jesus."
~ Galatians 3:28

Spiritual Vitamin

Have you been affected by racial tension lately? Prejudice is real. Racial tension is running rampant in our world today. This was never God's intention. When God created man, He intended us to live in harmony because we are all one in Christ Jesus. Unfortunately because of the enemy, the human race has not yet figured out how to peacefully co-exist. There are some who feel superior to others and those persons feel the need to oppress and control their fellow man. When God looks at you, He doesn't see you. He sees His Son. While there are many imperfections in man due to sin, there are no imperfections in Christ. He is perfect in every way, completely free of sin, guilt or shame. God is the ultimate power and He alone has the right to exercise control. Love is still the answer and will always cover a multitude of sins. The answer to our racial problems is the same as it always was, love. You have heard this and deep down inside, you know it is true -- only love will conquer hate. Take time today to apply love to a situation where hate exists. You will see the mighty hand of God move to miraculously turn things around.

Affirmation Prayer: Heavenly Father, You are no respecter of person and You regard no color. I am fearfully and wonderfully made and I am Your special creation. Help me to understand that You made me to love and not to hate, in the name of Jesus, Amen.

Daily Bread: 1 Chronicles 16:37-43; 1 Chronicles 17 – 18; 1 Corinthians 1:1-17; Proverbs 19:3-12

Blowin' in the Wind
August 4

Scripture: "The wind blows where it wishes, and you hear the sound of it, but cannot tell where it comes from and where it goes. So is everyone who is born of the Spirit."
~ John 3:8

Spiritual Vitamin

Can you feel God's Holy Spirit? God's Holy Spirit has been known to manifest Himself as wind. When we think of wind, we also think of breath. Wind is something that can be felt but not seen. *Have you ever allowed Him to take you to a place of perfect peace and serenity?* If not, you are missing out on a life-altering experience. There is a freedom associated with wind because as the passage in John 3 says, the wind blows where it wishes. It doesn't ask or need the permission or consent of man. It is controlled by Almighty God and He alone has rule and authority over this element. To demonstrate the power of wind, all one has to do is watch a sailboat on the water. As it moves about, it is controlled by the wind. *Is your spirit free?* If not, allow the power of the Holy Spirit to engulf you and blow the negative forces out of your life. Once you become free from mental and emotional anguish, you will find that you are free to walk in God's purpose and calling on your life. Take time today to experience the power afforded to you by God's Holy Spirit. You will never be the same.

Affirmation Prayer: Heavenly Father, what a consolation it is to know that You have provided a Comforter for me. He has directed, instructed and corrected me when I needed it the most. Help me to be open to the leading of Your Spirit, in the name of Jesus, Amen.

Daily Bread: 1 Chronicles 19 – 21; 1 Corinthians 1:18-31; 1 Corinthians 2:1-5; Psalm 91:1-8

Selwyn B. Cox

Put Your Body In It
August 5

Scripture: "Or do you not know that your body is the temple of the Holy Spirit who is in you, whom you have from God, and you are not your own?"
~ 1 Corinthians 6:19

Spiritual Vitamin

Do you listen to your body? As a human being, you tend to pay more attention to your body than you do to your soul. One reason for this is that the body is tangible, the soul is not. The body can be seen and felt; the soul cannot. Humans have the bad habit of over-feeding the body while starving the soul. *Why do you think your soul needs less food than your body?* While your body craves physical food, your soul craves spiritual food, which is the Word of God. When you read God's Word, you nourish your soul. When you spend quiet, meditative moments in His Presence, you nourish your soul. When you pray and engage in meaningful dialogue with God --- pouring out your heart to Him, you nourish your soul. Don't take the chance of becoming spiritually malnourished. Eat some soul food! Your soul cannot exist on a diet of carnality, so allow the Holy Spirit to change you from a person who is ruled by the flesh into a person who is ruled by God's Spirit. Take time today to read God's Word; allow the Holy Spirit to nourish your whole being, body and soul!

Affirmation Prayer: Heavenly Father, my body is the temple of Your Holy Spirit. I am not my own. I ask that You help me not to rely on my own will but on the power of Your Holy Spirit. Please lead, guide and direct me forever, in the name of Jesus, Amen.

Daily Bread: 1 Chronicles 22 – 23; 1 Corinthians 2:6-16; Psalm 91:9-16

Breathe Again
August 6

Scripture: "The Spirit of God has made me, And the breath of the Almighty gives me life."
~ Job 33:4

Spiritual Vitamin

Do you take time to breathe again? Today's scripture verse is a very powerful reminder of just how much you mean to God. He loves you so much that He used His own breath to give you life. God Himself breathed life into man. Within the Creation process, He could have used anything to bring man to life. Instead, God used Himself. He also repeated this process when you needed a sacrifice for your sin. God used Himself again; this time in the form of His Son, Jesus. When Jesus departed the earth, He sent the Holy Spirit as your Comforter. Not only does the breath of God give you life, it also gives you the power to **speak life**. You are not a victim of circumstance. Empowered by God's Holy Spirit, you can speak life to those "dead" things; things like financial lack, failing health or a troubled marriage relationship. Use the breath that God has given you to speak life. In this way, you accomplish the purposes of God. I believe He had an awesome plan in mind when He created you and it was for this particular moment in time. Take heart and refuse to be discouraged. Take time today to thank God for breathing the breath of life into you and for giving you the power, through His Holy Spirit, to speak life into any dead thing that attempts to come against the plan of God.

Affirmation Prayer: Heavenly Father, thank You for breathing life into me. I do not take it for granted. I rejoice because You gave me life, something that would not be possible without You. Help me to praise you forevermore, in the name of Jesus, Amen.

Daily Bread: 1 Chronicles 24 – 25; 1 Chronicles 26:1-19; 1 Corinthians 3; Psalm 92:1-15

Bustin' Loose
August 7

Scripture: "Now the Lord is the Spirit; and where the Spirit of the Lord is, there is liberty."
~ 2 Corinthians 3:17

Spiritual Vitamin

Today is the National Day of Forgiveness. The spirit of unforgiveness has the potential to influence every human being. In some cases, that influence has even turned into control. It is an individual's responsibility to maintain control of him or herself and to only be under the influence of God. If there is something in your life that is negatively influencing and affecting you and causing you to make the same mistakes over and over again, then you have to find a way to free yourself from whatever that is. For many of us, it is unforgiveness. Don't allow the enemy to ensnare and entangle you with his lies; bust loose, shake off and walk away from any and all demonic activity or forces that attempt to put you in bondage. Bondage is not just physical in nature; it can also be mental and/or emotional. You don't have to live this way. Bust loose from anger, jealousy, fear, depression, rage, slander, bitterness and the like. You are a child of the King and these negative attitudes and emotions have no place in your life. Take a stand for yourself. Don't allow any and everything into your life. Put some boundaries in place and draw the line on the enemy. Take time today, through the power of the Holy Spirit, to break free from the chains that keep you under the influence of unforgiveness. God will reward your efforts.

Affirmation Prayer: Heavenly Father, I repent of the sins that I have committed and I stand against all sin. Thank You for Your cleansing and forgiveness. Make me willing to forgive others, as You have forgiven me, in the name of Jesus, Amen.

Daily Bread: 1 Chronicles 26:20-32; 1 Chronicles 27; 1 Corinthians 4; Proverbs 19:13-22

Circle of One
August 8

Scripture: "God sits above the circle of the earth. The people below seem like grasshoppers to him! He spreads out the heavens like a curtain and makes his tent from them."
~ Isaiah 40:22 NLT

Spiritual Vitamin

Are you doing your part? From a human standpoint, it takes many people to make up a circle. But with God, He alone has the ability within Himself to be a circle of One. The Trinity of God is made up of God the Father, God the Son and God the Holy Spirit and is a circle of One. The body of Christ has many members but each member is a part of the same body. Each of us serves a specific purpose within the body. In order for the body to function as designed, each part must perform the job for which it was created. Hands cannot be ears; ears cannot be eyes; and arms cannot be feet. *What part were you created to play?* The only way an individual part can complement the body is by successfully carrying out its designed task. *What were you created to do? Can God trust you to do the job He created you to do? Does He have to constantly usher you back into your proper place?* Don't try to be something other than what you were made to be. Take time today to examine which part of the body you were created to serve. You won't be able to fulfill your purpose until you know.

Affirmation Prayer: Heavenly Father, thank You for being my circle of One. You take such good care of me and give me everything I need! Let me not stand in the way of Your purpose and plan for me, in the name of Jesus, Amen.

Daily Bread: 1 Chronicles 28 – 29; 1 Corinthians 5; Psalm 93:1-5

Daydreaming and Thinking of You
August 9

Scripture: "This Book of the Law shall not depart from your mouth, but you shall meditate in it day and night, that you may observe to do according to all that is written in it. For then you will make your way prosperous, and then you will have good success."
~ Joshua 1:8

Spiritual Vitamin

Sometimes, I find myself daydreaming and thinking of God. *Can you identify?* When you daydream, you tend to think of things in a different state than what they currently are. You can imagine something as you wish it were, rather than how it really is. If you spend a good deal of your time daydreaming, you should carefully examine your reasons for doing so. Ecclesiastes 5:3a (NIV) says "a dream comes when there are many cares." *Do you have many cares? Are you taking the weight of the world on your shoulders?* You don't have to live like that. Jesus gave you permission to cast your cares on Him. He didn't say for you to gently place your cares on Him, He said for you to *cast* them on Him. To cast is to throw something forcefully in a specified direction. *So, what are you waiting for?* Cast your cares on the Lord. You don't have to waste your time daydreaming about the way you wish things were. You can follow the plan of God and call those things which do not exist as though they did (Romans 4:17). Take time today to line up with the Word of God and make those dreams into realities.

Affirmation Prayer: Heavenly Father, I dream about the day when I will be with You in paradise. I am in line with Your will and have surrendered my ways. Help me to constantly think of You, in the name of Jesus, Amen.

Daily Bread: 2 Chronicles 1:1-17; 1 Corinthians 6; Psalm 94

(Everything I Do) I Do It For You
August 10

Scripture: "Likewise the Spirit also helps in our weaknesses. For we do not know what we should pray for as we ought, but the Spirit Himself makes intercession for us with groanings which cannot be uttered."
~ Romans 8:26

Spiritual Vitamin

Do you feel that God does everything for you and is it good? Yes, God does everything for you. He wakes you up every morning. He provides the things you will need to make it from the start of your day to the end of your day. He provides food, clothing, shelter and so much more. Not only does He provide your natural needs, He longs to provide your spiritual needs as well. God stands by, waiting to hear you call out to Him for assistance. When you do, the Holy Spirit speaks to your spirit throughout the day, leading and guiding you through every decision that you will have to make. He helps you through moments of crisis and weakness, even during moments when you find it difficult to pray. It is then that Jesus prays for you. He is your intercessor. *Isn't that a powerful thought?* Jesus prays for you! Everything God does, He does it for you. He has seen every yesterday and every tomorrow. You can only see one day at a time but God has seen the completed canvas of your entire life. Because of this, it's best to trust Him with the details of everyday life. Take time today to consider all that God is doing for you and give Him thanks and praise.

Affirmation Prayer: Heavenly Father, thank You for helping me in my weakness. Let everything I do glorify You, in the name of Jesus, Amen.

Daily Bread: Ecclesiastes 1 – 2; Ecclesiastes 3:1-22; 1 Corinthians 7:1-16; Psalm 94:12-23

Inseparable
August 11

Scripture: "If we live in the Spirit, let us also walk in the Spirit."
~ Galatians 5:25

Spiritual Vitamin

Do you feel that something has separated you from God? It should bring you comfort to know that once you become a part of the family of God, you and God are inseparable. There is nothing that can ever separate you from His love. Jesus made a great sacrifice on your behalf. What He did on the cross has expunged your record, so your sins no longer have the power to disqualify you from going into the Presence of God. With heartfelt repentance, you now have access to the throne of God. Because your sins have been forgiven, you don't need someone to speak to God on your behalf. You can now go and talk to Him yourself. What an awesome opportunity! With the help of your Savior, Jesus Christ, there is nothing standing between you and God and nothing can separate you from His love. God longs to spend time with you and He waits for any opportunity to do so. He longs to hear your voice cry out to Him in worship. When you worship God, the Holy Spirit connects your spirit with God's Spirit. Your worship produces a fragrance and when you open your heart and freely worship God, He can smell your fragrance. Take time today to send a sweet-smelling savor and aroma into the nostrils of God. Worship Him in spirit and in truth.

Affirmation Prayer: Heavenly Father, thank You for the opportunity to live in Your Spirit. Because of what You have done, we are inseparable. Help me to do the things that reflect Your character. Order my steps, in the name of Jesus, Amen.

Daily Bread: Ecclesiastes 4 – 6; 1 Corinthians 7:17-35; Proverbs 19:23-29; Proverbs 20:1-4

Jesus Will
August 12

Scripture: "Nevertheless I tell you the truth. It is to your advantage that I go away; for if I do not go away, the Helper will not come to you; but if I depart, I will send Him to you."
~ John 16:7

Spiritual Vitamin

Are you having difficulty finding help? When no one else will help you, Jesus will. As a matter of fact, when He left earth, He promised to send a Helper. This Helper is the Holy Spirit. When no one wants to hear your heart, the Helper does. When no one else is there for you, the Helper is. When everyone else walks away, the Helper remains. Knock on the door of heaven and you will always get an answer. The Helper is never too busy to hear what you have to say. If you are experiencing discouragement today, fear not. You have an all-powerful God on your side, who loves you more than you can imagine. Even if you have done something wrong, repent and ask for God's forgiveness. He will immediately restore you to a place of peace and He will send His Holy Spirit (the Helper) to comfort you. You don't have to be held hostage by people or past mistakes. Go directly to God and allow Him to restore your soul. God is everything you will ever need. Stop putting all your trust in man. The best thing to do is to trust God. Take time today to praise God because what people won't do for you, the Helper will!

Affirmation Prayer: Heavenly Father, thank You for establishing order in my life. First, Jesus died to save me and then He returned to You so that the Comforter would come to teach me how to live. What abundant blessings and provision I now enjoy. Keep me grateful, in the name of Jesus, Amen.

Daily Bread: Ecclesiastes 7 – 8; Ecclesiastes 9:1-12; 1 Corinthians 7:36-40; 1 Corinthians 8:1-13; Psalm 95:1-11

Just a Closer Walk With Thee
August 13

Scripture: "I say then: Walk in the Spirit, and you shall not fulfill the lust of the flesh."
~ Galatians 5:16

Spiritual Vitamin

Do you want a closer walk with God? If you do, you must delve into His Word. Not only must you read it, but meditate, ponder on and study it to gain a deeper understanding and revelation of what God has to say to you. Figure out what it means to you as an individual. Your relationship with God can continue to grow deeper and deeper for as long as you live. In your earthly experience, you will never reach a place where you know enough about God. You will always need the leading of the Holy Spirit as you study, meditate and learn more and more of His Word. As you live your life on a daily basis, you will discover new things about yourself and new things about God. God left His Word as a road map to guide you through the ups and downs of life. The Bible is the best self-help book there is. Each time you open up the Word of God, you have the opportunity to see hidden treasures and mysteries and to benefit from the way in which God thinks. God doesn't desire to hide things from you. He wants to share as much of Himself as you are ready to handle. Take time today to do what is necessary to gain a closer walk with God.

Affirmation Prayer: Heavenly Father, I want a closer walk with You. Teach me how to draw closer to You so that I live daily in Your Presence, in the name of Jesus, Amen.

Daily Bread: Ecclesiastes 9:13-18; Ecclesiastes 10 – 12; 1 Corinthians 9:1-18; Psalm 96:1-13

Let's Do It Again
August 14

Scripture: "Rejoice in the Lord always. Again, I will say, rejoice!"
~ Philippians 4:4

Spiritual Vitamin

Have you been touched by the Holy Spirit? If you have had an encounter with the Holy Spirit, you know how amazing that feels. The Holy Spirit is the third person of the Trinity and is the One Jesus promised to send as the Comforter. Once you have your first encounter with the Holy Spirit, you will always anticipate and expect the next encounter. The Holy Spirit's touch is unexplainable. You lose yourself and in a way, it feels like you have had an out of body experience. This is not something that is restricted to a particular time or place. You don't have to be in church and it doesn't have to be on Sunday. You can experience a touch from the Holy Spirit wherever you are. You must quiet yourself and get into a mind-set of worship. Repent of your sins, ask God to remove distractions and surrender yourself to Him. Invite the Holy Spirit in. This sets the atmosphere for fellowship and communion with God. You must let the experience happen. Don't rush through it; stay there and bask in His glory. Take time today to make a petition to God – "I've felt Your Holy Spirit before and the experience was amazing. I anxiously await a time when we can do it again!"

Affirmation Prayer: Heavenly Father, You and I together, have made it through the trials of yesterday. Today, let's do it again. Keep revealing Your loving kindness and tender mercies to me each and every day, in the name of Jesus, Amen.

Daily Bread: 2 Chronicles 2 – 4; 1 Corinthians 9:19-27; 1 Corinthians 10:1-13; Psalm 97:1-12

Can You Feel It?
August 15

Scripture: "We love Him because He first loved us."
~ 1 John 4:19

Spiritual Vitamin

Can you feel God's love for you? God knows how best to love you because He is your Creator. He is familiar with each one of your needs. You will never find the depth of love you receive from God anywhere else. *Isn't it amazing that we spend more time yearning for the love of people than we do seeking the love of the Father?* The Holy Spirit can enable you to feel the love of God in your heart. Unfortunately, we spend very little time allowing the Holy Spirit to do this. A great deal of effort gets poured into cultivating human relationships, often at the expense of your relationship with God. Maybe it's because God doesn't force His way into your life. He patiently waits for you to choose Him. There is no expiration date on His love for you. He knows that sometimes, you will not immediately respond to Him; so He waits. He knows that sometimes you will place other things in front of Him; so He waits. He knows that you will occasionally place other people in front of Him; so He waits. He waits because He's determined to win your heart; not by force but by proving to you how deep His love really is. *How can you resist a love like this?* Take time today to surrender to the tugging of God on your heart so that you can feel the love He has for you.

Affirmation Prayer: Heavenly Father, I can feel Your love for me. I sometimes do not live as if I am grateful. Forgive me when it looks like I am taking Your love for granted and help me not to do that, in the name of Jesus, Amen.

Daily Bread: 2 Chronicles 5:1-14; 2 Chronicles 6; 2 Chronicles 7:1-11; 1 Corinthians 10:14-33; Proverbs 20:5-14

Perfect Gift
August 16

Scripture: "Then Peter said to them, "Repent, and let every one of you be baptized in the name of Jesus Christ for the remission of sins; and you shall receive the gift of the Holy Spirit."
~ Acts 2:38

Spiritual Vitamin

When was the last time you received a gift? Undoubtedly, you have received many gifts during the course of your life. Some hold higher and more meaningful significance than others. In times past, you may have opened a package and once you saw what was inside, thought you had obtained the perfect gift. But there is one gift that surpasses them all. That is the gift of the Holy Spirit. You obtain this gift as a result of being in a relationship with God. When you surrender your life to God, through repentance, you gain the right to become a Kingdom citizen. God becomes your Father, Jesus Christ becomes your Savior and the Holy Spirit becomes your Comforter. After you repent and are baptized, you receive the gift of the Holy Spirit. Under His influence, your steps are ordered. Your faith allows Jesus and the Holy Spirit to operate on your behalf carrying out the will of God in your life. As a born again, blood washed believer in Jesus Christ, you now have the perfect gift, the Holy Spirit. Take time today to embrace all the benefits that come along with having this precious gift.

Affirmation Prayer: Heavenly Father, thank You for the gift of the Holy Spirit. I repent of my sins and am asking for Your forgiveness. Make me worthy of such a priceless treasure, in the name of Jesus, Amen.

Daily Bread: 2 Chronicles 7:12-22; 2 Chronicles 8 – 9; 1 Corinthians 11; Psalm 98:1-9

Power of Love
August 17

Scripture: "But love your enemies, do good, and lend, hoping for nothing in return; and your reward will be great, and you will be sons of the Most High. For He is kind to the unthankful and evil."

~ Luke 6:35

Spiritual Vitamin

Do you know the power of love? The desire to be loved is a basic human need. It is something we all have in common and no one is exempt. The desire is so deeply rooted that it sometimes leads you to search for love in places where you have no business looking. When the people you have pulled into your inner circle disappoint you, you may become angry and unforgiving. This is where you must call upon the power of the Holy Spirit. True love will cover sin and is a powerful force. There is no situation that cannot be solved using the power of love. Mankind was born for fellowship with God and one another. The enemy knows how true this is, which is why his greatest tactic is to keep you at odds with others. Do not allow him to rob you of your right to have peaceful, loving relationships with your family members and friends. No one has been good all the time and every human being has made mistakes. When you have received forgiveness for the things you have done wrong, you should be willing to extend forgiveness to those who need it from you. Take time today to examine where there may be brokenness among your relationships and ask the Holy Spirit to help you to apply a generous amount of forgiveness and love to each one.

Affirmation Prayer: Heavenly Father, please help me to forgive my enemies. Help me to forgive my siblings, my spouse, and all of my acquaintances, in the name of Jesus, Amen.

Daily Bread: Song of Solomon 1 – 4; 1 Corinthians 12:1-26; Psalm 99:1-9

(I Need A) Refill
August 18

Scripture: "And do not be drunk with wine, in which is dissipation; but be filled with the Spirit."
~ Ephesians 5:18

Spiritual Vitamin

Have you ever felt empty inside? Sooner or later, you will run low of something you need. Whether it's something natural or spiritual, this fact holds true. At some point, you will need a refill. The best example of this is when you are in a restaurant enjoying a meal and your server comes to the table, sees that your glass is empty and says *"do you want a refill?"* This is what the Holy Spirit does. He knows what you are dealing with each day. The Holy Spirit sees how much it takes for you to keep going and when you are running low. Just at the right moment, when it seems you are about at the end of your rope, He steps in and asks *"do you want a refill?"* The Holy Spirit's touch is to your spirit what a cold glass of water is to your body on a hot summer day; SO refreshing! When you are running low, go to the Holy Spirit for a refill. Don't deny yourself a drink of the Living Water. Without it, you take the chance of becoming spiritually dehydrated, which is not beneficial to your soul. Take time today to go to the fountain of God's grace and take a long, refreshing drink.

Affirmation Prayer: Heavenly Father, sometimes I feel depleted and empty. I make myself available to You. I need a refill. Fill me with Your Presence, in the name of Jesus, Amen.

Daily Bread: Song of Solomon 5 -8; 1 Corinthians 12:27-31; 1 Corinthians 13:1-13; Psalm 100:1-5

Seek and Ye Shall Find
August 19

Scripture: "Ask and it shall be given to you; seek and you will find; knock and it will be opened to you."
~ Matthew 7:7

Spiritual Vitamin

What are you looking for? God wants you to search for Him with your whole heart. He longs to reveal Himself to you in a life-changing way but He doesn't barge into your life uninvited. If you have an earnest expectation of seeing God, He will allow Himself to be discovered by you. *What kind of life are you expecting?* Jesus came to give you abundant life; a life of more than enough. When you allow yourself to be led by God's Holy Spirit, your life will be filled with many wonderful promises and spiritual gifts. If you need something, ask God. You won't receive what you want if you do not ask. Don't let this be true of you. Ask God for the things you want and need, but make sure your requests are according to His perfect will for your life. God loves you too much to give you something that will destroy you. Do not allow the doors of opportunity in your life to remain closed. You have to knock on each door and be in the right posture to receive what is waiting inside. Take time today to lay your requests before God and let Him bless your life with the answers you seek.

Affirmation Prayer: Heavenly Father, thank You that You have closed certain doors only to open other doors and windows that have blessed me beyond measure. I went seeking one thing, but because of Your grace, found something so much better. Help my wants and desires to match up with Your will for me, in the name of Jesus, Amen.

Daily Bread: 2 Chronicles 10 – 12; 1 Corinthians 14:1-19; Proverbs 20:15-24

Sending My Love
August 20

Scripture: "But the Helper, the Holy Spirit, whom the Father will send in my name, he will teach you all things and bring to your remembrance all that I have said to you."
~ John 14:26 ESV

Spiritual Vitamin

What do you need to learn about love? Every day, Gods sends you His love in tangible ways; in a beautiful sunrise; a cool crisp winter breeze or even in the picturesque view of freshly fallen snow. You have seen each of these elements of nature at one time or another. *The question is, did you recognize it as a love letter from God?* When you love someone, you should regularly tell them how you feel. *Do you love God?* If so, then tell Him. Express your love and gratitude to God for all that He's done to sustain your life. He is the only reason you exist and are still alive today. There is nothing you can do to keep the blood running warm in your veins or to keep your heart beating. The Holy Spirit is within you and is helping you to feel the love of God. God is sending you His love. For all He does for you, He requires very little of you. Even though His Son had to die on the cross for your sins, He doesn't hold you hostage with guilt and shame. Instead, He showers you with marvelous blessings as only He can. Take time today to enjoy the ways in which God sends you His love then send your love to someone else, so they too can experience this wonderful feeling.

Affirmation Prayer: Heavenly Father, thank You for sending Your love to me. Help me enjoy all the ways You care for me and to notice the beauty in every *little* thing, in the name of Jesus, Amen.

Daily Bread: 2 Chronicles 13 – 15; 1 Corinthians 14:20-40; Psalm 101:1-8

Shine
August 21

Scripture: "For it is the God who commanded light to shine out of darkness, who has shone in our hearts to give the light of the knowledge of the glory of God in the face of Jesus Christ."
~ 2 Corinthians 4:6

Spiritual Vitamin

Is God's light shining through you? The word shine brings to mind brightness, illumination and light. This is in complete contrast to darkness. There are two forces in this world — good and evil. Everyone on earth is ruled by one or the other. The Kingdom of God rules those who have accepted Jesus Christ as their Savior and the kingdom of darkness rules those who have not yielded to the Lordship of Christ, who are outside of the ark of safety. When you accept Jesus as your Savior, the Holy Spirit comes to live on the inside of you. Because we are spirit beings, we are able to feel and respond to the Holy Spirit. God placed a light inside of you and He wants that light to shine. *Are you willing to shine your light for Christ?* If you let God use you, others will be drawn to Him. Take time today to allow the "Son" to shine in your life. He will draw those around you into the knowledge of Him.

Affirmation Prayer: Heavenly Father, thank You for commanding light to shine out of my darkness. Now, I am able to shine my light for You. Let it never be hidden or obscured, in the name of Jesus, Amen.

Daily Bread: 2 Chronicles 16 – 17; 2 Chronicles 18:1-27; 1 Corinthians 15:1-34; Psalm 102:1-11

The Impossible Dream
August 22

Scripture: "But He said, "The things which are impossible with men are possible with God.""
~ Luke 18:27

Spiritual Vitamin

Do you dream the impossible dream? Nothing is impossible for God. The Creator of the universe has everything at His disposal. He does not operate within the same limitations as man. When you dream, you allow your mind to visit a place that your body has not yet been able to go. Guided by the Holy Spirit, your spiritual vision greatly aids in the dream process. If you can see something with your spiritual eyes, it is very likely that you will be able to believe that particular thing into existence. Spiritual vision and faith go hand-in-hand. You need to employ the power of the Holy Spirit to activate both. If you can see something in your spiritual imagination, then your imagination can send a signal to your brain that will help to bring whatever is imagined into physical being. *Why not dream your way into your next miracle?* With man, a certain dream may be impossible, but with God, there is no such thing. God has the power to make all things possible, according to His will. His power cannot be understood with the human mind. Take time today to dream, and not just a small dream. Dream big and watch God go to work on your behalf.

Affirmation Prayer: Heavenly Father, with You on my side, no dream is impossible. You empower me to accomplish my dreams and for that, I thank You. Help me to always celebrate the awesomeness of Your power, in the name of Jesus, Amen.

Daily Bread: 2 Chronicles 18:28-34; 2 Chronicles 19 – 20; 1 Corinthians 15:35-49; Psalm 102:12-17

The Spirit Is In It
August 23

Scripture: "Do you not know that you are the temple of God and that the Spirit of God dwells in you?"
~ 1 Corinthians 3:16

Spiritual Vitamin

As this month begins to wind down, I want to encourage you to open your heart to God's Holy Spirit within. You are not your own. You do not own yourself and your life does not belong to you. God paid an extremely high price to purchase you back from the enemy following the fall of man. He not only created you but He said you are fearfully and wonderfully made. Your body is the temple of the Spirit of God. *Do you take care of your body as if you realize this fact?* The best way you can honor God is by living like you understand that His Spirit is living on the inside of you. Give control of your life over to Him and what He does will completely amaze you. You will no longer have to figure out what you should be doing at any given time. God's Spirit is always there, ready to lead, guide, direct and protect you in whatever way is needed. *Is your temple clean?* Just as you clean your physical house, it is necessary to clean your spiritual house. Don't be negligent when it comes to properly nourishing and caring for your temple. After all, it's the house of God and you owe it to God to keep His house clean. Take time today to thank God for having the desire to dwell on the inside of you.

Affirmation Prayer: Heavenly Father, thank You for wanting to dwell within me. Continue to fill me with joy and Your presence, in the name of Jesus, Amen.

Daily Bread: 2 Chronicles 21 – 23; 1 Corinthians 15:50-58; 1 Corinthians 16:1-4; Proverbs 20:25-30; Proverbs 21:1-4

This Too Shall Pass
August 24

Scripture: "For our light affliction, which is but for a moment, is working for us a far more exceeding and eternal weight of glory, while we do not look at the things which are seen, but at the things which are not seen. For the things which are seen are temporary, but the things which are not seen are eternal."
~ 2 Corinthians 4:17-18

Spiritual Vitamin

Is there a storm passing through your life? No matter what you are going through, you have already won. When I speak in terms of winning, please understand that I am not saying the situation will work out the way you expect. On the contrary, the results may actually be the opposite of what you were hoping or praying for or expecting. In the end, God, through the power of His Holy Spirit, makes sure that everything works out for your good. While all things may not, in and of themselves be good, God can cause them to work out for good as it pertains to you. He watches you every single day of your life. You are never out of His reach and He is never unaware of what is happening to you. Don't let the circumstances of life weigh you down. If something is going wrong, just know that "this too shall pass." You have had hard times before and because of God, you came out victorious. If He did it before, He'll do it again. God delights in blessing you and seeing you happy. If you walk in His will, there's nothing He will not do for you. Take time today to trust God to deliver you out of anything that is causing you suffering, pain or hardship. Worship and praise Him and watch Him go to work on your behalf.

Affirmation Prayer: Heavenly Father, I am grateful that the good in my life outweighs the bad. Because You are so great, I refuse to complain. Never let me doubt whether You will bring me through anything that I encounter, in the name of Jesus, Amen.

Daily Bread: 2 Chronicles 24 – 25; 1 Corinthians 16:5-24; Psalm 102:18-28

To God Be the Glory
August 25

Scripture: "So whether you eat or drink or whatever you do, do it all for the glory of God."
~ 1 Corinthians 10:31

Spiritual Vitamin

Is your life glorifying God? Man does not deserve the credit for what God does; all the glory belongs to God. Aside and apart from Him, mankind has no power. Man's power only comes through the Holy Spirit. Empowered by the Holy Spirit, there's nothing you cannot do. Your total existence should bring glory to God. Everything you think, say and do should be a reflection of His goodness in your life. *Can those who know you well say that you are a shining example of the Lord Jesus Christ?* If you are honest with yourself, you can say that sometimes, you have been a product of your environment. When you are in the company of those who do not claim Christ as their Savior, you may have attempted to dim your light in order to keep your unsaved acquaintances from being uncomfortable. This type of behavior does not bring glory to God. On the contrary, when you are in the company of those who do not know Christ, is when you should allow your light to shine the brightest. Not in a way that will bring shame to them but more so in an attempt to enable the light of Christ to bring warmth to their souls. Take time today to change any behaviors in your life that do not bring glory to God.

Affirmation Prayer: Heavenly Father, You deserve all my praise. To You, be the glory. Change any attitudes or behaviors in me that do not honor and exalt You, in the name of Jesus, Amen.

Daily Bread: 2 Chronicles 26 – 28; 2 Corinthians 1:1-11; Psalm 103:1-12

Unforgettable
August 26

Scripture: "See, I have inscribed you on the palms of My hands; Your walls are continually before Me."
~ Isaiah 49:16

Spiritual Vitamin

Do you really know who you are? You are one of Jesus' amazing miracles! Psalm 111:4 (GW) says, "He has made his miracles unforgettable. The Lord is merciful and compassionate." To God, you are unforgettable. Your name is engraved in the palm of God's hand. He can't ever forget you and He won't let you go. At times, there will be struggle and busyness in your life and you may feel like you are alone. This is the furthest thing from the truth. The Holy Spirit is within you. God will not abandon or overlook you. You are not second best and should never feel as though you need to be in the shadow of any other human being. Step into the light! God knows you, He accepts you and He values you. As far as God is concerned, no one can replace you and you are a one of a kind Designer's original. There is never a justification for a child of God to struggle with issues of low self-esteem. This is what the enemy wants. Don't listen to him. Your Creator adores you. When you know that, you don't worry about feeling unloved or unwanted. Take time today to thank God that He regards you as unforgettable.

Affirmation Prayer: Heavenly Father, You are unforgettable. I know that I am not forgotten because you know my name. I am amazed that You love me so much. Help me to be worthy, in the name of Jesus, Amen.

Daily Bread: 2 Chronicles 29–31; 2 Corinthians 1:12-23; Psalm 103:13-22

War
August 27

Scripture: "For we do not wrestle against flesh and blood, but against principalities, against powers, against the rulers of the darkness of this age, against spiritual hosts of wickedness in the heavenly places."
~ Ephesians 6:12

Spiritual Vitamin

Who or what are you fighting? Your fight is not against another human being. Your fight is against the enemy of all humanity — satan. It is his desire to ruin your relationship with God. If satan can keep you bound mentally, he can keep you bound emotionally and physically. You can only do as much as your mind will allow you to think and speak into existence. If you think you can do something, you can. Likewise, if you think you cannot do something, chances are you won't even try. Maybe no one ever told you before but you are in a war; not a natural war but a spiritual one. You are involved in a fight for your soul. Just as with Peter, satan desires to sift you as wheat. *Will you let him?* Whenever what you are doing is outside of the will of God, you are assisting the enemy with furthering his plan to destroy you. Please stop and think about that for a moment. Flesh and spirit will never agree, which is why you must choose your spirit over your flesh. Employ the Holy Spirit to help you to put off anything that is against the Word of God or that directs you to disobey what God is telling you to do. Take time today to declare war on the enemy. Then, you will be empowered to overcome all the fiery darts he throws your way.

Affirmation Prayer: Heavenly Father, the battle is not mine, You have already won and I am celebrating. No devil in hell can stop me, now that I am Your child, in the name of Jesus, Amen.

Daily Bread: 2 Chronicles 32 - 33; 2 Corinthians 2:1-11; Proverbs 21:5-16

Wind Beneath My Wings
August 28

Scripture: "They that wait upon the Lord shall renew their strength; they shall mount up on wings as eagles; they shall run and not be weary; they shall walk and not faint."
~ Isaiah 40:31

Spiritual Vitamin

Who is your hero? Everyone has someone in their life they look up to and/or admire. Some have even gone so far as to say that person is their hero. *Is there someone in your life who inspires you and pushes you forward?* God wants to be this person for you because more than anyone else you know, He longs to see you succeed. He wants you to excel in every area of your life. He put a divine plan in place that will ensure this happens. But you must follow His plan. With God, failure is not an option. But many times, we don't do things God's way and this is when the results we receive are less than desirable. God loves to be worshiped and He loves praise. When you worship and praise Him, He shows up on your behalf. If you are struggling with something, stop trying to work out all the details and give it over to God. See yourself on the other side of the situation and start praising and worshiping God for a victorious outcome. Before you know it, there will be a shifting in the atmosphere around you. The Holy Spirit will help you with your struggle. The circumstances may not change immediately, but your perspective certainly will. Take time today to ask God to be the wind beneath your wings. He'll make sure you soar to the highest of heights in your relationship with Him.

Affirmation Prayer: Heavenly Father, help me to trust You enough to allow You to be the wind beneath my wings. Let me run and not be weary, let me walk and not faint, in the name of Jesus, Amen.

Daily Bread: 2 Chronicles 34 - 35; 2 Corinthians 2:12-17; 2 Corinthians 3:1-6; Psalm 104:1-18

Windows of Hope
August 29

Scripture: "Now hope does not disappoint, because the love of God has been poured out in our hearts by the Holy Spirit who was given to us."
~ Romans 5:5

Spiritual Vitamin

No situation is hopeless. No matter what you go through or face in this life, you will never be without hope. God has promised to take care of you. This is why God has given you His Holy Spirit. *Are you living within the benefits afforded by this gift?* If not, you are living beneath your privilege. Faith and hope go together. If you can use your faith to believe that something will come to pass, you can also employ hope along with your faith and let it provide a strong foundation on which your faith can rest. Hopeful people are happy people. God has given the gift of hope and He wants you to use it. When you are tempted to allow the burdens and cares of life to begin to weigh you down, stop and remember that there's hope. Faith moves God. Never stop believing that God has your best interest at heart, in every way and at all times. The next time you feel down, ask the Holy Spirit to guide you to a better place. See the situation from another point of view and gain a fresh perspective. Take time today to linger at the window of hope. Let what you see inspire you to give hope to others.

Affirmation Prayer: Heavenly Father, thank You for pouring Your love into me. Because of You, no situation is hopeless because the Holy Spirit helps me see clearly. You have given me hope; help me to live and walk in it, in the name of Jesus, Amen.

Daily Bread: 2 Chronicles 36; 2 Corinthians 3:7-18; Psalm 104:19-30

You're All I Need To Get By
August 30

Scripture: "And my God shall supply all your need according to His riches in glory by Christ Jesus."
~ Philippians 4:19

Spiritual Vitamin

Do you have all that you need? Mankind was not created to exist alone. People need people. God created you for fellowship with Himself and others. God is all you need to get by but He wants you to build human relationships with like-minded, Godly individuals. When you experience emotional pain, it is tempting to just go within and decide not to extend yourself to others, in an attempt to protect your feelings. This is not God's design. Rather, this is where forgiveness comes into the picture. Once you accept Christ, you put on what I'd like to refer to as Christ's "character coat". Galatians 5:22-23 says "But the fruit of the Spirit is love, joy, peace, longsuffering, kindness, goodness, faithfulness, gentleness and self-control. Against such there is no law." If you accept Jesus Christ, you must agree to put on the coat. God wants you to forgive those who have harmed you and use the supernatural power of His Holy Spirit to love them in spite of what they have done. God's Holy Spirit helps you lead a holy life. Holiness is not to be confused with weakness. On the contrary, forgiveness actually requires a great deal of strength. Following forgiveness, you can redefine the parameters of relationships to put measures in place that will create a healthier and more emotionally safe environment for yourself as well as the other person. When you don't place unrealistic expectations on others, everyone is free to be themselves. Take time today to free someone in your life from trying to be who you think they should be and allow them to be who they really are.

Affirmation Prayer: Heavenly Father, thank You for being all I need to get by. Make me willing to always trust You, in the name of Jesus, Amen.

Daily Bread: Micah 1 – 4; 2 Corinthians 4; Psalm 104:31-35

You Light Up My Life
August 31

Scripture: "In Him was life, and the life was the light of men."
~ John 1:4

Spiritual Vitamin

Is there someone in your life who makes you smile every time you think of them? You love them more than you can put into words and in your eyes, they can do no wrong. This individual makes you feel better about anything you might be going through and in your opinion, they will never let you down or disappoint you. If you need them, you believe they will always be there, day or night, without hesitation or restriction. *Who plays this role in your life?* It is my intention to cause you to consider giving this position to God. He alone is the only One who can perfectly fit this description and meet every requirement without fail. God is the only person who can meet the demands of "always". He's always there; He always comes through for you; He's always on time; and He always cares. No one can light up your life like God can. God gives you His light through the Holy Spirit. This light can never be diminished by situations or circumstances and is not controlled by anything or anyone outside of God Himself. Take time today to follow God's path of light and outshine the enemy's darkness.

Affirmation Prayer: Heavenly Father, You light up my life. Make me willing to shine Your light into darkness wherever I encounter it, in the name of Jesus, Amen.

Daily Bread: Micah 5 – 7; 2 Corinthians 5:1-10; Proverbs 21:17-26

MONTHLY REFLECTIONS

September: Self-Preservation (Learning to Survive Crisis)

Strength for the Journey

Heavenly Father:

You are everything to me. In You, I live and move and have my being. I will not be afraid of the terror by night, for You have given me angels to watch over me. Please forgive me for trying to survive moments of crisis without consulting You. Now, You are teaching me how to survive moments of crisis as they present themselves in my life. Because of You, I have the assurance that if I keep my mind stayed on You, I will be in perfect peace. Keep me assured that You are always with me and nothing can harm me. Remind me that You are my sustainer. In the midst of trials and darkness, You are my strong tower and protector. Teach me to trust in You always, in the name of Jesus, Amen.

September

Self-Preservation (Learning To Survive Crisis)

During the month of September, you will go on a journey, learning how to survive personal crisis through self-preservation. Self-preservation is defined as the protection of oneself from harm or death, especially regarded as a basic instinct. My focus as it relates to the theme for this month is geared not toward physical death but more so to protect yourself from spiritual death. You must be willing to do the inner work that is necessary in order to keep yourself spiritually healthy, whole and safe. In your pursuit of spiritual wholeness, you will not completely avoid conflict and crisis, so it is best to learn how to deal with these things by exercising your faith and trust in God. As you demonstrate calm in the midst of chaos, you send a message to the enemy and those around you about how much you believe in the saving power of God. Like me, you will learn that it is never your responsibility to settle the score; let God do that for you. As others watch you walk through your difficulties with your faith intact, you encourage them to believe they can do the same. It is my prayer that you will use this month's devotionals to aid you in gaining insight on how to survive crisis while exercising your faith in God.

Quote: "You're safe not because of the absence of danger, but because of the Presence of God." --- Author Unknown

"For You formed my inward parts; You covered me in my mother's womb. I will praise You, for I am fearfully and wonderfully made; Marvelous are Your works, And that my soul knows very well."
~ Psalm 139:13-14

All Things Are Working For My Good
September 1

Scripture: "And we know that all things work together for good to those who love God, to those who are the called according to His purpose."
~ Romans 8:28

Spiritual Vitamin

How are things going for you right now? It is no secret that everything that happens in your life will not be good. But, there is good news concerning this fact. Even though bad things will sometimes happen to you, God has created a way to work those bad things out for your good; but there is something you must do. You must remain in faith and expectancy and refuse to give in to the temptation to murmur and complain. During the hard times, you will be tempted to give up and the enemy will try to convince you that you have no one on your side. That is a lie. God is on your side! God allows you to experience the bitter with the sweet. There are lessons to be learned even in the worst of times. God's Word says that ALL things work together for good to those who are the called according to His purpose. If you love God, He has promised to take care of you. *Do you love God?* Then you don't have to worry about anything that you're currently going through because you have God's promise to work it out for your good. Stand firm and do not waver. God will come through and bring you out when the time is right. Take time today to glorify God for His provision, even when times are hard.

Affirmation Prayer: Heavenly Father, Your presence in my life causes all things to work for my good. Teach me how to glorify You in a way that is pleasing in Your sight, in the name of Jesus, Amen.

Daily Bread: Isaiah 1 – 2; 2 Corinthians 5:11-21; Psalm 105:1-11

A Long Walk
September 2

Scripture: "You shall walk in all the way which the Lord your God has commanded you, that you may live and that it may be well with you, and that you may prolong your days in the land which you shall possess."
~ Deuteronomy 5:33

Spiritual Vitamin

When was the last time you took a long walk? Everyone knows that walking is good for you. On a cool, spring evening, it feels great to take a long walk, by yourself or in the company of someone you love. This is from a natural perspective and pertains to walking as a verb. But let's examine this term from a spiritual perspective, where it pertains to the word "walk" as a noun; let's examine your walk with God. In simple terms, your walk with God is your relationship to and connection with Him. God's Word gives commandments that He wants His children to follow, which can be referred to as walking in His way. Please be advised that God's way will be in stark contrast to your way. What you want to do most often will be vastly different than what God wants you to do, so you have a choice to make. *Are you going to walk in the ways of God? Can you give up your plans and the desire to do things your way in order to see what God has for you? Why don't you take a walk with God?* Not a short, fast-paced and hurried walk, but a slow, long walk, with your hand in His, telling Him all that's on your heart and allowing Him to tell you what's on His. Take time today for a long walk with your Father. It will do you a world of good.

Affirmation Prayer: Heavenly Father, You are the object of my faith and every day I am walking with You, which is the best exercise for my soul. Help me to stay on the path of Your choosing, in the name of Jesus, Amen.

Daily Bread: Isaiah 3 – 4; Isaiah 5:1-7; 2 Corinthians 6:1-18; Psalm 105:12-22

Are You Gonna Go My Way?
September 3

Scripture: "Jesus said to him, "I am the way, the truth, and the life. No one comes to the Father except through Me."
~ John 14:6

Spiritual Vitamin

Before you were created in your mother's womb, the plan for your life was already in the mind of God. *Isn't that mind-blowing?* He knew what your abilities, talents and gifts would be and He knew the purpose for which you have been made. He knew who your parents would be and how you would look. When you were born, you were a manifestation of what had already been created in His mind. He chose someone to care for you and to nurture you into adulthood. At that time, that person made all the decisions concerning you until such time as you could do so for yourself. *Now that you are able to make your own decisions, what kind of choices are you making?* God wants you to surrender your life to the Lordship of Jesus Christ and to do things His way. *Will you do that or would you rather go your own way?* In order for the plan of God to continue to manifest in your life, you must be obedient to what He tells you to do. In order to hear from Him, you must be quiet and listen for that still, small voice. Take time today to learn what God expects from you and make the decision to go His way, rather than your own.

Affirmation Prayer: Heavenly Father, You are gracious and mighty and I choose to do Your work and walk Your way. Keep me in the center of Your will, in the name of Jesus, Amen.

Daily Bread: Isaiah 5:8-30, Isaiah 6 – 7; Isaiah 8:1-10; 2 Corinthians 7:1-16; Psalm 105:23-36

Brand New Me
September 4

Scripture: "that you put off, concerning your former conduct, the old man which grows corrupt according to the deceitful lusts, and be renewed in the spirit of your mind, and that you put on the new man which was created according to God, in true righteousness and holiness."
~ Ephesians 4:22-24

Spiritual Vitamin

Labor Day is the first Monday in September and is recognized as a day dedicated to the social and economic achievements of American workers.

Are you the same person you have always been? When you accept Christ, you become a new person. The old, sinful, disobedient, defiant person you were before has to take a back seat to the new, submitted, obedient you in Christ. According to Ephesians 4:22-24, you must put off your old self, which is corrupt through deceitful desires. You are directed to deny yourself and to take on the personhood of Jesus, adopting His character, His attitudes and His way of thinking. You must set aside what you want and focus on what God wants for you. If you allow Him to, God will remove self-centeredness and selfish desires from you and replace them with an uncommon care, concern and love for others. There is an old you that needs to die and a new you that will then come alive in Christ. When you accept Him, by faith in what He has done on the cross, there is a brand new you. The old you is crucified; he or she is gone. The new you is the one who contains the spirit and light of God, which He then uses to draw others to Himself through you. Each person has a light. Take time today to allow your light to shine, so that someone else can find their way to Christ.

Affirmation Prayer: Heavenly Father, under the influence of Your Holy Spirit, I am a brand new me. The old me is gone. Help me continue to walk in the newness of life, in the name of Jesus, Amen.

Daily Bread: Isaiah 8:11-22; Isaiah 9; Isaiah 10:1-19; 2 Corinthians 8:1-15; Proverbs 21:27-31; Proverbs 22:1-6

Express Yourself
September 5

Scripture: "In all things showing yourself to be a pattern of good works; in doctrine showing integrity, reverence, incorruptibility."
~ Titus 2:7

Spiritual Vitamin

You have the right to express yourself; working and serving is a good way to accomplish this. You have the right to speak your mind and let others know how you are feeling. When you disagree with something, it is okay to respectfully say so. Along with the right to express yourself comes the responsibility to do it in a manner that will not be harmful to others. You have the right to speak the truth but you must speak the truth in love. There is a kind and considerate way to say anything that needs to be said. If your highest goal is to be pleasing to God in all that you do and say, you will not find it hard to say things in a kind and considerate way. You will never intentionally set out to hurt another person's feelings and your behavior and conversations will reflect that as your true desire. Learn to put your feelings into constructive words that edify and build up rather than in hurtful words that wound and tear down. If you allow Jesus to be the Lord of your life, your speech will be seasoned with grace. Take time today to express yourself, speaking the truth in love.

Affirmation Prayer: Heavenly Father, thank You for the spiritual gifts You have given me that allow me to express myself. Show me the best ways to use these gifts, in the name of Jesus, Amen.

Daily Bread: Isaiah 10:20-34; Isaiah 11 − 13; 2 Corinthians 8:16-24; 2 Corinthians 9:1-5; Psalm 105:37-45

Found a Cure
September 6

Scripture: "The Lord will preserve him and keep him alive, and he will be blessed on the earth; You will not deliver him to the will of his enemies. The Lord will strengthen him on his bed of illness; You will sustain him on his sickbed."
~ Psalm 41:2-3

Spiritual Vitamin

Are you currently struggling with illness? The human body is subject to various physical and emotional illnesses, among which are cancer, heart disease, diabetes, rejection, loneliness and depression. Several of these illnesses have gone without a cure in the natural sense, but I want to let you know that in the spiritual sense, Jesus IS the cure for whatever ails you. He was wounded for your transgressions, bruised for your iniquities and by His stripes, you are healed. When you are born into the family of God and you allow Jesus to become your Lord and Savior, no matter what ailments you're facing, you have found a cure. With Him in your life, you will never again have to experience shame, guilt, despair, defeat or discouragement. You can take all of your cares to the Lord in prayer and leave them with Him, knowing that He will work them out for you. God is more concerned about what is going on in your life than you can understand or even comprehend. Sometimes, you may think He's unaware, but this couldn't be further from the truth. To prove my point, God knows the number of hairs on your head. If he would take the time to know that information, then He will take the time to oversee every other detail as well. Take time today to celebrate the fact that there's nothing wrong with you that your Heavenly Father cannot cure.

Affirmation Prayer: Heavenly Father, Your Word is the cure to anything that ails me. Help me search Your promises each time I am in need, in the name of Jesus, Amen.

Daily Bread: Isaiah 14 – 16; 2 Corinthians 9:6-15; Psalm 106:1-15

Free Your Mind
September 7

Scripture: "And do not be conformed to this world, but be transformed by the renewing of your mind, that you may prove what is that good and acceptable and perfect will of God."
~ Romans 12:2

Spiritual Vitamin

Do you entertain thoughts that hurt or thoughts that heal? Your thoughts rule your life. Everything you do begins in your mind as a thought, which is why your thoughts are extremely important. *What types of thoughts do you entertain? Are they thoughts of good, wholesome, positive things or are they thoughts of bad, unwholesome, negative things?* Philippians 4:8 says "finally, brethren, whatever things are true, whatever things are noble, whatever things are just, whatever things are pure, whatever things are lovely, whatever things are of good report, if there is any virtue and if there is anything praiseworthy — meditate on these things." You can be free from mental wickedness but you must meditate on the Word of God. You can be free from negative self-talk and what others think of you by seeking the face of God each day. You can't think positive and negative thoughts at the same time. One will win over the other. Take time today to immerse your mind into the Word of God, so that what you focus on will be positive and pure.

Affirmation Prayer: Heavenly Father, thank You for freeing my mind. Help me to keep my mind stayed on You, in the name of Jesus, Amen.

Daily Bread: Isaiah 17 — 19; 2 Corinthians 10; Psalm 106:16-31

Get Here
September 8

Scripture: "Show me Your ways, O LORD; Teach me Your paths. Lead me in Your truth and teach me, For You *are* the God of my salvation; On You I wait all the day."
~ Psalm 25:4-5

Spiritual Vitamin

How much do you know about God? God wants you to know and discern His will and purpose for your life. He wants you to get to a place in Him where you are able to rise above the situations and circumstances of life. He wants to take you to a place of peace, faith and trust in Him. Before He can do this, you must be willing to seek Him with your whole heart. God is waiting for you and has issued an invitation for you to come; He says "there is something I have prepared for you; a level that I want you to attain in Me; I am here waiting for you and I need you to get here, to this place where you can know and understand Me and what it is I want to do in your life." *Do you want to go?* If so, you must lighten your load. There are things you cannot take into the Presence of God. Sin is one of those things. If there is something you are actively and willingly engaged in that you know is against the Word of God, be willing to lay it at the feet of Jesus and repent, so that you can move forward and walk into your destiny. Take time today to follow the path of righteousness, so that you can get to where God is.

Affirmation Prayer: Heavenly Father, I desire to be with You. Show me how to get to You when the way does not seem clear, in the name of Jesus, Amen.

Daily Bread: Isaiah 20 – 23; 2 Corinthians 11:1-15; Proverbs 22:7-16

Gimme a Break
September 9

Scripture: "Come to Me, all you who labor and are heavy laden, and I will give you rest. Take My yoke upon you and learn from Me, for I am gentle and lowly in heart, and you will find rest for your souls. For My yoke is easy and my burden is light."
~ Matthew 11:28-30

Spiritual Vitamin

Do you need a break? Sometimes in life, you will feel overwhelmed. You will feel like you need a break. During times like this, you need to know what to do in order to protect yourself from an emotional breakdown. The answer is clearly written in Matthew 11. Jesus invites you to come to Him. He promises to give you rest. He extends an offer that is difficult to refuse. He wants to make a trade with you. He has agreed to take your heavy burden and load and in return, give you His gentleness and His load, which He says is light. *Why would one reject an offer like this?* Yet so often, this is exactly what you do. You reject the offer and assistance of God because you feel that your way of dealing with the situation is better than the way He will handle it. This couldn't be further from the truth.

Anything you can do, God can do better! If you are overwhelmed, it's time for you to stop. Go to God and allow Him to give you a break, a rest or an intermission, where you can have a chance to catch your breath. Take time today to relax in the arms of God. He will replenish your strength and put you back in the race more energized and prepared than you were before.

Affirmation Prayer: Heavenly Father, thank You for the opportunity to come to You when I need a break. You are always ready to refresh me. Teach me how to rest in You, in the name of Jesus, Amen.

Daily Bread: Isaiah 24 – 26; 2 Corinthians 11:16-33; Psalm 106:32-39

Give Me Some Time
September 10

Scripture: "making the best use of time, because the days are evil."
~ Ephesians 5:16 ESV

Spiritual Vitamin

Within a 24-hour period, how much time do you give to God? God is asking for more of your time. Given the hectic schedule you already keep, you don't see how it is possible for you to give Him more of your time. Let me give you a few suggestions. If you start your day with God, He will order your steps and keep you away from the traps and pitfalls that are so apt to steal your time. You will be calm, focused and settled within your spirit, which will allow you to concentrate and think clearly. This way, you will know which tasks are a good use of your time and which tasks are simply time wasters. You give time and attention to many things throughout your day. *Is God on the agenda?* You may have several people who want to meet with you. If you first meet with God, He will align your day and give you time to do everything else that He wants done within the allotted time. Take time today to unplug from the busyness of life and give God more of your time.

Affirmation Prayer: Heavenly Father, thank You for my life. You have given me a chance to make a difference in this world. Show me the best use of my time, in the name of Jesus, Amen.

Daily Bread: Isaiah 27 – 28; 2 Corinthians 12:1-10; Psalm 106:40-48

911
September 11

Scripture: "He who dwells in the secret place of the Most High shall abide under the shadow of the Almighty."
~ Psalm 91:1

Spiritual Vitamin

Have you ever called 911? What happened on this day in the history of America will never be forgotten. During this tragic event, many lives were lost and even the ones not lost were forever changed. This heinous act is one of the results of what happens in a heart where hatred resides. The enemy (satan) is described in scripture as a thief, who comes to steal, kill and destroy. This is his ultimate and highest goal. But Jesus said that He has come so you might have life and life more abundantly. Your safety is connected to abiding in the Presence of God. God is with you in EVERY circumstance, no matter how dark the details. You will not see Him with your physical eyes, which is why you must use your spiritual eyes. Your self-preservation depends on your ability to trust that God will deliver you out of every evil attack that attempts to come your way. Stand on your faith no matter what, and never waver because God cannot lie. If He said He'll be there, He will. Even in the emergencies of life such as unexpected death or loss or illness, God is present. God was there on September 11th and He's still here today. Every person who lost his or her life that day will be remembered in the hearts and minds of their loved ones. The enemy did not win that day and he never will. God's purposes will always prevail. Take time today to trust God in the 9-1-1 situations of your life.

Affirmation Prayer: Heavenly Father, in every emergency, I can go to the secret place and abide under Your shadow. Teach me how to cast my cares upon You, in the name of Jesus, Amen.

Daily Bread: Isaiah 29 – 30; 2 Corinthians 12:11-21; Psalm 107:1-9

Have You Ever?
September 12

Scripture: "Have you not known? Have you not heard? The everlasting God, the Lord, The Creator of the ends of the earth, neither faints nor is weary. His understanding is unsearchable."
~ Isaiah 40:28

Spiritual Vitamin

You go to church on Sundays. Throughout the week, you occasionally pickup your Bible and read a few passages. You've even committed a few of those passages to memory. *But have you ever taken the time to really listen to what God is trying to tell you?* God speaks to you each and every day. He talks to you in various ways: through nature, from within your spirit and even through other people. *Can you hear Him?* God wants a deep, personal and meaningful relationship with you. He wants the lines of communication to be wide open, so that you can hear Him and so that you are assured He is hearing you. Giving God a total commitment will allow Him to work in your life in ways you cannot imagine. When your spirit is connected with His Spirit, there is nothing to hinder your progress. You will be able to experience the peace of God and live joyously within your calling and purpose. Take time today to examine yourself to identify what stands between you and a deeper relationship with God.

Affirmation Prayer: Heavenly Father, I have heard that You are everlasting and that Your understanding is unsearchable. Help me give up self-reliance for total dependence on You, in the name of Jesus, Amen.

Daily Bread: Isaiah 31-32; 2 Corinthians 13; Proverbs 22:17-27

I Can See Clearly Now
September 13

Scripture: "For now we see in a mirror, dimly, but then face to face. Now I know in part, but then I shall know just as I also am known."
~ 1 Corinthians 13:12

Spiritual Vitamin

What seems unclear to you at the moment? Sometimes, things are just not clear. Facts and details can get so tangled and confused that you may not know which way is up. In order to be able to see things clearly, naturally as well as spiritually, you need the help of the Lord. 1 Samuel 12:16 says "Now then, stand still and see this great thing the Lord is about to do before your eyes!" God wants to do so much in your life. He has many wonderful things in store for you. *Is what you're doing helping or hindering the move of God in your life?* When you fully surrender to God, He is able to cause your perception to become crystal clear. You begin to understand things that you couldn't understand before. Wrong motives can cloud your judgment. But right motives will create an atmosphere that is conducive to more positive perception, thanksgiving and praise. Take time today to allow God to remove the blinders from your eyes, so that you can clearly see what He is trying to show you.

Affirmation Prayer: Heavenly Father, because of Your love for me, I can see clearly now. Keep my mind and vision clear, so that I can hear You clearly and obey, in the name of Jesus, Amen.

Daily Bread: Isaiah 33 – 35; Galatians 1; Psalm 107:10-22

I Don't Love You Anymore
September 14

Scripture: "If someone says, "I love God," and hates his brother, he is a liar; for he who does not love his brother whom he has seen, how can he love God whom he has not seen?"
~ 1 John 4:20

Spiritual Vitamin

Have you ever heard or said, I don't love you anymore? These are sobering words to hear — I don't love you anymore. There is no way to avoid the hurt and pain that would come along with hearing these words. You never want to hear someone say they don't love you anymore. Many times, a person won't say the words directly but their actions will instead convey the message. Perhaps you know what I'm talking about. The good news is that you will never hear these words from God. He will never stop loving you, even if you stop loving Him. There is nothing you can do to influence God's decision to love you. He made the choice long before you were even born. God's promise to love you follows you from earth into eternity. God's love is the most important love to have in your life. If you have His love, then you have all the love you need, with or without a romantic love in your life. Take time today to accept God's unconditional love, then you will be equipped to make an important declaration to the enemy. Rather than telling people these hurtful words, you can declare them to the one that deserves to hear them the most, the enemy. Those words -- "I don't love you anymore!"

Affirmation Prayer: Heavenly Father, I am in awe of how much You love me. You have engraved me in the palm of Your hand and will never stop loving me. Help me celebrate this miraculous truth, especially when I feel unloved by those around me, in the name of Jesus, Amen.

Daily Bread: Isaiah 36– 37; Galatians 2; Psalm 107:23-32

Satisfaction Guaranteed
September 15

Scripture: "For He satisfies the longing soul, and fills the hungry soul with goodness."
~ Psalm 107:9

Spiritual Vitamin

Retail companies make promises when trying to sell their products. Many of them use the words "satisfaction guaranteed or your money back." This is an attempt to make you confident that their product works before you even have a chance to try it out for yourself. *Has anyone witnessed to you about the goodness of God? If so, did what they said to you convince you of His goodness and make you want to try Him for yourself?* The only way to be truly satisfied in this life is to give control over to God and allow Him to manifest His plan for you. His guarantee is the only one that is fool-proof. When you surrender yourself to Christ, there will be no tricks or schemes and you will never be left holding an empty bag. What God promises, He delivers. Psalm 145:16 (ESV) says, "you open your hand; you satisfy the desire of every living thing." This perfectly describes God. If you are reading this and you are unsaved, take time today to accept God's offer of salvation. If you have already done this, then commit to witnessing to others so that they might become partakers of this offer, satisfaction guaranteed.

Affirmation Prayer: Heavenly Father, thank You for satisfying the longings of my soul and for filling me with goodness. Give me a heart of thanksgiving for what You have done, in the name of Jesus, Amen.

Daily Bread: Isaiah 38 – 40; Galatians 3:1-9; Psalm 107:33-43

I've Got Love On My Mind
September 16

Scripture: "Then make me truly happy by agreeing wholeheartedly with each other, loving one another, and working together with one mind and purpose."
~ Philippians 2:2 NLT

Spiritual Vitamin

Is love on your mind? When your number one priority is love, it influences every area of your life. Where you may once have been very disgruntled and argumentative, the spirit of love changes those negative characteristics into positive ones. You no longer seek to be right all the time or to be the one to "win" the argument. When you've got love on your mind, your ultimate goal is whatever is best for the greater good of everyone involved. You don't demand your own way anymore, you want to see the will of God performed. Love will make you do things differently than you once did. Your personality will change and those closest to you will know that something has happened on the inside of you. That is your opportunity to testify to the goodness of the Lord. Only God can change you from the inside out and cause you to leave behind your old habits and desires of the flesh. Take time today to demonstrate a Godly love and to keep love in the forefront of your mind.

Affirmation Prayer: Heavenly Father, my desire is to make You happy by the way I live my life. Help me to love my fellow man and work together with them with one mind and purpose, in the name of Jesus, Amen.

Daily Bread: Isaiah 41 – 42; Galatians 3:10-25; Proverbs 22:28-29; Proverbs 23:1-9

Keep On Smiling
September 17

Scripture: "A glad heart makes a happy face; a broken heart crushes the spirit. For the despondent, every day brings trouble; for the happy heart, life is a continual feast."
~ Proverbs 15:13, 15 NLT

Spiritual Vitamin

What do you do when faced with negativity? There will be days in your life when things happen that won't make you smile. There will be situations and circumstances that will cause your eyes to fill with tears and your faith to be tested. But during these times, you have the option to reach deep down on the inside of yourself, into that place of knowing, and pull the resolve of God into the situation. You already know how much God loves you; you know that He is there with you in every moment. You know that He will never let you down and you also know that He will not leave you. So, with all of that knowledge, in the end, there really is no reason to doubt, worry or fear. God is there so smile, and through it all, keep on smiling because He has everything under control. Proverbs 17:22 says "a merry heart does good, like medicine, but a broken spirit dries the bones." Keep your heart merry and don't allow the things of the flesh to damper your spirit. Take time today to relax, reflect and smile. God is taking great care of you.

Affirmation Prayer: Heavenly Father, thank You for a happy heart, which makes my life a continual feast. Thank You that no matter what, I can keep on smiling. Please let my behavior and appearance reflect the fact that I am in communication with You, in the name of Jesus, Amen.

Daily Bread: Isaiah 43 – 44; Galatians 3:26-29; Galatians 4:1-20; Psalm 108:1-5

Let the Sun Shine In
September 18

Scripture: "Let your light so shine before men, that they may see your good works and glorify your Father in heaven."
~ Matthew 5:16

Spiritual Vitamin

Do you know there's a light inside of you? Let me remind you, every human being has a light on the inside of them. God knows it's there because He placed it there Himself. He intends for you to let that light shine. Light is not meant to be hidden. It is meant to be shared and enjoyed by those around you. Once you discover your individual purpose, it brings you satisfaction to work in the area of your calling and your light begins to shine. You find that the best way to take care of yourself is to do what you were put on earth to do. After discovering your purpose you will be the happiest you've ever been. That will bring you your highest level of joy. When you realize what God has empowered you to do and you do it, you will have joy that can't be tampered with or taken away. Let the light of Christ shine in your life and empower you to shine your light onto others. Take time today to let the "Son" shine in and create a warmth in your soul that will draw others to Him through you.

Affirmation Prayer: Heavenly Father, thank You for Your light that shines brightly on me and for the light You've placed within my soul. Help me to let my light shine on others, in the name of Jesus, Amen.

Daily Bread: Isaiah 45 – 46; Galatians 4:21-31; Galatians 5:1-6; Psalm 108:6-13

You're So Vain
September 19

Scripture: "If your first concern is to look after yourself, you'll never find yourself. But if you forget about yourself and look to me, you'll find both yourself and me."
~ Matthew 10:39 MSG

Spiritual Vitamin

Who is at the top of your priority list? Life will be difficult if your first and only priority is you. God never intended it to be that way and He did not create you to be stuck on self. In a world of selfies and social media, the temptation is great but you must avoid it. You were made for fellowship with God and to be a blessing to others. There are gifts and talents within you, not so that you can become vain and conceited, but so that you can share them with others. The longer you live, the more you will begin to realize that everything is not about you. You will find your highest happiness when you learn how to get your mind off yourself — what you want, what you need, what's going on with you — and onto what others want, what they need and what's going on with them. Learn to receive your satisfaction from the things that please God rather than the things that please self. Take time today to safeguard yourself from the effect of vanity, self-centeredness and pride.

Affirmation Prayer: Heavenly Father, at times in my life, I have been vain. I have attempted to take the glory that belongs to You alone. Forgive me, in the name of Jesus, Amen,

Daily Bread: Isaiah 47 — 48; Galatians 5:7-26; Psalm 109:1-20

No More Tears
September 20

Scripture: "And God will wipe away every tear from their eyes; there shall be no more death, nor sorrow, nor crying. There shall be no more pain, for the former things have passed away."
~ Revelation 21:14

Spiritual Vitamin

How do you handle sadness? Life shows us there are many things in your human experience that will bring you to tears. Sometimes, they will be tears of joy and other times, they will be tears caused by hurt and pain. The good news is that there is a day coming when you won't have to cry any more. The Word says that God will wipe every tear from your eyes. You won't have to experience the loss of death or sorrow. You won't have to experience any more pain. This sounds like something every person will enjoy. It lends itself to the notion that the uncertainties of life will no longer have control over you but that you will be in a safe place, where God Himself is in control. In heaven, there will be no reason to cry because in heaven, there is no sadness. God will remove devastation and irritation from within your midst. The human conditions and afflictions that you experience now will no longer be a factor. Tears and the reasons why you shed them are only temporary. Psalm 30:5 says "for His anger is but for a moment, His favor is for life. Weeping may endure for a night, but joy comes in the morning." Take time today to give God praise that, in your heavenly experience with Him, there will be no more tears.

Affirmation Prayer: Heavenly Father, I cried many tears in the past and You have dried them all. Help me to rejoice because I am free, in the name of Jesus, Amen.

Daily Bread: Isaiah 49 – 51; Galatians 6; Proverbs 23:10-18

Real Love
September 21

Scripture: "For God so loved the world that He gave His only begotten Son, that whoever believes in Him should not perish but have everlasting life."
~ John 3:16

Spiritual Vitamin

Every human being has a need for love. This is something every person has in common. We all want to be loved. When you receive the love you desire, it gives you a sense of fulfillment and peace within yourself. When you are not receiving that love, you tend to feel that you have to go out looking for it and in many cases end up with something counterfeit rather than something authentic. There are a few things you must do before you go looking for love. First, you need to learn to accept the love of your heavenly Father, which will supersede any human love you will ever find. Then, you need to learn to love yourself. Receiving God's love and cultivating self-love are the best ways to experience real love. God will never let you down and you won't purposely let yourself down. When you make a mistake, you can go to God, repent and He will make things right again. Then, when you are ready to permit the love of another human being into your life, it will be a love without unrealistic expectations. Take time today to accept and receive the love of God for yourself first, then you will know how to love those around you.

Affirmation Prayer: Heavenly Father, You have shown me real love. You've set the standard for my life. Let me not give my attention to anything other than real love in every area of my life, in the name of Jesus, Amen.

Daily Bread: Isaiah 52 – 54; Ephesians 1; Psalm 109:21-31

Starting Over Again
September 22

Scripture: "Do not remember the former things, nor consider the things of old. Behold, I will do a new thing. Now it shall spring forth; shall you not know it? I will even make a road in the wilderness and rivers in the desert."
~ Isaiah 43:18-19

Spiritual Vitamin

How do you feel about starting over again? Most people dread the thought of starting over. Whether it be a new job, a new place to live or a new relationship, there are many elements about these things that can bring fear and uneasiness to you. *Do you share the negative side to this or have you mastered keeping your thoughts positive and upbeat?* God is a God of progression and is always providing opportunities for you to move to a higher level in Him. According to Isaiah, God, will do a new thing. You cannot embrace the new thing God is attempting to do in your life with an old mindset. You must allow His Holy Spirit to renew your mind, making it possible for you to willingly embrace what God is trying to do. You may not understand at first, but pray and ask Him for a revelation of His latest move in your life. God does not desire to keep secrets from you. He wants to share what He's doing with you but you must be in the right frame of mind to receive what He's going to say. Take time today to get comfortable with starting over again, realizing that newness is not a bad thing.

Affirmation Prayer: Heavenly Father, today I walk in the newness of life because You have given me another chance. Teach me how to live in a way that demonstrates my appreciation, in the name of Jesus, Amen.

Daily Bread: Isaiah 55 – 57; Ephesians 2; Psalm 110:1-7

Stop for Love
September 23

Scripture: "Depart from evil and do good; seek peace and pursue it."
~ Psalm 34:14

Spiritual Vitamin

Are you taking good care of yourself? You must do what is necessary to take care of yourself --- mentally, physically, emotionally and spiritually. Every choice that you make will influence one or more of these areas in your life. From time-to-time, there will be moments of crisis in your life over which you have no control. On the other hand, some crisis are self-imposed. It is as a result of the way you think and can be as a result of unresolved hurt and/or pain from your past. If you are guilty of imposing crises onto yourself, please do what is necessary to stop. God's love for you requires you to have a love for yourself. He hurts when He sees you make choices and decisions that will negatively impact your life. He sent His Son so that you could have abundant life and not so that you could wander aimlessly around. You have an obligation to take good care of yourself and God will show you how to do that. You must go to Him, get to know His voice, spend time with Him and allow Him to guide you. Take time today to give yourself some love; stop looking outside of yourself for what is already contained within.

Affirmation Prayer: Heavenly Father, I have been guilty of making choices that have caused me trouble and pain. I agree to stop behaving in this way, because it is damaging to me. Help me to walk away from any behavior that is hurting me, in the name of Jesus, Amen.

Daily Bread: Isaiah 58 – 59; Ephesians 3; Psalm 111:1-10

Victory Shall Be Mine
September 24

Scripture: "No, despite all these things, overwhelming victory is ours through Christ, who loved us."
~ Romans 8:37 NLT

Spiritual Vitamin

Are you fighting a battle in your life right now? Before the battle began, you've already won. That should give you a deep sense of joy and contentment. As a matter of fact, you don't even have to fight the battle because God has promised to do that for you. Your best method of self-preservation is to hide yourself in God. So closely follow, listen to and obey God that the enemy can't even get close to you. No matter how hard the fight, victory is yours to enjoy. God will never allow the enemy to defeat you. Never! At times, it may look like the enemy is winning, but nothing could be further from the truth. This is when it is necessary to walk by faith and not by sight. You will discover, if you haven't already, that it's not always what it looks like. The enemy is good at deception and lies. This is what he does best. In every situation you will face in this life, victory shall be yours. Take time today to celebrate the provision that has already been put into place for you to win, no matter what the struggle.

Affirmation Prayer: Heavenly Father, living with You at the center of my life ensures me that victory shall be mine. Show me how to walk in that victory, in the name of Jesus, Amen.

Daily Bread: Isaiah 60 – 62; Ephesians 4:1-16; Proverbs 23:19-28

What's Going On?
September 25

Scripture: "The thief does not come except to steal, and to kill, and to destroy. I have come that they may have life, and that they may have it more abundantly."
~ John 10:10

Spiritual Vitamin

The state of affairs in the world in which we live would cause anyone to pause and ask "what's going on?" In the daily news, there are stories of abuse, death, disaster, political corruption and a lack of integrity just about everywhere you look. Sometimes, you will hear certain things and wonder what you should do. The answers are not too far out of your reach. God's Word explains everything you need to know for your earthly existence. He has made it clear that the enemy has some power in the earth realm and because of that, certain things will be allowed to take place that are associated with the kingdom of darkness; but take heart. God has all power. The enemy's power will never be greater than the power of God! All you really have to do is go to God in prayer and talk to Him about how you feel regarding the things that are going on in the world. He hears your prayers and He does what is necessary to answer them. Sometimes, you will see His hand moving and at other times, you will not, but you will receive the answers you seek. Take time today to cry out to God about what's going on in your world and watch Him show up where resolution once seemed impossible.

Affirmation Prayer: Heavenly Father, when I look at the evil practices of those in this world, I sometimes wonder "what's going on?" Yet, I am confident that the enemy is already defeated. I will calmly and confidently look forward to the time of Your Son's return, in the name of Jesus, Amen.

Daily Bread: Isaiah 63 – 65; Ephesians 4:17-32; Psalm 112:1-10

Worth Fighting For
September 26

Scripture: "Blessed are the peacemakers, for they shall be called sons of God."
~ Matthew 5:9

Spiritual Vitamin

Do you need to reconcile with someone? Reconciliation is important to God. One solid proof of this fact is that it was one of the reasons why God sent Jesus, to reconcile us to Himself after sin entered the world during the fall of man. When man sinned, God did not just throw up His hands and say, "oh well, I guess I'll just let them go". No, He devised a plan to get you back. He thought you were worth fighting for! Through this act, He has demonstrated the power of exercising this kind of love. *Since He did it on your behalf, can you now extend this same courtesy to someone in your life?* Some relationships are worth saving. Don't let pride, anger and selfishness cause you to lose valuable connections with your loved ones. Everyone's time on earth is temporary and all of us have the responsibility of making the best use of the time we have. Don't allow the enemy to rob you of that time and of the relationships that will make that time worthwhile. Fight for what is important to you. Take time today to consult God concerning what is worth fighting for and then go out and win the war through prayer.

Affirmation Prayer: Heavenly Father, thank You for accepting me back into Your Presence after I went willingly into sin. Because of what Jesus did for me, I know that my soul is worth fighting for. Help me to teach what I've learned to others, in the name of Jesus, Amen.

Daily Bread: Isaiah 66; Ephesians 5; Psalm 113:1-9

You Can't Always Get What You Want
September 27

Scripture: "You want what you don't have, so you scheme and kill to get it. You are jealous of what others have, but you can't get it, so you fight and wage war to take it away from them. Yet you don't have what you want because you don't ask God for it."
~ James 4:2 NLT

Spiritual Vitamin

Do you have a spirit of entitlement? You can't always get what you want, but you can always get what God wants for you! Maybe you should read that again, a bit more slowly this time. The simplest way to get what you want in life is to line-up your will with the will of God. That way, anything you request will promote the plan He has as well as aid you in becoming the best person you can be. When you are in line with God's will, you won't ask for things that are outside of His design for your best life. God wants nothing but the best for you and His plan includes what is needed to bring that to pass. The hardest thing you have to do is overcome the doubt and learn to trust that God knows what He's doing. *When will you learn that God knows how to take care of you better than you will ever know how to take care of yourself?* Take time today to think about ways in which you can give up your rights and accept the will of God for your life, so that in the end, you can always get what you want.

Affirmation Prayer: Heavenly Father, when things are not going my way, I am reminded that what looks like tragedy most often turns out to be triumph. Help me to trust that You alone know what is best for me, in the name of Jesus, Amen.

Daily Bread: Nahum 1 – 3; Ephesians 6; Psalm 114:1-8

Everything I Need
September 28

Scripture: "The Lord is my shepherd, I lack nothing. He makes me lie down in green pastures, he leads me beside quiet waters, he refreshes my soul."
~ Psalm 23: 1-3a NIV

Spiritual Vitamin

What do you need to be happy? Every individual must examine what they need in order to be happy. I believe the best way to know is to consult with God. Since He made you, He alone knows what is needed to cause a lasting joy and fulfillment within your soul. There are spaces within you that only God can fill. Tangible things cannot suffice for longings of the soul. Spiritual things must be employed in cases of this nature. God truly is all you need to be happy but the only way you will ever really know that is to develop a strong relationship with Him. God has always longed to be first in your life and He still does. Often, you put other people and things in front of Him. If this is so with you, please take the time to rearrange your priorities. Put God first, willingly and joyfully. It will be the best decision you will ever make. God will teach you how to love yourself and then, how to love others. Your relationships will be peaceful, full of harmony and happiness. The spirit of offense will be removed from you and you will no longer experience thoughts of revenge and vengeance. Take time today to accept the Lord as your shepherd and you will have everything you need.

Affirmation Prayer: Heavenly Father, thank You for providing all my needs. You are the Good Shepherd. Help me realize the depth of Your love, care and provision for me, in the name of Jesus, Amen.

Daily Bread: Zephaniah 1 – 3; Philippians 1:1-26; Proverbs 23:29-35; Proverbs 24:1-4

You're Gonna Make It After All
September 29

Scripture: "Have I not commanded you? Be strong and of good courage; do not be afraid, nor be dismayed, for the Lord your God is with you wherever you go." ~ Joshua 1:9

Spiritual Vitamin

As the end of the month draws near, I want to encourage you to continue practicing the art of self-preservation as it pertains to learning how to survive crisis. There have been times in your life when you thought you would not make it. You were convinced that it was over for you. But then, God came through in a way you never saw or expected. He did battle on your behalf and brought you out of the darkness into His marvelous light. When you have God on your side, the odds can never be stacked against you. 1 John 4:4 says "you are of God, little children, and have overcome them, because He who is in you is greater than he who is in the world." *Do you believe that?* If you do, then you have a continuous cause to celebrate. The circumstances of life will never defeat you. You must commit this to memory so that the next time a troubling situation arises, you can meditate on that fact rather than becoming disheartened and overwhelmed. Stop doubting and giving in to fear. God is moved by faith. Declare war on the tumultuous situations in your life and employ the tools that God has made available to you to help you defeat the evil one. Take time today to celebrate --- why, you ask --- because despite what you once thought, you're going to make it after all!

Affirmation Prayer: Heavenly Father, when my faith gets weak, I sometimes doubt whether I can handle what's happening in my life. Strengthen my faith and help me to believe when you tell me that I'm going to make it after all, in the name of Jesus, Amen.

Daily Bread: Jeremiah 1 – 2; Philippians 1:27-30; Philippians 2:1-11; Psalm 115:1-11

Lose My Mind
September 30

Scripture: "Finally, brethren, whatever things are true, whatever things *are* noble, whatever things *are* just, whatever things *are* pure, whatever things *are* lovely, whatever things *are* of good report, if *there is* any virtue and if *there is* anything praiseworthy --- meditate on these things."
~ Philippians 4:8

Spiritual Vitamin

Have you been converted? There is a very simple way to find out the answer to this question. If you are reacting rather responding, the answer is no. Jesus was never on "get back" and He never set out to get even or settle the score. His time was consumed with following the will of the Father. He wasn't consumed with the plots, schemes and plans that others were attempting to develop against him. Take a lesson from Jesus and stop being tossed and driven by your emotions; get off the roller coaster and save yourself! Put on the Fruit of the Spirit, especially self-control, before you lose your mind. There is nothing in this world worth sacrificing your sanity and you should never allow anyone or anything to push you over the edge. If God's Holy Spirit is in control of your being, you won't find it hard to rest in Him when you experience various trials and tribulations. You already know how important it is for you to take care of yourself physically, but you must not neglect your mental and emotional health in the process. Take time today to think, concentrate and meditate on the things of God.

Affirmation Prayer: Heavenly Father, thank You for mental and emotional stability. Remind me that I don't have to be swayed by the plans and plots of the enemy, in the name of Jesus, Amen.

Daily Bread: Jeremiah 3 – 4; Philippians 2:12-30; Psalm 115:12-18

Selwyn B. Cox

MONTHLY REFLECTIONS

October: Serenity (Having Peace That Passes Understanding)

Strength for the Journey

God, grant me the serenity to accept the things I cannot change, courage to change the things I can and wisdom to know the difference. Living one day at a time, enjoying one moment at a time, accepting hardship as the pathway to peace; taking as He did, this sinful world as it is, not as I would have it; trusting that He will make all things right if I surrender to His will, that I may be reasonably happy in this life and supremely happy with Him forever in the next. Amen
--- Reinhold Neibuhr (Serenity Prayer, full version)

October

Serenity (Having Peace That Passes Understanding)

During the month of October, you will go on a journey, learning about the process of obtaining serenity and a peace that surpasses understanding. Serenity is defined as the state of being calm, peaceful and untroubled. Serenity is truly a gift from God and something only He can provide. It will not just come to you, you must actively pursue it and once you find it, you must be deliberate about holding on to it. There will be several daily attempts made by the enemy to rob you of your peace. You must protect it at all costs. You have a divine right to serenity and it is a priceless treasure, offered to you by your heavenly Father. It is my prayer that you will use this month's devotionals to take advantage of the offer. With peace aboard your life, you will have endless encounters with all the other Fruit of the Spirit (see Galatians 5:22-23).

"You will keep him in perfect peace whose mind is stayed on you because He trusts in you."
~ Isaiah 26:3

At Your Best (You Are Love)
October 1

Scripture: "Do your best to present yourself to God as one approved, a worker who has no need to be ashamed, rightly handling the word of truth."
~ 2 Timothy 2:15 ESV

Spiritual Vitamin

Are you at your best? You were created with the necessary components to become the best you that you can be. When God made you, He left nothing out. You are packed full of what is needed to have a successful life in Christ Jesus. There are gifts and talents that are yet untapped so you must go on a quest to learn how to uncover what is hidden within. It is necessary to spend time with yourself and God so He can reveal the things He knows about you that you do not yet know about yourself. With God at the center of your life, you will be at your best. Without Him in your life, you will never be able to achieve what He had in mind when He created you. When you do the very best you can, it brings an element of peace to your spirit. You realize you do not have to compete. You are not consumed with being better than anyone else; you are content being the best person you can possibly be. Do yourself a favor and operate within the calling and purpose for your life; in other words, stay in your lane. This is a sure-fire way to be at your best. Take time today to read God's Word. Allow Him to uncover the mysteries within His Word and celebrate the discovery of the true you.

Affirmation Prayer: Heavenly Father, under the influence of Your Holy Spirit, I will always operate at my best. Renew my mind that I may uncover the mysteries You have in store for my life, in the name of Jesus, Amen.

Daily Bread: Jeremiah 5; Philippians 3; Psalm 116:1-11

Selwyn B. Cox

Quiet Storm
October 2

Scripture: "He calms the storm, so that its waves are still."
~ Psalm 107:29

Spiritual Vitamin

Do you live your life in a quiet storm? This seems like an oxymoron because in the natural sense, most storms are not quiet. In a natural storm, there is lots of loud thunder and the sound of hard rain can be heard, showering down from the skies. But there is another storm that is quiet, and although it cannot be heard with the physical ear, it has the power to impose dangerous and/or deadly consequences. This is the storm of the heart; where silent suffering goes on. When something is bothering you, it is best to face it head on and find a way to get it out in the open. Talk about your pain with someone who has your best interest at heart and who will keep what you have shared in confidence. Suffering in silence can make you physically sick. Strokes, heart attacks, high blood pressure and other related illnesses can be a result of silent suffering. You owe it to yourself to take advantage of the way of escape God has provided for you from the trials and hardships of life. You don't have to suffer in silence. Pray to your heavenly Father about the things that concern you. He is waiting to meet with you. Take time today to sit in the throne room of God and ask Him to quiet your storm.

Affirmation Prayer: Heavenly Father, let Your favor be upon me and allow me to experience peace in my spirit, no matter what is going on around me. Assure me that you can quiet my storm, in the name of Jesus, Amen.

Daily Bread: Jeremiah 6; Jeremiah 7:1-27; Philippians 4; Proverbs 24:5-14

Harvest for the World
October 3

Scripture: Then He said to His disciples, "the harvest truly is plentiful, but the laborers are few."
~ Matthew 9:37

Spiritual Vitamin

The word harvest is defined as the process or period of gathering. When something is gathered, it is joined together. When people love each other the way God intended, they are joined together. At the Rapture, those who love God and have accepted His Son Jesus as their Savior will be gathered to be taken to their heavenly home to live with God. This will be a harvest for the Kingdom of God. But we don't have to wait for the Rapture to take place before we gather. As members of the body of Christ and the Kingdom of God, we can decide right here on earth to spread the love of God so that there can be a harvest for the world. It is possible to change the world, one soul at a time. You can make a difference in the lives of those closest to you by encouraging everyone with whom you are personally connected, to establish a relationship with Christ. Your witness has the power to influence others for the cause of Christ. *When was the last time you shared the story of your conversion with someone else?* Take time today to talk about God's light and love that are on the inside of you and light the way for new believers to be born.

Affirmation Prayer: Heavenly Father, empower me to always speak of You so that I may reap a harvest of souls for Your Kingdom, in the name of Jesus, Amen.

Daily Bread: Jeremiah 7:28-34; Jeremiah 8; Jeremiah 9:1-16; Colossians 1:1-23; Psalm 116:12-19

Everything Will Be Alright
October 4

Scripture: "Though the mountains be shaken and the hills be removed, yet my unfailing love for you will not be shaken nor my covenant of peace be removed," says the Lord, who has compassion on you."
~ Isaiah 54:10

Spiritual Vitamin

When your life is wrapped up in God, you are safe and protected and there is no need for worry or concern of any kind. *Would you slowly read that first sentence again?* Now, take a deep breath and really focus and concentrate on what that means. This is not the first time you have been told this. You already know that you are not supposed to worry, but you do it anyway. You worry because you choose to do so. God never asked you to worry; instead, He asked you to have faith. God never asked you to be in control of your own life. He volunteered the services of His Son to handle the details for you. In order for this to happen, you must surrender the control you think you have and allow Christ to step in. He would be happy to become your Savior and Lord. You do not have the power to change your circumstance but you do have the power to pray and believe that God will do what is best for you. *When someone tells you everything will be alright, do you believe them? Can you believe me?* Take time today to put your faith into operation, then relax and trust that everything really will be alright.

Affirmation Prayer: Heavenly Father, I realize that fear is the complete opposite of faith. Help me to pray and not fear and to trust that You will make everything alright, in the name of Jesus, Amen.

Daily Bread: Jeremiah 9:17-26; Jeremiah 10: Jeremiah 11:1-17; Colossians 1:24-29; Colossians 2:1-5; Psalm 117:1-2

Finally
October 5

Scripture: "Finally, my brethren, be strong in the Lord and in the power of His might."
~ Ephesians 6:10

Spiritual Vitamin

Do you trust that God knows where you are? Everything God intends for you to have will reach you if you line up with His will for your life. You cannot be out of place and expect God to re-route your blessings. Your blessings have been strategically placed along the path God intends for you to take. In order to get them, you must remain on and follow His path. It takes determination, faith, belief and trust in God to stay on the right road. Relying on God's strength rather than your own can aid you in this process. Through submission to His will, allow God to take control and to demonstrate His plans and purposes through you. You were created to be used by God and to bring glory to His name. You may think it's too late and that you have done too many things wrong. This could not be further from the truth. Your mistakes will never supersede the power and ability of God. Jesus Christ has taken all of your sins to the cross and you have been forgiven. *Why not decide to turn toward God and finally begin to receive all that He has to give you?* Take time today to repent of your sins and begin a new life in Christ --- it is never too late to begin again.

Affirmation Prayer: Heavenly Father, thank You for equipping me with strength and power. I repent of every sin. Make me willing to receive You as Savior and Lord, in the name of Jesus, Amen.

Daily Bread: Jeremiah 11:18-23; Jeremiah 12 – 13; Colossians 2:6-23; Psalm 118:1-16

His Eye Is On the Sparrow
October 6

Scripture: "Look at the birds of the air, for they neither sow nor reap nor gather into barns; yet your heavenly Father feeds them. Are you not of more value than they? Which of you by worrying can add one cubit to his stature?"
~ Matthew 6:26-27

Spiritual Vitamin

God is a God of detail. *Did you know that? Better yet, do you believe it?* Every living thing in creation was made by Him. Even the smallest creature enjoys the love, care and concern of God. Man is the most special of God's creation because man was made in the very image of God. In comparison to humans, many creatures are small in size, for example, the birds. But even as small as they are, they still have the attention and concern of God. If He is concerned about the birds, certainly He is concerned about you. The birds were not made in His image, but you were. You were made in the likeness of God and His eye is on you each and every day. You are never out of the sight or reach of God and you will never be. *Isn't that good news?* Let me reemphasize even when you take a path that seems to be leading you away from God, He is still able to reach you and bring you back to Himself. God is watching over you. Whether you like it or not, He loves you so deeply that He relentlessly pursues you, not wanting to let you go. Take time today to relax and allow God's peace to surround you; the same peace He provides for all creatures of the earth.

Affirmation Prayer: Heavenly Father, thank You for watching over me. I give You praise and thanks for Your great love. Forever keep me in Your care, in the name of Jesus, Amen.

Daily Bread: Jeremiah 14 – 15; Colossians 3; Proverbs 24:15-22

How Excellent Is Thy Name
October 7

Scripture: "O Lord, our Lord, how excellent is Your name in all the earth!"
~ Psalm 8:9

Spiritual Vitamin

How do you feel about your name? Your name is the method by which people communicate with you and is used for the purpose of identification. When you were born, the first gift your parents gave you was your name. Every name is significant and while this is true, no name is more significant, higher or greater than the name of God. As a matter of fact, His name is excellent. There is power in His name. You have heard it time and time again, but it really is true — there IS power in the name of Jesus. Power to help you do whatever you need to do. God's name carries great weight and power in the spirit realm. When you come under attack from the forces of darkness, you can simply call on the name of the Lord and be rescued by His supernatural strength and power. God's name means many things and as you grow closer to Him, you will begin to experience Him according to the meaning of those names. Jehovah Jireh is the Lord who provides. Jehovah Shalom is your peace. Jehovah Nissi fights for you. Take time today to get to know God according to His names and experience the life-changing power that experience will provide.

Affirmation Prayer: Heavenly Father, how excellent is Your name. Allow me to get to know You better according to the attributes in Your Word, in the name of Jesus, Amen.

Daily Bread: Jeremiah 16 – 17; Colossians 4:1-18; Psalm 118:17-29

How Sweet It Is
October 8

Scripture: "I do not turn aside from your rules, for you have taught me. How sweet are your words to my taste."
~ Psalm 119:102-103a ESV

Spiritual Vitamin

Are you living a peaceful life? Peaceful living is sweet. There is no greater contentment to have than a clean, pure and faith-filled heart. If you have found that place in your life, you are experiencing not only happiness, but a profound sense of joy. Your attitude and disposition do not change when the various circumstances in your life do. You are so rooted and grounded in God's Word that you know He is aware and actively involved in everything that goes on in your life. For this reason, there is no need for you to worry because God is at the controls, making sure the outcome is what He desires to take place in this particular season of your life. How sweet it is to be loved by an all-powerful God! A God whose love you cannot and did not earn, yet He showers it upon you every single day you live and breathe. It is not too much to worship and praise a God who takes such wonderful care of you, even when you decide to do what He has asked you not to do. He even made provisions for the times you would sin and gave you provisions to get back into the good grace of God. Take time today to taste the sweetness and contentment of a life surrendered to God.

Affirmation Prayer: Heavenly Father, You have changed my life. You have not treated me like an orphan but Your very own. Now, my life is rich and sweet. Help me to lift my hands and thank You, in the name of Jesus, Amen.

Daily Bread: Jeremiah 18 – 20; 1 Thessalonians 1; 1 Thessalonians 2:1-16; Psalm 119:1-8

I Can't Stop Loving You
October 9

Scripture: The Lord has appeared of old to me, saying: "Yes, I have loved you with an everlasting love; therefore with lovingkindness I have drawn you."
~ Jeremiah 31:3

Spiritual Vitamin

Have you stopped loving someone or yourself? With humans love is a choice, but I want to say it again, with God it's a promise. Human beings fall in and out of love at will. When someone is doing what you want them to do, it is easy to remain in love with them. But when they do things that hurt and betray you, you start to feel differently about them. You allow their actions and behavior to dictate the way you feel about them. Thankfully, this is not so with God. His decision to love you covers every aspect of your being and behavior. He loves you when you are right and He loves you when you are wrong. This is unconditional love. *Can you do this same thing for someone in your life?* All too often, we stop loving the people in our lives because of external things. *When was the last time you attempted to see inside the heart of someone who hurt you?* It has been said that it is easy for people who are hurt themselves to hurt others. *Can you see how true this is?* Make a determination that you will not stop loving those close to you because of their bad choices and decisions. Take time today to look beneath the surface and help them get to the root of the problem instead of deciding to walk away.

Affirmation Prayer: Heavenly Father, You have chosen me and saved my soul. Because of this, I cannot stop loving You. Let me always be a reflection of Your goodness, in the name of Jesus, Amen.

Daily Bread: Jeremiah 21 – 22; Jeremiah 23:1-8; 1 Thessalonians 2:17-20; 1 Thessalonians 3; Psalm 119:9-16

I Don't Feel No Ways Tired
October 10

Scripture: "And let us not grow weary of doing good, for in due season we will reap, if we do not give up. So then, as we have opportunity, let us do good to everyone, and especially to those who are of the household of faith."
~ Galatians 6:9-10 ESV

Spiritual Vitamin

Are you tired of doing good because you are not seeing the results you wanted to see? You should never get tired of doing good. Never allow the enemy to have the satisfaction of making you abandon your good nature because you feel it is not worth the effort to bless those to whom God sends you. Often, we wait for the response of those we are sent to bless and if their response is less than favorable, we become disheartened in our efforts to bless them. This should not be the case. What you are doing, you are not really doing for them; you are doing it for God. Do not allow your soul to become weary. Jeremiah 31:25 ESV says, "for I will satisfy the weary soul, and every languishing soul I will replenish." If you feel yourself becoming weary, go to God and let Him replenish your soul. Don't listen to the enemy when he tries to tell you that your work is in vain. This couldn't be further from the truth. No, it's actually his work that's in vain because Christ has already won the victory over him. Don't let satan pass off his defeated condition onto you. With Christ, you have already won. Take time today to do good for others and God will greatly reward you.

Affirmation Prayer: Heavenly Father, sometimes the good I attempt to do is misunderstood. But I will never tire of working for You. Every day, provide Your brand new mercies to empower me to move forward, in the name of Jesus, Amen.

Daily Bread: Jeremiah 23:9-40; Jeremiah 24; Jeremiah 25:1-14; 1 Thessalonians 4; Proverbs 24:23-35

I Love Your Smile
October 11

Scripture: "Then our mouth was filled with laughter, and our tongue with singing. Then they said among the nations, "The Lord has done great things for them."
~ Psalm 126:2

Spiritual Vitamin

Do you smile often? A smile has the ability to change the dynamics of a situation. It also has the power to change how you feel. No matter what's going on in your life, if you can find the strength to simply smile, you will begin to feel better about your circumstances. The details of the situation may not be conducive to smiling but if you meditate on the fact that God has whatever is wrong under His control, then that should give you a reason to smile. God loves your smile. After all, He is the One who gave you that smile. It brings Him delight to see the smile upon your face. According to Psalm 126, it is God who puts laughter in your mouth and singing on your tongue. In Philippians 4, you are reminded to rejoice in the Lord always. This is because God knows that rejoicing brings hope and hope is something you will need in order to be able to endure your earthly experience. Your smile is not only for you, it is a gift to those around you. It is to be used for the purposes of uplifting, supporting and encouraging someone else. Take time today to share your smile with someone around you. It just may be the thing that brightens their day.

Affirmation Prayer: Heavenly Father, You have smiled on me and set me free. I am now able to smile inside and out. Let my smile draw others to You, in the name of Jesus, Amen.

Daily Bread: Jeremiah 25:15-38; Jeremiah 26; 1 Thessalonians 5; Psalm 119:17-24

I Need Thee
October 12

Scripture: "Let us therefore come boldly to the throne of grace, that we may obtain mercy and find grace to help in time of need."
~ Hebrews 4:16

Spiritual Vitamin

Do you realize how much you need God in your life? You cannot live this earthly experience alone. There will be times when you wish you could, but that is not in the plan of God. At different places along your journey, you are going to need the help and assistance of others. There will be situations when people can assist you and there will be situations when they cannot. It is during those moments that you must go to God. When you need divine intervention, go into the throne room of God. Lay your problems, concerns and cares at the feet of our heavenly Father. He is always available to spend time with you. He's never too busy and He'll never turn you away. He knows that you need Him in every area of your life. He loves it when you come to Him with your cares and concerns. You will be able to do absolutely nothing without the help of God. *Isn't it interesting that some people think they don't need Him? Have you realized that you do?* You will struggle through life, experiencing frequent trials and tribulations without the assistance and wisdom of God. But you don't have to do that. Take time today to cry out to God, telling Him how much you want and need Him in your life.

Affirmation Prayer: Heavenly Father, I cry out with a loud voice, I need You every hour, every minute, every second of the day. Thank you for always being there for me. Help me make a commitment to do as You command, in the name of Jesus, Amen.

Daily Bread: Jeremiah 27 – 28; Jeremiah 29:1-23; 2 Thessalonians 1; Psalm 119:25-32

It's Gonna Be Alright
October 13

Scripture: "Now to Him who is able to do exceedingly abundantly above all that we ask or think, according to the power that works in us."
~ Ephesians 3:20

Spiritual Vitamin

Have you mastered the art of resting on the promises of God? The Word of God tells you not to worry. God has promised to take good care of you. What God has promised, He delivers and He has never gone back on His Word. He is so much greater than any of us can understand with our finite minds. He has everything you need at His disposal and can speak your miracle into existence, just like that! Whenever something unexpected or unfortunate happens in your life, you can rest assured that with God on your side, everything is going to be alright. God will make a way for you and your family to survive crisis and hardship. You are never left alone to figure out what you should do about a problem or situation. Just pray and receive the wisdom and assistance of Almighty God. After God tells you what to do, don't be afraid to spring into action. Do what He says and you will see things quickly change for the better. If not with the situation itself, then at least with your perspective concerning the details. Take time today to celebrate the fact that no matter what's going on, God has promised you that "it's gonna be alright!"

Affirmation Prayer: Heavenly Father, I see the light at the end of the tunnel. I see the rainbow at the end of the storm. You have assured me that everything is going to be alright. Help me to believe, in the name of Jesus, Amen.

Daily Bread: Jeremiah 29:24-32; Jeremiah 30; Jeremiah 31:1-14; 2 Thessalonians 2; Psalm 119:33-40

It Is Well
October 14

Scripture: "For thus says the Lord: "Behold, I will extend peace to her like a river, and the glory of the nations like an overflowing stream; and you shall nurse, you shall be carried upon her hip, and bounced upon her knees."
~ Isaiah 66:12 ESV

Spiritual Vitamin

Can you say these words and mean them? It is well. There is freedom in being able to say this phrase and mean it because in reality, it really is well. No matter what "it" is, if God is in control of your life, it is well. God is not unaware concerning any particular detail of your life. He has seen every day of it from beginning to end. He knows every mistake you will make and has decided to forgive and love you anyway. It is well. That alone is a huge indication of the level of love God has for you. Some of the sins that you are forgiven for have not even been committed yet. *Did you get that?* The thing you haven't even done yet has already been forgiven by God. It is well. If that isn't love, I don't know what is. In the natural, the sun will not shine every day. There will be clouds and there will be rain. Yes, there will be days when you would like to run away from it all but in those moments, realize that you are trying to control the situation rather than resting on what God has said. It is well. Take time today to give complete control over to God. Then you will know in your heart of hearts that it is well!

Affirmation Prayer: Heavenly Father, when peace comes over me and I am able to feel Your love, I am grateful. Help me rest in knowing that it is well with my soul, in the name of Jesus, Amen.

Daily Bread: Jeremiah 31:15-40; Jeremiah 32:1-25; 2 Thessalonians 3; Proverbs 25:1-10

Jesus Loves Me
October 15

Scripture: "And whatever you ask in My name, that will I do, that the Father may be glorified in the Son."
~ John 14:13

Spiritual Vitamin

Do you know that Jesus loves you? Does that mean anything to you? In a world that is full of constant change, especially in relationships, you should find comfort in knowing that Jesus loves you. Because you cannot see Him with your physical eyes, maybe you don't know the magnitude of what that really means. So often, people are more consumed with who does not love them that they miss the opportunity to celebrate who does. There is no love more priceless than the love of God. You didn't do anything to earn it yet you will never lose it. God demonstrated this great love for you by sending His only Son to take the punishment for your sin and die in your place. Jesus is God's prized possession, His Son and the Savior of the world. He gave up His best for mankind when mankind was at its worst. This act is beyond logical comprehension. Most of us don't do our best for people when they are not acting as we would like. God looks beyond every fault, sees and meets every need. Take time today to celebrate the love God has for you and in turn, give love to someone else in need.

Affirmation Prayer: Heavenly Father, how grateful I am that You have loved me in spite of my secret sins. You know everything yet You continue to shower Your love and blessings on me. Make me worthy of Your grace, in the name of Jesus, Amen.

Daily Bread: Jeremiah 32:26-44; Jeremiah 33 – 34; 1 Timothy 1; Psalm 119:41-48

Keep Smiling
October 16

Scripture: "The Lord make His face shine upon you, and be gracious to you; The Lord lift up His countenance upon you, and give you peace."
~ Numbers 6:25-26

Spiritual Vitamin

Are you smiling, no matter what? Some situations in your life will not make you smile. In fact, there will be times when smiling will be the last thing on your agenda. It is then when you must reach deep within your inner self and pull out what God has spoken into your spirit. God has made His intentions clear toward you. Nothing is hidden that you are not allowed to search for and uncover. The mysteries of God will be revealed to you as you go deeper in your search of Him. You are God's child, He loves you and wants nothing more than a strong, personal connection with you. So relax, take a deep breath and smile. For your own sake, find something to smile about, every single day that you live and breathe. Show God how much faith you have in Him by how well you wait on Him when things are not as you wish they were. An abundance of faith opens the door to an abundance of peace. This peace will allow you to keep smiling, no matter what else the circumstances of life may be telling you to do. *Will you believe what you can see with your natural eyes or will you look through the eyes of faith?* Take time today to quiet your thoughts, relax and smile.

Affirmation Prayer: Heavenly Father, because You are so powerful and loving, I can keep smiling through the trials of life. Help me to see clearly what You have preordained for my life, even in times of uncertainty, in the name of Jesus, Amen.

Daily Bread: Jeremiah 35 – 37; 1 Timothy 2; Psalm 119:49-56

Living On A Prayer
October 17

Scripture: "pray without ceasing."
~ 1 Thessalonians 5:17

Spiritual Vitamin

Do you have a strong prayer life? Prayer is one of the greatest tools you have. In order to know this, you must become acquainted with the proper way to use this tool and then commit to using it often. It seems that some have complicated prayer beyond what God intended. Prayer is a conversation with God. First you talk, then you listen. If you only do one without the other, the process is not complete. *Speaking in human terms, would you want to have a conversation with someone who only talked but then didn't want to listen to what you had to say?* Sadly, this is sometimes how we treat God. Don't spend a long time telling God everything that is wrong in your life and what you want Him to do about it and then end the conversation and walk away. By all means, tell God what you need but first, give Him adoration, confess your sins, thank Him for what He's already done and then, tell him what you need. This formula for prayer is known as ACTS (adoration – confession – thanksgiving – supplication). Take time today to strengthen your relationship with God through the process of prayer.

Affirmation Prayer: Heavenly Father, I acknowledge You as my Abba Father, my daddy, my papa, my rock, my shield and my protection. I hallow Your holy and righteous name. Strengthen my connection to You, in the name of Jesus, Amen.

Daily Bread: Jeremiah 38 – 40; 1 Timothy 3; Psalm 119:57-64

I Luh God
October 18

Scripture: "So he answered and said, "You shall love the Lord your God with all your heart, with all your soul, with all your strength, and with all your mind, and your neighbor as yourself.""
~ Luke 10:27

Spiritual Vitamin

Do you love God? God is asking you to love Him more than you love anything else. 1 John 2:15-17 (ESV) says, "do not love the world or the things in the world. If anyone loves the world, the love of the Father is not in him. For all that is in the world — the desires of the flesh and the desires of the eyes and the pride of life — is not from the Father but is from the world. And the world is passing away along with its desires, but whoever does the will of God abides forever." God paid a high price to buy you back from the clutches of sin, and all He is asking for in return is your love and obedience. He extends His love to you in a way that can change your life, if you would permit it to do so. In return, He deserves your praise, worship, devotion and loyalty. You demonstrate your love to God through your obedience to His Word. *How well are you doing with listening to and obeying God?* This is an indication of how much you love Him. God has perfected the art of loving you. Take time today to let Him teach you how to love Him in return and share that knowledge with others.

Affirmation Prayer: Heavenly Father, I proclaim and declare my love for You. Make my life a reflection of this declaration, as a witness to those around me, in the name of Jesus, Amen.

Daily Bread: Jeremiah 41 — 42; 1 Timothy 4; Proverbs 25:11-20

On the Ocean
October 19

Scripture: "Who else has measured the waters in the hollow of His hand? Measured heaven with a span?"
~ Isaiah 40:12a

Spiritual Vitamin

Isn't the ocean a miraculous creation? God is a Master Creator. He made everything with His own hands and the power of His voice. He made the elements and He made mankind. The ocean is one of the wonders of the world. It is living and active and moves at the direction and command of God. The movement of the ocean communicates various messages to us. One message is that in certain circumstances, we have no control. When out in a vessel on the ocean, man has no control over the movement of the water. Sometimes the waves roll and gently turn, as they meet the sand on the shore and at other times, the waves seem to crash and pound onto the sand, as if in an uproarious rage. The times of our lives can be much the same; sometimes calmly and gently rolling along and at other times, crashing and pounding as if in a rage. Through it all, God is in total and complete control. On the more peaceful side, the ocean can have a soothing, calming effect on the human senses. You can sit and watch it with a sense of wonder and appreciation for the abilities of God. Take time today to plan a trip to the ocean. Once there, clear your mind and just bask in the beauty of it all.

Affirmation Prayer: Heavenly Father, You alone can measure the expanse of the ocean. Teach me to appreciate the beauty of everything in nature that You have made, in the name of Jesus, Amen.

Daily Bread: Jeremiah 43 – 45; 1 Timothy 5; Psalm 119:65-72

What A Wonderful World
October 20

Scripture: "Then God saw everything that He had made, and indeed it was very good. So the evening and the morning were the sixth day."
~ Genesis 1:31

Spiritual Vitamin

God said "let there be" and there was. Everything that He made was made for the appreciation and enjoyment of man. God wasn't thinking of Himself when He made the world. He was thinking of you and me. He knew what your senses would need in order to experience wonder and delight and that is how He created the things He made. The view of the countryside from the top of a mountain, seeing the clouds from an airplane window or an evening sunset bursting with color all create some type of emotional response within us. As you get older, you must work to maintain an appreciation for the wonders of God. The longer you live in this world, the better the chance you will begin to take things for granted. Sometimes, it happens unconsciously but you must work to prevent it at all costs. Life is a gift and must be celebrated on a daily basis. The reality of it all is that someone dies every day and if you are not that someone today, then that is a cause to celebrate. Don't allow the tactics of the enemy to rob you of your joy and cause you to miss out on the wonders of life that God is trying to show you. Take time today to thank God you're still here because no matter what's going on, you live in a wonderful world.

Affirmation Prayer: Heavenly Father, thank You for the wonderful world in which I live. Make me grateful and show me ways to care for it, in the name of Jesus, Amen.

Daily Bread: Jeremiah 46 – 47; 1 Timothy 6; Psalm 119:73-80

On Bended Knee
October 21

Scripture: "that at the name of Jesus every knee should bow, of those in heaven, and of those on earth, and of those under the earth."
~ Philippians 2:10

Spiritual Vitamin

Do you think you need validation from another human being? Jesus did not need human validation. His identity has been validated by God. If you have accepted Jesus as your Savior, your identity has been validated by God as well. Jesus received the stamp of approval from God. God has stated that He is not only pleased but "well" pleased with Jesus. There are some who do not accept Jesus for who God says He is and they need to realize that their unacceptance will not change the facts. Bowing is a sign of reverence and respect. Jesus deserves that reverence and respect from us because of what He freely surrendered on our behalf. To sacrifice certain things for the sake of someone else is one thing, but to sacrifice everything is another thing completely. Jesus did nothing but good to and for everyone He encountered. Yet, as a reward, what He received in return was ridicule, scorn and death. There was no reason for Jesus to die — except one — us. He did it for you and He did it for me. The way I see it, we owe Him something for all He's given us. We can start with praise and worship, on bended knee. Take time today to get down on your knees and thank God for what He's given you through His Son.

Affirmation Prayer: Heavenly Father, You have made each limb of my body. I will bow down and worship You, for You deserve all glory, honor and praise. Help me to be willing to pray each day, on bended knee, in the name of Jesus, Amen.

Daily Bread: Jeremiah 48; 2 Timothy 1; Psalm 119:81-88

Paradise
October 22

Scripture: "He has made everything beautiful in its time. Also He has put eternity in their hearts, except that no one can find out the work that God does from beginning to end."
~ Ecclesiastes 3:11

Spiritual Vitamin

What is paradise to you? If you asked several people to define the word "paradise", you would receive several different responses. One dictionary definition of paradise describes it this way, "heaven as the ultimate abode of the just." *What is your definition of paradise? Is it some far away, tropical destination with white sand, blue water and palm trees? Or can it be a state of mind?* I would like to challenge your thinking today. I believe you can visit a place of mental paradise while experiencing physical conditions that are exactly the opposite. *How would you do that?* By simply activating your faith. You have been told, by God Himself through His Son Jesus, that you will never be left alone. *What do you need to do in order to believe that?* You do not serve a God who is with you only in moments of pleasure and joy. He doesn't get up and walk out when things get hard. This is when He draws closer. *Can you feel Him?* If not, you need to adjust your position because He is right where He said He would be. Take time today to spend a few moments in paradise, in the company of Almighty God.

Affirmation Prayer: Heavenly Father, Paradise awaits me. Grant me momentary glimpses of it while I walk out my faith in You, in the name of Jesus, Amen.

Daily Bread: Jeremiah 49; 2 Timothy 2; Proverbs 25:21-28; Proverbs 26:1-2

Peace Be Still
October 23

Scripture: "Then He arose and rebuked the wind, and said to the sea, 'Peace, be still!' And the wind ceased and there was a great calm."
~ Mark 4:39

Spiritual Vitamin

The disciples were afraid because their boat was being tossed to and fro in the middle of a storm. Jesus was on the boat with them, but He was asleep. *Have you ever wondered about this passage of scripture? How is it possible that everyone on board was awake and afraid, yet Jesus was asleep?* There are a few indications here. One, if something is not troubling to Jesus, it should not be troubling to you. When you see Jesus get worried, that is when you should get worried. If He doesn't get worried, neither should you. Jesus has the ability to SPEAK peace. He doesn't need to physically do anything, all He has to do is speak. What power! He has given us power and authority over situations. *When was the last time you spoke peace to your own situation? If you do not have the knowledge to be the captain, why are you trying to sail the boat?* Let Jesus be the captain. He has much more experience with these types of things than you do. Become a passenger and enjoy the ride. Take time today to exercise your God-given rights. Speak peace into your life and watch things change for the better.

Affirmation Prayer: Heavenly Father, You have spoken peace into every circumstance of my life. Continue to grant me peace as I let You lead me through each day, in the name of Jesus. Amen.

Daily Bread: Jeremiah 50; 2 Timothy 3; Psalm 119:89-96

Quiet Time
October 24

Scripture: "But you, when you pray, go into your room, and when you have shut the door, pray to your Father who is in the secret place and your Father who sees in secret will reward you openly."
~ Matthew 6:6

Spiritual Vitamin

Do you need some quiet time? Most people think they have to wait until their vacation time in order to enjoy this luxury. That is not the truth. You don't have to wait for a yearly vacation to experience quiet time. All you have to do is agree to unplug and disconnect from the hustle and bustle of life for a specified period of time. You can carve out quiet moments every day but you must be intentional about this practice. Just as you plan other items on your calendar, plan your quiet time. In scheduling the time you spend with others, don't forget to schedule time to spend with yourself and God. Each day, there will be many demands that will be placed upon you and because of those demands, you will be required to pour out of your spirit. When you do that, you become depleted and need to get replenished. You must spend time with God and His Holy Spirit for this to take place. Learn to meditate on the Word of God, not just read it in passing. Soak it in and really allow it to penetrate your spirit. This will provide you with great comfort and strength. Spend some quiet time with God and use it to your advantage.

Affirmation Prayer: Heavenly Father, thank You for the gift of quiet time. Let me not forget to take advantage of it on a regular basis, in the name of Jesus, Amen.

Daily Bread: Jeremiah 51; 2 Timothy 4; Psalm 119:97-104

Remember the Time
October 25

Scripture: "I will remember the deeds of the Lord; yes, I will remember your wonders of old."
~ Psalm 77:11 ESV

Spiritual Vitamin

A great storyteller makes use of the line --- "do you remember the time when ....." --- and they go on to add names and specific details to the rest of the story. I have one for you. *Do you remember the time when God brought you out of that seemingly impossible situation that you thought would be the end of you?* If you haven't yet experienced that moment, in the words of the seasoned saints, "just keep on living." Sooner or later, it will come. God's deliverance creates opportunities for testimonies to be shared. So often, rather than keeping the details of His deliverance alive, we choose to keep silent and not share what He's done. We quietly thank Him and try to move forward as if nothing has occurred. This is wrong on many levels. When you don't share what God has done for you, it's hard for others to have the necessary evidence for the hope they need in their own lives. Everyone is struggling with something and many people are too prideful to share their struggle or ask for help. When you share your victories, you will inspire someone else who is going through the same thing. Take time today to "remember the time" and share the details of the story for the benefit of others.

Affirmation Prayer: Heavenly Father, I recall many times in my past when You have delivered and helped me. Let me be willing to share these memories as testimonies to Your goodness, in the name of Jesus, Amen.

Daily Bread: Jeremiah 52; Titus 1; Psalm 119:105-112

Rhythms of Life
October 26

Scripture: "For I have come down from heaven, not to do My own will, but the will of Him who sent Me."
~ John 6:38

Spiritual Vitamin

The word rhythm is defined as a strong, regular, repeated pattern of movement or sound. *As it pertains to you, is your life a strong, regular, repeated pattern of movements?* You have established certain habits and patterns and they govern how you spend the hours of your day. These habits fall into one of two categories: Godly or ungodly. Hopefully, there are more Godly rhythms (patterns and habits) in your life than ungodly ones, but you must be the judge of that. *As it pertains to sound, what is the rhythm of your life? Are there strong, regular, repeated patterns of sound or a bunch of cracked notes and broken chords?* If there are more cracked notes and broken chords, it doesn't have to be this way. God can turn the sound of your life into a beautiful symphony. The soundtrack of your life can produce beautiful music if you are living within God's purpose and allowing Him to conduct the orchestra. He knows what is needed and when. He knows when it's time for the drums and when it's time for the piano and He never confuses the two. Allow God to write the song and it will play in perfect harmony. Take time today to listen to the sounds of your life and make adjustments where necessary.

Affirmation Prayer: Heavenly Father, I set my pace for the day in prayer and quiet moments of solitude. Keep me in sync with You, in the name of Jesus, Amen.

Daily Bread: Habakkuk 1 – 3; Titus 2; Proverbs 26:3-12

Sittin' Up In My Room
October 27

Scripture: "There is therefore now no condemnation to those who are in Christ Jesus, who do not walk according to the flesh, but according to the Spirit."
~ Romans 8:1

Spiritual Vitamin

Is your bedroom a special place? The bedroom is one of the most private places in your home. It is the room that most people who visit you do not see. It is this room where you are the most vulnerable. Your guard is down when you are in your room. This is the place you feel safe and secure. I want to bring an important point to your attention. There can be a false sense of security when you are in your room, if you have not secured the rest of your house. In order for your room to be safe, the door to your house must be locked. According to the Word of God, the enemy will come to steal, kill and destroy. The only thing that will deter him is the Word of God and the blood of Jesus. Thieves can break into a physical door but no thief can break through the protection of God or the blood of Jesus. Just as good locks and security systems secure your physical house, the Word and the whole armor of God protect your spiritual house. Take time today to make sure your spiritual house is as secure as your physical house.

Affirmation Prayer: Heavenly Father, thank You that I am not condemned because I am in Christ. Help me take the necessary steps to protect my spiritual house, in the name of Jesus, Amen.

Daily Bread: Lamentations 1 – 2; Titus 3; Psalm 119:113-120

Take Me To The King
October 28

Scripture: "From the end of the earth I will cry to You, when my heart is overwhelmed; Lead me to the rock that is higher than I".
~ Psalm 61:2

Spiritual Vitamin

You want people in your inner circle who will pray for you when things are not going well in your life; someone who will notice when things are off and you're not quite yourself. You want someone close to you who will not always need all the intricate details of the problem but who will simply go to God on your behalf. You need someone who will intercede for you; in other words, someone who will take you to the King. You need someone who doesn't mind spending time on their knees on your behalf, who expects nothing in return. They want to see you at your best and they know there is only one way you can truly be that way – with God's help. *Don't you want someone in your life who will pay enough attention to you to know when something is wrong?* We could all benefit from having a person like this in our lives. Not an individual who wants all the details of the problem so that they can go and tell everyone they know, but rather someone who will take it all to our heavenly Father, the King. He's a great keeper of secrets and He'll never use the unholy details of your life to shame or embarrass you. Take time today to examine your inner circle. Make sure you are linked up with people who know how to pray, so they can talk to God on your behalf, especially when you can't talk to Him for yourself.

Affirmation Prayer: Heavenly Father, thank You for welcoming me into Your Presence when things are not going well. Help me to accept Your help in the name of Jesus, Amen.

Daily Bread: Lamentations 3 – 4; Philemon 1; Psalm 119:121-128

Walk By Faith
October 29

Scripture: "For we walk by faith, not by sight."
~ 2 Corinthians 5:7

Spiritual Vitamin

Are you walking by faith? It takes concentrated effort not to believe the things you see with your natural eyes. Let me remind you, you must make a firm decision not to listen to the enemy when he comes to you with all of his stories and lies. Often throughout the moments of your day, he will tell you all kinds of lies about God and your relationship with God. You will be told that God does not love you and that He is not going to help you with what you're going through. You will be told that you are not good enough for God to be concerned about you. When this happens, you must allow God to build your faith in Him by resting on His promises. You must keep your mind in a positive place and do everything you can to keep your hands clean and your heart pure. You must walk by faith. You must employ the services of your spiritual eyes rather than your natural eyes, because in reality, it's not always what it looks like. You have the power to choose obedience, no matter what. Take time today to make whatever changes are necessary to allow you to walk by faith.

Affirmation Prayer: Heavenly Father, I am at the place in my life wherein I have made a conscious decision to believe all of Your Word or none of Your Word. I believe it ALL. Help me to walk by faith, in the name of Jesus, Amen.

Daily Bread: Lamentations 5; Hebrews 1; Psalm 119:129-136

Yes You Can
October 30

Scripture: "For we do not have a High Priest who cannot sympathize with our weaknesses, but was in all points tempted as we are, yet without sin. Let us therefore come boldly to the throne of grace, that we may obtain mercy and find grace to help in time of need."
~ Hebrews 14:15-16

Spiritual Vitamin

As the end of the month draws near, I want to encourage you to hold on to your serenity, learning to enjoy the peace that surpasses all understanding. This is your God-given right. Be positive and have peace about your circumstances. Someone has told you that you can't make it. I have a different message — yes, you can! Someone told you that you can't become the person God created you to be. I have a different declaration — yes, you can! If you have taken the necessary steps to accept Jesus Christ as your Savior and allow Him to be the Lord of your life, then there is nothing that can stop you from having an abundant life and being all that God has called you to be. Activate the Word of God in your life. You must understand that abundance is not always about money and wealth; there is so much more to life. There are many people in the world who have enough money but not enough peace, not enough joy, not enough love and they are most miserable. Money alone cannot make you happy. Everything you need to live a life of prosperity and wealth is connected to God. Take time today to say yes to God's will for your life and celebrate the victory you have in Him.

Affirmation Prayer: Heavenly Father, I used to feel as if You could not understand how I felt. But now, I know that You can. Help me to activate Your Word in my life, in the name of Jesus, Amen.

Daily Bread: Obadiah 1; Hebrews 2; Proverbs 26:13-22

When October Goes
October 31

Scripture: "To everything there is a season, a time for every purpose under heaven."
~ Ecclesiastes 3:1

Spiritual Vitamin

Are you constantly changing? Change is inevitable. There is nothing you can do to escape the effects of it. Some changes you will welcome, while other changes you will despise. I challenge you to try to find a way to embrace change so that you will find a sense of peace about it rather than a sense of dread. *Since it is out of your sphere of control anyway, why not rest in God and let Him do the heavy lifting?* God is right there with you through all of the different seasons of life and the good news is that HE is the one thing that will never change. Amidst all of the chaos, ups, downs, trials and tribulations, He is your constant. I'll say that again, God is your constant. That should bring you peace and a sense of comfort. Knowing that you have a living, loving God who will never change should provide you with a profound peace and an assurance that helps you rise above your temptation to fear and worry. Stop trying to be in control of everything. Take time today to let go and let God. Once you see the outcome, you will be glad you did.

Affirmation Prayer: Heavenly Father, I am powerless without You, I am not connected unless I am plugged into You. Thank You for being my life's power source, in the name of Jesus, Amen.

Daily Bread: Joel 1 – 2; Hebrews 3; Psalm 119:137-144

Selwyn B. Cox

MONTHLY REFLECTIONS

November: Service (To God and Others)

Strength for the Journey

Heavenly Father,

You are the supplier of all my needs and the keeper of my soul. I desire to serve you until the day I die. At times, I have become disobedient by being too busy to serve You. I repent and ask for Your forgiveness. I am on assignment for You and today I report for duty. I will be devoted to the work You have assigned me to do. Please use me as You see fit. I cannot accomplish my assignment without Your strength and power. Distractions may come but I will look to You for the help I need to remain focused. Lead me to those who can best benefit from my gifts and talents. You have set high standards for me and I will strive each day to attain the level of success that You have already ordained. Bless the work of my hands, in the name of Jesus, Amen.

November

Service (To God and Others)

During the month of November, you will go on a journey, learning how to answer the call of duty as you provide service to God and others. Service is defined as the action of helping or doing work for someone else. God has a job for you to do. There is something you were sent here to fulfill and you have been given the necessary tools to perform the task. You were not created for nothing, you were created to serve. You have a responsibility to meet. Even Jesus said He came to serve, not to be served! If the only begotten Son of God took up the mantle of servanthood, there is no excuse for anyone else. How well you serve others shows your level of appreciation and gratitude for what God has equipped you to do. Don't squander your talents; protect them and use them wisely. Keep your tools handy at all times because you never know when they'll be needed. It is my prayer that you will use this month's devotionals to help you become deliberate about providing service to God and others.

Quote: "The best way to find yourself is to lose yourself in the service of others." --- Mahatma Gandhi

"For even the Son of man did not come to be served, but to serve, and to give His life a ransom for many."
~ Mark 10:45

A Different World
November 1

Scripture: "God saw that human evil was out of control. People thought evil, imagined evil --- evil, evil, evil from morning to night. God was sorry that he had made the human race in the first place; it broke his heart. But Noah was different. God liked what he saw in Noah."
~ Genesis 6:5-6, 8 MSG

Spiritual Vitamin

Are you good to other people? When we are good to each other, we make the world a better place. Jesus said He did not come to be served, but to serve and to give His life as a ransom for many (Matthew 20:28). If the Son of God can humble Himself to serve humanity, there is no excuse for anyone else. With all that's going on in our world today, there are many chances and opportunities to make a difference in the life of someone else. The sincere desire to serve is inspired by love. One thing the world is lacking is love. This is because of the enemy's influence to do evil things. In order to make a difference, we must choose good over evil and love over hate. This would be a different world if human beings loved each other the way God intended. Once you learn how to receive God's grace and love for yourself, it should be easier to pass on that same grace and love to those around you. Take time today to do more than you did yesterday to make a difference in the lives of others.

Affirmation Prayer: Heavenly Father, thank You for Your brand new mercies You provide every day. You have changed my life and I live in a different world filled with joy and happiness. Show me how to make a difference in the lives of others, in the name of Jesus, Amen.

Daily Bread: Joel 3; Hebrews 4:1-13; Psalm 119:145-152

Close the Door
November 2

Scripture: "And to the angel of the church in Philadelphia write, 'These things says He who is holy, He who is true, "He who has the key of David, He who opens and no one shuts, and shuts and no one opens."
~ Revelation 3:7

Spiritual Vitamin

Does sin have an open door in your life? Close the door to sin and everything else that's ungodly in your life. The only way you can be prepared and ready to be of service to others is to be sanctioned with purpose and vision. This empowerment must come from God and you obtain it by spending time with Him and in His Word. If you attempt to perform Kingdom duties and tasks in your own strength, you will grow weary and disappointed. But if you rely on the strength of God, you will never faint. Close the door to negativity and doubt. Don't allow the enemy to cause you to believe that your efforts are in vain. Just because you can't see a change with your natural eyes doesn't mean there is no change. God works in the spirit realm. He is a God of progression and He doesn't intend for things to remain the same. Close the door to anything that is contrary to the purpose of God for your life. Take time today to do what is necessary for God to operate as He desires in your life today, without limitations or restrictions.

Affirmation Prayer: Heavenly Father, I now understand when doors open and close in my life. I realize Your work. Let me enter each open door with thanksgiving and praise and accept each closed door with confidence, knowing that it will work together for my good, in the name of Jesus, Amen.

Daily Bread: Ezekiel 1 – 3; Hebrews 4:14-16; Hebrews 5:1-11; Psalm 119:153-160

Don't Ask My Neighbor
November 3

Scripture: "Do not say to your neighbor, "Go, and come back, and tomorrow I will give it," when you have it with you."
~ Proverbs 3:28

Spiritual Vitamin

Can others feel comfortable coming to you with questions or concerns? Be approachable so that people feel free to come to you rather than going to ask others about you. Jesus was approachable. He welcomes those who have problems and concerns into His Presence. He never leaves anyone the way He found them. He changed their situation. He does the same thing today. Whenever you go to God in prayer, something changes; and, when it does, you owe it to God and others to share what He has done. Every human encounter is an opportunity to share a testimony. *Do you talk about God's goodness to other people or are you ashamed to mention that He's your Savior?* When you allow Jesus to be the Lord of your life, you don't mind opening yourself up and sharing who you really are with others. Don't make people feel that they have to ask others about you; make them feel comfortable coming to you themselves. Don't make them go elsewhere seeking information that is best received from you. Take time today to welcome someone into your presence and share something new and exciting about yourself.

Affirmation Prayer: Heavenly Father, since you sealed me with a guarantee of one day reigning with You for eternity, teach me to take time to share my faith today, in the name of Jesus, Amen.

Daily Bread: Ezekiel 4 – 6; Hebrews 5:12-14; Hebrews 6:1-12; Proverbs 26:23-28; Proverbs 27:1-4

Do You Love Me?
November 4

Scripture: "He said to him the third time, "Simon, son of Jonah, do you love Me?" Peter was grieved because He said to him the third time, "Do you love Me?" And he said to Him, "Lord, You know all things; You know that I love You." Jesus said to him, "feed my sheep.""
~ John 21:17

Spiritual Vitamin

Have you had to ask someone if they love you? If you have to ask, then you have your answer. There is one person whom you will never have to ask this question. You already know who it is. God not only spoke His love but He has proven it through His actions. I can't say it enough, He did so by sending His only Son Jesus to die for our sins. Not only was Jesus God's only Son, but He was completely innocent of any wrong doing. Yet He was crucified on a cross for your sins and mine. He never resisted what the Father required of Him because His highest goal was to please God. This is true love. *What is your highest goal?* When true love is in operation, it can be seen and felt by those to whom it is directed. Genuine love cannot be a secret because it can't be hidden. Something so powerful can never hide. A person's action and behavior will always speak louder than their words. All you have to do is pay attention. You should never have to ask someone you're close to if they love you. Read the handwriting on the wall. Take time today to evaluate how well you show your love for others and if there is more that you can do.

Affirmation Prayer: Heavenly Father, I want to share true love with others because You command me to do so in Your Word. Please put someone in my path today who needs to know that they are loved, in the name of Jesus, Amen.

Daily Bread: Ezekiel 7 – 9; Hebrews 6:13-19; Hebrews 7:1-10; Psalm 119:161-168

Every Praise
November 5

Scripture: "I will praise You, O Lord my God, with all my heart, and I will glorify your name forevermore."
~ Psalm 86:12

Spiritual Vitamin

God deserves every praise. We are good at praising people but should be better at praising God. It seems there is a disconnection in the human understanding of how to praise God. Let's use a simple example. As parents, we teach our toddlers how to do things for the first time. When they master the skill we are teaching, we praise them for being able to do what we have taught. We clap and laugh and cheer for them, telling them what a great job they have done. *If we can do that for our children, why can't we do it for the great and awesome God who so generously provides everything we need?* When we go to football games, we praise the team through our cheers and applause. When we go to parties and social events, we praise the honorees through our words of kindness and support. But then, we go to church and sit on the pew as if we are glued to the seat, mouths closed and arms folded, as if there is nothing going on. Jesus said the rocks would cry out if we don't praise Him. Take time today to let your voice be heard. Don't let a rock cry out for you.

Affirmation Prayer: Heavenly Father, You have done so much for me. Help me to always be willing to give You the praise, just for who You are, in the name of Jesus, Amen.

Daily Bread: Ezekiel 10 – 12; Hebrews 7:11-28; Psalm 119:169-176

Got Me Working Day and Night
November 6

Scripture: "To everything there is a season, a time for every purpose under heaven."
~ Ecclesiastes 3:1

Spiritual Vitamin

Do you wish the day was longer? There are 24 hours in a day and a lot that needs to done during that time. Let's say you need at least eight hours of sleep to be well rested. That leaves you with 16 hours to do everything else that needs to get done. Ecclesiastes says there is a time for everything. That means there is a time to work and a time to rest. *Is it a wise use of your time to work both day and night?* Yes, you must work, but there are other things you must do as well. God wants you to include time to serve Him and those to whom He calls you to help. There is a formula to follow to be prepared to meet the demands of time. First, you must spend one-on-one time with God in worship and prayer, so that He can fill you with His Presence. This is the only way you can gain the strength that will be needed for the journey ahead. Then, you will be prepared for the work He will give you to do, both secular and sacred. Ask God to show you how to create the proper balance in your life, so that you can serve Him and others in a way that is pleasing to Him. Take time today to learn how to become a better steward of your time.

Affirmation Prayer: Heavenly Father, surely You have given me gifts and talents. Help me to use them to edify You and to bless Your people. I will work while it is day, in the name of Jesus, Amen.

Daily Bread: Ezekiel 13 – 15; Hebrews 8; Psalm 120:1-7

If I Can Help Somebody
November 7

Scripture: "But whoever has this world's goods, and sees his brother in need, and shuts up his heart from him, how does the love of God abide in him?"
~ 1 John 3:17

Spiritual Vitamin

There is something you can do to help someone else. You have the resources to assist those whom God wants you to help. You are gifted with the necessary skills to meet the needs of the people to whom you are sent or who are sent to you. The issue is less about your ability to help but more about your willingness to do so. You can help somebody else; the question is *"will you help them?"* When you use your time to help others, it causes you to sacrifice time you could spend on yourself. If you are self-absorbed, this will not appeal to you. On the other hand, if you have realized what a privilege it is to be used by God, then you will have no problem doing it. The next time you consider the cost of helping someone else, also consider the cost that Jesus had to pay to help you. What He did didn't cost Him something, it cost Him everything! Jesus paid with His life. *What higher price can someone pay that is greater than that?* Take time today to help somebody. You will be the better because of it and God will be pleased.

Affirmation Prayer: Heavenly Father, to gain this world's possessions and keep them all to myself would be a travesty. Please help me to give freely and tirelessly offer help to my brothers and sisters, in the name of Jesus, Amen.

Daily Bread: Ezekiel 16; Hebrews 9:1-15; Proverbs 27:5-14

If I Could
November 8

Scripture: Jesus said to him, "if you can believe, all things are possible to him who believes."
~ Mark 9:23

Spiritual Vitamin

Is there something you want to do but you can't see how to do it? Every person has experienced this dilemma at one time or another. Rather than agonizing over whether or not you can accomplish something, just pray about it and consult God as to whether it is in His will for you. If it is, He will empower and strengthen you to be able to get it done. *Did you know that God is the God of the impossible?* Because everything is at His disposal, He can create things with His voice. After all, in the book of Genesis, He did say "let there be" and there was. What He could do back then, He can still do right now. *What do you wish you could do?* With God's help, you can! One thing God wants you to do is to help and serve others. He has equipped you with certain gifts and abilities that will aid you in doing so. Activate your faith and be ready to follow His instructions. He will tell you exactly what to do. Speak positive, faith-filled words that will inspire you to get the job done. Let your faith infuse you with positive energy. Change "if I could" to "I know I can" and go forward. Let us say over and over again, God has empowered you to accomplish what He created you to do. He's waiting for you to take the next step. Take time today to push fear aside and obey God's call to service.

Affirmation Prayer: Heavenly Father, I believe the infallible Word of God. I know that You have covered me with Your protection. Help me to bury all fears and fervently exercise my faith, in the name of Jesus, Amen.

Daily Bread: Ezekiel 17 – 18; Hebrews 9:16-28; Psalm 121:1-8

If You Asked Me To
November 9

Scripture: "If you ask anything in My name, I will do it."
~ John 14:14

Spiritual Vitamin

Are you doing what God has asked you to do? God wants His children to obey His Word and behave as Christ demonstrated during His public ministry. Every person knows right from wrong and because of free will, has the ability to decide which one will be their master. There are two forces in the world, good and evil. *Which one do you more closely identify with?* If we are honest, most of us would admit that we more readily do what other people ask us to do than what God asks us to do. This should not be the case. God asks us to love others as we love ourselves. God asks us to pray for those who use us and who treat us unkindly. God asks us to be willing to make peace with those who offend us. *Are we doing what He asks?* Before you say it's hard, let me challenge your way of thinking. In your own strength, yes, it is hard but in God's strength, nothing is hard. *The question is, will you continue to move in your own strength or will you employ the strength of God?* Take time today to become strengthened and empowered by God so you are able to do what He asks.

Affirmation Prayer: Heavenly Father, thank You for hearing and answering my prayers. Help me to pray Your will for my life and the lives of those around me, in the name of Jesus, Amen.

Daily Bread: Ezekiel 19; Ezekiel 20:1-44; Hebrews 10:1-18; Psalm 122:1-9

If You Want Me To Stay
November 10

Scripture: "Joyful are people of integrity, who follow the instructions of the Lord. Joyful are those who obey His laws and search for him with all their hearts."
~ Psalm 119:1-2 NLT

Spiritual Vitamin

Is God welcome in your life or are you living like you don't want Him involved? God wants to be everything to you but He will not force His way into your life. Jesus will "knock" on the door of your heart. This is powerful and profound because in reality, He doesn't have to knock; He has the power to walk through the door, but He doesn't. He waits for you to invite Him in. If you want God in your life, ask Him to come in. If you want Him to stay, give Him charge over you. God loves you more than you know how to love yourself and He wants to remain with you forever. His commitment is not like another human being's commitment; that is, based on something you do or don't do. In human relationships, if you want people to stay in your life, you have to do things to keep them happy and satisfied. With God, all you have to do is accept His love and obey His Word. Take time today to show God that you want Him to stay in your life by the way you allow your light to shine through service to Him and others.

Affirmation Prayer: Heavenly Father, my name is engraved in the palm of Your hand. As long as I obey Your Word, I will never walk alone. I can never be plucked out of Your hand, in the name of Jesus, Amen.

Daily Bread: Ezekiel 20:45-49; Ezekiel 21; Ezekiel 22:1-22; Hebrews 10:19-39; Psalm 123:1-4

I Give Myself Away
November 11

Scripture: "And do not present your members as instruments of unrighteousness to sin, but present yourselves to God as being alive from the dead, and your members as instruments of righteousness to God."
~ Romans 6:13

Spiritual Vitamin

Happy Veteran's Day! Today in the USA, we salute and celebrate all the men and women who perform faithful and dedicated service to our country. Thank You! Each one of us could take a service note from our veterans because serving is something God wants each of us to do. When you empty yourself onto others, God will refill you. Give of your time, give of your talents and give of your treasure. Nothing speaks love better than showing up in person to show support for someone else. Every material resource can be replenished except time. Money when spent, can be replaced, regained or re-earned. Talents once used, can be re-used; but time, once spent, cannot be recovered. Your time is the most valuable asset you have. *How are you spending your time? Are you doing more wasting of time than spending?* If you are not making a lasting imprint on the hearts of those around you, perhaps the answer is yes. God desires to use you but He will not use you by force. Be willing to give yourself away and God will use you for His glory. As you pour into others, God will pour into you. Take time today to identify those to whom you will lend your talents, gifts and treasure.

Affirmation Prayer: Heavenly Father, I was an empty pitcher until You began to pour into my life. Now, my cup runs over. I give myself away, in service to others. Let me never be selfish about my gifts, in the name of Jesus, Amen.

Daily Bread: Ezekiel 22:23-31; Ezekiel 23; Hebrews 11:1-16; Proverbs 27:15-22

I'm On Your Side
November 12

Scripture: "The Lord is on my side, I will not fear. What can man do to me?"
~ Psalm 118:6

Spiritual Vitamin

Do you know that God is on your side? No matter what you face in this life, you have someone with you who is mighty and powerful. You have someone whose love for you is greater than you can imagine or comprehend. When you get into trouble, you tend to seek the comfort of the human touch. But God's touch goes beyond that which is human. His hand reaches into the very heart and soul of man. God is on your side, so you have no reason to fear. Knowing this, you are now equipped to share this knowledge with others. Tell someone else that God is on their side too. You may be afraid to do so at first, but don't give in to fear. Fear is the enemy of faith. Don't let fear rob you of the chance to make someone's life better. Help them recover their joy by reminding them that God is on their side. Their situation may not be good but God remains able to do all things but fail. Show them how to trust that wherever they are, God is there as well. Teach someone how to trust Him from their heart rather than just their mouth. Live like you are the child of a King and show someone else how to do the same. Take time today to celebrate the fact that God is on your side.

Affirmation Prayer: Heavenly Father, I am a royal priesthood because You established me to be so. You have built a fence all around me and the enemy cannot harm me. Keep me strong in You and in the power of Your might, in the name of Jesus, Amen.

Daily Bread: Ezekiel 24 – 25; Hebrews 11:17-40; Psalm 124:1-8

In the Upper Room
November 13

Scripture: "and be renewed in the spirit of your mind."
~ Ephesians 4:23

Spiritual Vitamin

Jesus and His disciples had an experience in the Upper Room. This was where they shared their last meal together and during this time, Jesus imparted more of His wisdom into them. There were many times when Jesus spoke to the disciples and they did not fully understand the meaning behind what He was saying. Had they grasped the deeper meaning behind His words, they would have dealt differently with His crucifixion. In order for that to happen, the skill of deeper listening would have needed to be employed. *How well are you listening to what God is saying to you today?* He wants to meet with you in the upper room. Not an upper level room within a building or structure but rather the upper room of your mind. He wants to renew your mind through His Word. Take time today to sit in quiet solitude, meditation and prayer so God can impart His wisdom into you and equip you for the journey ahead.

Affirmation Prayer: Heavenly Father, my most intimate time with You is when I am all alone. I can feel Your Presence, I can hear Your voice and I am equipped with supernatural strength. Help me carry out the tasks that You have preordained for me each day, in the name of Jesus, Amen.

Daily Bread: Ezekiel 26 – 27; Hebrews 12:1-13; Psalm 125:1-5

I Pray
November 14

Scripture: "bless those who curse you, and pray for those who spitefully use you."
~ Luke 6:28

Spiritual Vitamin

Do you find it easy to pray for other people or are most of your prayers self-directed? Christians have a responsibility to intercede for others in prayer. One of the reasons some don't pray for others is that they don't want God to bless other people more than He blesses them. This type of heart is not pure before God. *What is the position of your heart when you pray for other people? Do you really want God to bless them with the things they desire?* It takes a mature Christian to earnestly pray for the needs of other people. It takes an even more mature Christian to genuinely celebrate when God answers those prayers and gives those individuals the things for which they've asked. Pray for other people. Celebrate with them when their prayers are answered. The statement is true, what goes around comes around. We mostly use this phrase in connection to negative things but it's also true concerning the positive. If you celebrate with and for someone else when something wonderful happens to them, someone will celebrate with and for you when it's your turn. Take time today to pray for someone else and then be genuinely happy for them regarding their latest blessing.

Affirmation Prayer: Heavenly Father, it is me. I am praying for the peace of Jerusalem and the sin-sick souls of the world. I rejoice because You hear my prayers. Assure me that You are working on my behalf, in the name of Jesus, Amen.

Daily Bread: Ezekiel 28 – 29; Hebrews 12:14-29; Psalm 126:1-6

I See You Brave
November 15

Scripture: "Be strong and of good courage, do not fear nor be afraid of them; for the Lord your God, He is the One who goes with you. He will not leave you nor forsake you."
~ Deuteronomy 31:6

Spiritual Vitamin

Everyone needs encouragement. Often, you can see in someone what that individual cannot see in themselves. When you recognize good qualities in another person, you should tell them what you see. Don't keep it to yourself because your words may be just what they need to gain the confidence and courage to do what God is telling them to do. Your encouragement could help them to be brave and empower them to take that next step along their journey to success. You have the power to strengthen someone else; don't hold back. Encourage others with all your heart. *Someone encouraged you when you needed it, so why not pay it forward?* Think back on how what they told you pushed you forward and helped you become who you are today. Take time today to say these words to someone who is going through something "no matter what you're facing, I see you brave!"

Affirmation Prayer: Heavenly Father, in the midst of my anxiety, You are there. In the midst of my joy, You are there. You are there in the midst of it all! Remind me to share You with everyone I know, so their joy may be full, in the name of Jesus, Amen.

Daily Bread: Ezekiel 30 – 31; Hebrews 13; Proverbs 27:23-27; Proverbs 28:1-6

It Takes Two
November 16

Scripture: "Two are better than one, because they have a good reward for their labor."
~ Ecclesiastes 4:9

Spiritual Vitamin

Are you operating within the will of God for your life? When operating within the will of God, you can accomplish anything. You might think you need a large cast of characters around you in order for you to be successful but that is not quite true. While God does indeed intend for you to be in connection to and in fellowship with other people, He never intended for you to rely on them as your source. They are not your source or resource for success. God is your source and together, the two of you can do great things! In order for you to make an effective impact on this world, it will take deliberate effort on your part. God will not do everything for you. He has already done what He said He would do. Now it's your turn. You have to be willing to let God use you to bless the lives of others. You have to stand confident and strong in the gifts and talents He's given you and use them to the best of your ability. If used for the glory of God, the results will astound you. Take time today to become a tool in the hand of Almighty God, to be used for the purpose of Kingdom building.

Affirmation Prayer: Heavenly Father, together, You and I equal a multitude. There is nothing too hard for us to conquer. You are the carpenter, I am your tool to use for Kingdom building. Use me for Your glory, in the name of Jesus, Amen.

Daily Bread: Ezekiel 32; Ezekiel 33:1-32; James 1; Psalm 127:1-5

I Walk the Line
November 17

Scripture: "If we live in the Spirit, let us also walk in the Spirit."
~ Galatians 5:25

Spiritual Vitamin

Do you feel like you're all alone? You're not, Jesus Christ is walking the line with you. For this reason, don't allow people to suffer alone; walk the line with them. Over the course of your life, someone was there for you in your time of need. Think about how good that felt and how much you were blessed because of it. *Don't you want to provide that same level of comfort to someone else?* Don't downplay your ability to be of assistance. You have the power to bless the lives of other people. You are an ambassador for Christ and the power of His Holy Spirit lives on the inside of you. *How does that make you feel?* You are equipped to be an agent of change. God wants to use you in a way that will make a difference in the lives of those around you. Don't be afraid to share out of the abundance of your heart. God knows what is needed in every situation and if He sends you to be a part of the solution, than what you're carrying will be what is needed to bring healing and freedom. Take time today to be a part of the solution for someone who is struggling with something beyond their control.

Affirmation Prayer: Heavenly Father, perseverance must finish its work so that Your plan for each life will be complete. Today, I will walk the line and assist someone through their struggles so that they will not lack any good thing. See us through, in the name of Jesus, Amen.

Daily Bread: Ezekiel 33:21-33; Ezekiel 34 – 35; James 2; Psalm 128:1-6

Love Is Like That
November 18

Scripture: "Be kindly affectionate to one another with brotherly love, in honor giving preference to one another."
~ Romans 12:10

Spiritual Vitamin

Love happens. It is a natural occurrence and there is nothing that will hinder the plan God put in place in regards to it. Every heart knows the feeling and is familiar with the joy that being loved can bring. Once you experience true love for yourself, it changes you. Love is like that. It is almost indescribable and sometimes takes you by surprise. Love and forgiveness are partners and need to remain together in order to keep relationships from falling apart. Forgiveness is the order of the day because it positions you to be an effective witness for God and enables you to better serve others and lead them to Him. If you love from a place of genuineness, then it will not be too hard to forgive. After receiving the grace of God for yourself, you will become empowered to apply His grace to the areas of offense in your own life. Love will make you forgive because love is like that. It makes your spirit man willing to pardon offenses when your natural man really doesn't want to do so. You will do it because you know that it is pleasing to God and because it's the right thing to do. Take time today to practice the art of forgiveness so that your prayers will not be hindered.

Affirmation Prayer: Heavenly Father, Your Word tells us that we are our brother's keeper and also that we should let brotherly love continue. I want to esteem others more highly than I do myself. Give me the strength to do it, in the name of Jesus, Amen.

Daily Bread: Ezekiel 36 − 37; James 3; Psalm 129:1-8

Love Is the Message
November 19

Scripture: "Love suffers long and is kind; love does not envy; love does not parade itself, is not puffed up; does not behave rudely, does not seek its own, is not provoked, thinks no evil; does not rejoice in iniquity, but rejoices in the truth; bears all things, believes all things, hopes all things, endures all things."
~ 1 Corinthians 13:4-7

Spiritual Vitamin

Do you read your Bible? The Bible is the greatest book ever written. There are many accounts contained therein but the bottom line message is love. Love is woven all throughout the scriptures from start to finish. Even when God's wrath came into play, it was because of His love. God knows the destructive results of disobedience, so He does what is necessary to protect His children from experiencing the total devastation of it. He will protect His investment at all costs. Everything you need to know about love is written in God's Holy Word. If you want to know how to love, study the lifestyle, behavior patterns and activities of Jesus Christ. His public, earthly ministry was to carry out the Word and will of God. He did everything the Father told Him to do, fully and completely and provided the perfect example for us to follow. Take time today to study God's message of love and apply its principles to your daily life, as you interact with others.

Affirmation Prayer: Heavenly Father, I am nothing without Your love and I can do nothing if I don't share Your love with others. While I have faith and hope, love is the greatest of them all. Don't ever let me forget that, in the name of Jesus, Amen.

Daily Bread: Ezekiel 38 – 39; James 4; Proverbs 28:7-17

One-on-One
November 20

Scripture: "fulfill my joy by being like-minded, having the same love, being of one accord, of one mind"
~ Philippians 2:2

Spiritual Vitamin

Do you spend time alone with God? In order to get to know someone better, you must spend time with them. As you and the other person share intimate information and details of your lives, a connection and bond are formed. It is also during this one-on-one time that an element of trust is built. Not the type of trust that creates an expectation but more so, the type that creates a sense of comfort and security. *Do you have a connection and bond with God?* If you do, then you have developed an element of trust for Him that cannot be matched as relates to human beings. When you are one-on-one with God, your focus is on Him and His focus is on you. You put away distractions and ignore the things that attempt to hinder your concentration because you realize that God deserves your full, complete and undivided attention. *Now that you know how to properly form a bond, will you seek someone who needs a loving human touch and help them?*
You can be of service to God by being of service to others. Somebody you know needs a helping hand. Take time today to be that helping hand and God will reward you for the sacrifice of your time.

Affirmation Prayer: Heavenly Father, You are my water when I am thirsty and my food when I am hungry. Nothing compares to the one-on-one time I spend in fellowship with You. Show me that this time is the most important part of my day, in the name of Jesus, Amen.

Daily Bread: Ezekiel 40; James 5; Psalm 130:1-8

Reach Out and Touch
November 21

Scripture: "But Jesus said, "Somebody touched Me, for I perceived power going out from Me.""
~ Luke 8:46

Spiritual Vitamin

Have you ever felt God's touch? Every human being needs the touch of God. Within His touch is the answer to all your needs. God is still in the healing business and His touch can cure your deepest need. After receiving your personal touch from God, you will then be empowered to touch the lives of others. There is nothing more rewarding than the feeling produced by lending a helping hand. Helping others brings joy to man and glory to God. People need other people and every human being is gifted with the ability to serve. Each person's method of serving may be different, but each of us possesses the knowledge and skill to be of service to those around us. *Will you reach out and touch the life of someone else with the skill that you've been gifted to perform?* Take time today to reach out and touch someone outside of your normal circle of influence. They will be pleased and God will be praised!

Affirmation Prayer: Heavenly Father, no one else can do the things You do. One touch of Your powerful hand performs miracles. You've healed the sick, raised the dead and turned water into wine. Thank You for Your continuous touch that gives me life everlasting. Help me to intentionally reach out and touch someone today, in the name of Jesus, Amen.

Daily Bread: Ezekiel 41 – 42; 1 Peter 1; 1 Peter 2:1-3; Psalm 131:1-3

That's What Friends Are For
November 22

Scripture: "A man who has friends must himself be friendly, but there is a friend who sticks closer than a brother."
~ Proverbs 18:24

Spiritual Vitamin

Are you a good friend? Be a better friend to others than they are to you. Serve as the example of what true friendship really means. Every one of us has a story of friendship gone wrong. With that occurrence, you have been given the opportunity to take lemons and make lemonade. Rather than continuing to play hurt tapes in your head over and over again regarding the offense, you can take the lessons learned and apply them to your own life and let them change the way you deal with others instead of becoming bitter regarding how they dealt with you. Friends are supposed to give love, support, kindness and consideration to those in their lives; that's what friends are for. *Would others says that you're a good friend?* It is your responsibility to make people feel valued, loved and appreciated. If you do that for others, someone will do that for you. Take time today to celebrate the gift of love and friendship and those whom God has placed in your life.

Affirmation Prayer: Heavenly Father, I know that I must first show myself to be friendly before I can have a friend. Please help me to show lasting love to those who come in my path. Help me to keep old friends and to make new ones, in the name of Jesus, Amen.

Daily Bread: Ezekiel 43 – 44; 1 Peter 2:4-45; Psalm 132:1-18

It's A Good Day
November 23

Scripture: "This is the day the Lord has made; we will rejoice and be glad in it."
~ Psalm 118:24

Spiritual Vitamin

This is the Thanksgiving season. During this time, we gather with our family and friends to give thanks to God for His bountiful blessings. For some, this is a good day, while for others, perhaps not so much. In reality, every day that God allows you to see is a good day. If He woke you up this morning, that means He still has purpose for your life. Maybe you struggle during the holiday season. Even if this day represents tremendous loss or disappointment for you, God's power is still able to save. If you are not connected to your family, this day might be difficult for you. I have a suggestion. *Why not provide service to someone else today, rather than spending it alone, focusing on what you don't have?* Maybe you can adopt a family for the day and spend it with them. Or, perhaps there is a community feeding going on at a location near you. *Why not go and serve?* Don't allow the enemy to rob you of an opportunity to be a blessing to someone else. Make this a good day for yourself and others. God is with you in whatever you're facing. *Can you sense His Presence?* Quiet yourself before God and cast your cares on your Savior Jesus. Then, become determined to enjoy this day. Take time today to find a place to serve and celebrate all that God has done.

Affirmation Prayer: Heavenly Father, thank You for everything You have done for me and my loved ones. I am grateful to be able to celebrate another Thanksgiving Day with those I love. Remind us of all we have and make us forever grateful, in the name of Jesus, Amen.

Daily Bread: Ezekiel 45 – 46; 1 Peter 3; Proverbs 28:18-28

This Little Light of Mine
November 24

Scripture: "Let your light so shine before men, that they may see your good works and glorify your Father in heaven."
~ Matthew 5:16

Spiritual Vitamin

Is your light shining brightly? There is a light down on the inside of you. God put it there when He created you. It was part of His master plan and He expects you to shine. Don't dim your light for any reason. If there are people in your life who feel threatened or intimidated by your light, then it wasn't meant for them. That's okay because your light is not meant for everyone; only those whom God has purposed for any given season of your life. Things and people change. For this reason, your light can never go dim unless you allow it to do so. One incredible thing about your light is that the bulb will never need changing because God is its source. He never runs out of energy and never needs to be recharged. God is self-sufficient and doesn't need anything outside of Himself to exist or operate. Take time today to warm someone else with the God-inspired light inside of you.

Affirmation Prayer: Heavenly Father, let the intent of my heart, my attitude, my walk and my talk be evidence of the light You have given me and may it shine brilliantly, in the name of Jesus, Amen.

Daily Bread: Ezekiel 47 – 48; 1 Peter 4; Psalm 133:1-3

Try a Little Tenderness
November 25

Scripture: "A soft answer turns away wrath, but a harsh word stirs up anger."
~ Proverbs 15:1

Spiritual Vitamin

Are you mean? Do you find it hard to speak kind words to others and to maintain good thoughts about them? If so, why don't you try a little tenderness? Don't live with such a high and lofty expectation of others. Allow people to be who they are and respect them for doing the best they can. Being kind never hurt anyone. *Are you a constant complainer?* God has been too good to you for you to behave poorly. You may have come through numerous trials and tribulations but the point of the matter is that you got through them. God didn't leave you where you were. He walked with you every step of the way and then carried you when the load was too much to bear. So, the next time something or someone brings the temptation for you to react in a negative manner, try a little tenderness instead. God will be pleased by your response. An old saying is "you draw more bees with honey than vinegar" and one of the perks to that is honey tastes so much sweeter. Take time today to be more tenderhearted with someone who needs your kindness.

Affirmation Prayer: Heavenly Father, please give me conviction and compassion to be patient with those who appear difficult or different. You want me to win souls for You; please help me to become a fisher of men, in the name of Jesus, Amen.

Daily Bread: Daniel 1; Daniel 2:1-23; 1 Peter 5; Psalm 134:1-3

Wake Up Everybody
November 26

Scripture: "And do this, knowing the time, that now it is high time to awake out of sleep; for now our salvation is nearer than when we first believed. The night is far spent, the day is at hand. Therefore, let us cast off the works of darkness, and let us put on the armor of light."
~ Romans 13:11-12

Spiritual Vitamin

Are you willfully practicing sin? Living in a state of sin can be compared to being physically asleep. When you are asleep, you are in a state of unconsciousness. You are alive but unaware of what is going on around you. You are not in control of what is happening inside of your physical body or even in your natural environment. In order for you to be able to effect change of any kind, you must wake up. This same principle is true in the spirit realm. You must not remain spiritually asleep. You have to wake up. You do this by accepting the finished work of Jesus Christ on the cross and allowing Him to become your Savior and Lord. There is work for you to do. Stop pulling the covers over the issues and situations in your life. It is time to address them. Jesus is coming back for His bride. *Who is that, you ask?* It is the body of Christ. *Are you a part of that body?* If you are, then He is your Bridegroom. Take time today to awake from a state of spiritual sleep and prepare to meet THE KING.

Affirmation Prayer: Heavenly Father, Your Word tells us that You are coming back for Your church, for Your Bride. I know that includes me. I am awake, alive, alert, and waiting for Your return. Help me to sound the alarm and tell others, in the name of Jesus, Amen.

Daily Bread: Daniel 2:24-49; Daniel 3:1-12; 2 Peter 1; Psalm 135:1-12

What A Friend We Have In Jesus
November 27

Scripture: "Greater love has no one than this, than to lay down one's life for his friends. No longer do I call you servants, for a servant does not know what His master is doing; but I have called you friends, for all things that I heard from My Father I have made known to you."
~ John 15:13, 15

Spiritual Vitamin

Is Jesus your best friend? This is a good time to center your thoughts on Jesus because He is the best friend you will ever have. There is no truer statement than that. No human being will be able to love you the way He does and no one will be more loyal than He is. It is never His desire to hurt or shame you in any way. He will never talk about you behind your back or betray your trust. If you tell Him something, it will remain between the two of you and He will not tell anyone else. When things go wrong, He will sit with you and talk to you about what needs to change in your life in a way that encourages you to submit to the will of God rather than attempt to justify and defend your bad choices and decisions. Most of all, when you are at your worst, He will not turn and walk away but will love you through it. He is determined to get the best out of you for the glory of the Father. *If Christ is willing to do all of this for you, can you be willing to try to do some of this for others?* Everyone needs help and everyone needs a friend. During this month of service, take time today to develop a lasting friendship with someone who needs your help. Jesus has done it for you, you can do it for them.

Affirmation Prayer: Heavenly Father, I have some acquaintances, I have some associates but I am confident that in You, I have a true friend. Thank You for loving me unconditionally. Help me to grow up in Your love and to willingly share it with others, in the name of Jesus, Amen.

Daily Bread: Daniel 3:13-30; Daniel 4:1-18; 2 Peter 2; Proverbs 29:1-9

What Have You Done For Me Lately?
November 28

Scripture: "I will bless the Lord at all times; His praise shall continually be in my mouth."
~ Psalm 34:1

Spiritual Vitamin

As the end of the month draws near, I want to encourage you to find new ways to provide service to God and others. *What have you done for Him lately? If God were to ask you this question, how would you respond? Would you even have an answer to give?* God created humans for His purpose and pleasure. What you do with your life shows God how appreciative you are that He took the time to create you. *Does the way you're living your life tell Him that you're grateful?* It makes God happy when He sees those who are blessed turn around and bless others. This is what He intended from the beginning. There is something for you to do for the Kingdom of God. *Are you doing it?* There is a long list of things that God has done for you. *The question is "what have you done for Him lately?" Is it a chore for you to go to church?* God asked that we not forsake the assembly of the saints. He knows that you need to be around other like-minded believers in order to stay encouraged. *Do you complain when asked to serve others?* This should not be. All of your efforts should not be self-directed. Reach out to someone else. A thriving, growing relationship with God begins with praise. Take time today to do something for God in exchange for all that He's done for you. After all, you can never repay all His goodness, but you certainly can die trying!

Affirmation Prayer: Heavenly Father, my greatest desire before leaving this earth is to become pleasing in Your sight. Search me and cast out any wicked ways. Let total praise drip from my lips, in the name of Jesus, Amen.

Daily Bread: Daniel 4:19-37; Daniel 5:1-16; 2 Peter 3; Psalm 135:13-21

He's All I Need
November 29

Scripture: "For his divine power has bestowed on us [absolutely] everything necessary for [a dynamic spiritual] life and godliness, through true and personal knowledge of Him who called us by His own glory and excellence."
~ 2 Peter 1:3 AMP

Spiritual Vitamin

Human beings use a number of things for inspiration and comfort. *What is your source of inspiration and where do you look for comfort?* If you are looking for inspiration in anything outside of God and His Word, you are setting yourself up for disappointment. God alone is all you need. You don't need the superficial things of this world to help you get through your times of testing and trial. All you need is God. You don't need alcohol, you don't need drugs or anything else to lift you out of darkness and despair. All you need is God. We all experience the ups and downs of life; things like depression, anger, sickness, divorce, broken families, abandonment, abuse, guilt and shame. Even when these things come into your life, God is all you need. When your time comes to be tested, don't panic. Just pray, read the Word and rest on the promises of God. Take time today to celebrate the fact that God truly is all you need.

Affirmation Prayer: Heavenly Father, You have given us over 7000 promises in Your Word. I will relish in Your precious promises and live one day at a time, knowing You are all I need to get by, in the name of Jesus, Amen.

Daily Bread: Daniel 5:17-31; Daniel 6:1-28; 1 John 1; 1 John 2:1-11; Psalm 136:1-12

You're Number One in My Book
November 30

Scripture: "Your eyes saw my substance, being yet unformed. And in Your book they all were written, the days fashioned for me, when as yet there were none of them."
~ Psalm 139:16

Spiritual Vitamin

Who is number one in your book? When someone is number one in your book, they are pretty important and high up on your list. You have a great deal of admiration for them and a high level of expectation from them. The person who is number one in your book would be someone you would call in times of crisis, when you are experiencing challenges and some element of critical change. This would be the person you feel can get you out of anything you've gotten yourself into and the one who will never let you down. In reality, God is the only One who can even come close to fitting this description. Even before your life began, He made you His number one priority. As Christians, we have a habit of saying that God is first in our lives, but our habits and actions say anything but. One way to demonstrate that God is number one in your book is to be willing to be of service to others. Obedience to God is a great way to show others how much you love Him. No one individual has done more for you than God and He deserves your loyalty and obedience. Take time today to make God number one in your book.

Affirmation Prayer: Heavenly Father, above any number in the address book for my family, friends and acquaintances, You hold the first spot. You are number one in my book. How great Thou art, in the name of Jesus, Amen.

Daily Bread: Daniel 7; Daniel 8:1-14; 1 John 2:12-27; Psalm 136:13-26

MONTHLY REFLECTIONS

December: Surrendering (Letting Go)

Strength for the Journey

Heavenly Father,

You are Almighty and Omnipotent. I praise and worship You for who You are. In this last month of the year, I ask that you forgive me for my past transgressions against You and now I surrender everything that is not like You. As the year comes to a close, help me to be willing to surrender my will and to let Your will be done in my life. I relinquish everything that I am accustomed to doing in my own strength and I ask for Your strength. Your anointing breaks all yokes of bondage. I ask You now to break every yoke of bondage the enemy has tried to enforce in my life. Set me free to do Your will. I ask that You bind all of satan's wicked schemes and tactics and prevent them from manifesting in my life. I willingly let go of everything that has had me bound and I surrender to Your promises, purpose and power, in the name of Jesus, Amen.

December

Surrendering (Letting Go)

During the month of December, you will go on a journey, learning how to surrender yourself to God and how to let go of anything that is not conducive to the betterment of your relationship with Him. Surrendering is defined as the action of ceasing resistance to and submitting to the authority of; in other words, when you surrender to God, you stop resisting Him and you freely and willingly submit to His authority. You no longer wrestle with what He tells you to do or debate about what He said in His Word. You simply accept it and go along with Him, trusting and believing that He knows what is best. When you surrender, you give up any and all rights that you once believed were yours to have and you give total and complete control of the outcome of the situation to God. You leave the choice to Him. It is my prayer that you will use this month's devotionals to aid you in learning how to rest on the promises of God because He can't take hold of something until you let it go.

Quote: "You will know you have fully surrendered when you can say these words to God: "any way it goes, either way it goes, as long as you don't let me go, I'll go with you!" --- Selwyn B. Cox

"Surrender your heart to God, turn to Him in prayer."
~ Job 11:13

All At Once
December 1

Scripture: "so Christ was offered once to bear the sins of many. To those who eagerly wait for Him He will appear a second time, apart from sin, for salvation."
~ Hebrews 9:28

Spiritual Vitamin

Are you feeling guilty about something? Everyone has done things for which they are ashamed. During the course of your life, you will miss the mark and disobey the Word of God. What is of the utmost importance is what you do after you transgress against God's Word. My suggestion is that you immediately repent. Cry out in heartfelt sorrow to God and receive His forgiveness, cleansing and restoration. All at once, surrender every bit of guilt and shame the enemy has placed upon you with his lies and deceit. God is not mad at you. Every sin you will ever commit has been taken to the cross and covered with the blood of Jesus. This is not a license to continue in sin. It is an opportunity to reflect on just how much God loves and values you. He wants you to honor and respect what Jesus did for you so much that it causes you to turn away from the temptations of sin. God is ready to give you another chance. *Do you want it?* Take time today to surrender, all at once, everything that would hinder your relationship with God.

Affirmation Prayer: Heavenly Father, thank You for offering Christ to bear my sins. I know that one day, He will come to take me home. Help me to live in anticipation of His return, in the name of Jesus, Amen.

Daily Bread: Daniel 8:15-27; Daniel 9:1-19; 1 John 2:28-29; 1 John 3:1-10; Proverbs 29:10-18

Bittersweet Symphony
December 2

Scripture: "No temptation has overtaken you except such as is common to man; but God is faithful, who will not allow you to be tempted beyond what you are able, but with the temptation will also make the way of escape, that you may be able to bear it."
~ 1 Corinthians 10:13

Spiritual Vitamin

In this life, you must learn to take the bitter with the sweet. There will be good days and there will be bad days. Your security lies in the fact that God has promised to be there through it all. You will not have a problem-free earthly experience, free from hardship of any kind. You must surrender this type of unrealistic expectation. Jesus' life was not free from trials and tribulations. He experienced them at their worst, yet He was able to overcome because He was committed to living out the will of God. Because He was successful in doing so, you can now do the same. Face good days with worship and face bad days with praise, because God knows how to handle both extremes. The tapestry of your life is not one continuous, smooth piece of fabric. It contains holes that need to be mended and snags that need to be smoothed. God is prepared and ready to do the necessary repairs, but He requires your permission. *Will you give it to Him?* Take time today to embrace the bittersweet symphony of your life. Before it's all said and done, perfect harmony will be the end result.

Affirmation Prayer: Heavenly Father, thank You for providing a way for me to escape temptation. It was difficult sometimes but You brought me through. Help me to remember that in times of testing, all I need to do is call upon You, in the name of Jesus, Amen.

Daily Bread: Daniel 9:20-27; Daniel 10; 1 John 3:11-24; 1 John 4:1-6; Psalm 137:1-9

Brokenhearted (It's Not Over)
December 3

Scripture: "The Lord is near to those who have a broken heart, and saves such as have a contrite spirit."
~ Psalm 34:18

Spiritual Vitamin

This is the beginning of Advent Season. Advent is a season observed in many Christian churches as a time of expectant waiting and preparation for the celebration of the Nativity of Christ at Christmas.

Undoubtedly, somewhere along the course of your life, your heart has been broken. If you have yet to experience this, the saints of old would say "just keep on livin." But, if you are like most, you have indeed experienced a broken heart. You have struggled to put the pieces back together and to erase all the unpleasant memories that continue to play inside your mind. Your life doesn't end when someone hurts or offends you. For this reason, you must surrender offenses. It is not wise to walk through your life holding grudges against people because of things they have done to hurt you or to cause you pain. Give your hurt and pain to God and let Him mend your broken heart. The person who hurt you does not have the power to heal you; you must go to God for that. The good news is mending hearts is one of His specialties. It has been said that, "He's a heart fixer and a mind regulator." Knowing this, the only reason to hold on to a broken heart is because of pride. *If you know your heart is broken and you know where to go to get it fixed, yet you do not go, what else would be the reason?* If you want to be made well, you need to go to the doctor. Take time today to make an appointment with the specialist. Dr. Jesus is waiting to see you now!

Affirmation Prayer: Heavenly Father, thank You for healing my broken heart. Teach me that when I am hurting, all I have to do is run into Your arms, in the name of Jesus, Amen.

Daily Bread: Daniel 11:1-35; 1 John 4:7-21; Psalm 138:1-8

(A Wonderful) Change
December 4

Scripture: "Jesus Christ is the same yesterday, today, and forever."
~ Hebrews 13:8

Spiritual Vitamin

Everything must change. This is without exception. Nothing is unaffected by change except God. Knowing this, it is wise to do yourself a favor and surrender the temptation to entertain struggle. When you develop a habit of welcoming struggle into your life, you are rarely able to see provision, even when it is freely offered to you. Under a spirit of struggle, you frequently engage in pity parties and develop a "woe is me" attitude. Your mood is often somber and you don't have much good to say about the things or people in your life. If this is you, I want you to know that you have been living this way too long and there is hope. Now it's time for all of that to change. Breakup with your love of struggle because it is not God's design for you. In order to receive and embrace all that He has for you, you must be agreeable to welcome change. If you think about it, the prospects can actually be very exciting. Take time today to surrender your will to God, then embrace and welcome change. He has some wonderful surprises in store for you.

Affirmation Prayer: Heavenly Father, this morning I took a good look into the mirror of my life. Wow, how things have changed. Some changes were due to mountain-top experiences while others were because of valley-low experiences. In hindsight, I realize that everything I experienced worked together for my good. Keep me mindful that You will never change, in the name of Jesus, Amen.

Daily Bread: Daniel 11:36-45; 1 John 5:1-21; Psalm 139:1-10

Come What May
December 5

Scripture: "These things I have spoken to you, that in Me you may have peace. In the world you will have tribulation; but be of good cheer, I have overcome the world."
~ John 16:33

Spiritual Vitamin

Is God in charge of the details of your life? When you know that God is in charge, you know you don't have to worry. When you know that you belong to God, you know that He will take care of you. Because of this, you can make the choice to surrender worry and frustration. The reason you can do this is because you realize that, come what may, you will be alright because God's hand is on your life. If you are submitted to His will, you walk a path that is safe and secure. God's eyes are never directed away from you. He sees every step you take and is in control of every detail of your life at all times. Even when you don't want God to be near you, still right there He remains. He won't force you into submission; He will patiently wait until you decide to give up the control you believe is yours to have. You will not have to endure hand to hand combat with God. He does not drag you into battle. He simply waits until you have exhausted yourself fighting a battle that He knows you cannot win. Take time today to remove your combat gear and let the Lord fight your battles. Come what may, your victory lies in Him.

Affirmation Prayer: Heavenly Father, through the many hard trials I have encountered, I am confident now that the battle is not mine. Come what may, You will give me victory. Make me grateful to You for fighting my battles, in the name of Jesus, Amen.

Daily Bread: Haggai 1; Haggai 2:1-23; 2 John 1:1-13; Proverbs 29:19-27

We Don't Say Goodbye
December 6

Scripture: "And let us not grow weary while doing good, for in due season we shall reap if we do not lose heart."
~ Galatians 6:9

Spiritual Vitamin

Are you growing impatient about something? The longer you have to wait for something to happen, the more you may begin to doubt that it ever will. This is why it is important to surrender doubt and resist the temptation to give up on your dreams. As long as you have breath in your body, you still have a chance to turn your dreams into realities. Don't say goodbye to your destiny because you are tired of waiting for something that has not yet happened or because you think it's too late. God is a redeemer of time. He knows how much time you have left to live out your purpose. You can be intentional about the way you spend your time. Be kind, gentle, patient and loving with yourself. Stop being so quick to criticize and beat yourself up for the season of life you are currently in. Sometimes lessons have to be repeated and tests have to be retaken in order to pass. If you have failed a test, go back over the material again. Recommit to the process and retake the test. Take time today to declare that you are in it to win it and decide that you will never give up.

Affirmation Prayer: Heavenly Father, there are times when I feel unappreciated for some of the good things I try to do for others. Please help me to never grow weary while doing good, in the name of Jesus, Amen.

Daily Bread: Zechariah 1 – 4; 3 John 1:1-14; Psalm 139:11-16

Don't Take It Personal
December 7

Scripture: "The discretion of a man makes him slow to anger, and his glory is to overlook a transgression."
~ Proverbs 19:11

Spiritual Vitamin

Are you easily offended? Everything is not meant to be a personal attack on you. Yes, there are times when the enemy will arrange circumstances that will be intended to interrupt the flow of blessings and the divine plan of God for your life. But this is not and can never be a 24-hour a day occurrence. God will never leave you in the hands of the enemy. Be assured that His rescue plan is already in operation. In order to see His plan manifest, you must surrender the victim mentality and the desire to always be right. When something goes wrong in your life, don't panic. Contrary to popular belief, everything is not about you. Don't over-analyze the details of the situation. God is a divine deliverer and He comes at exactly the right time. Learn to accept what God allows and go with the flow. The pilot flies the plane, not the passenger, so sit back, buckle up and enjoy the ride. Take time today to change courses and stop taking things so personally. No matter what's going on, God will see you through.

Affirmation Prayer: Heavenly Father, often times when things didn't go my way, I felt victimized. I took it personally as if no one else was experiencing crisis. I viewed myself as a target. I had a pity party. Show me that I am victorious in You. Allow me to exchange the victim mentality and instead, embrace the mentality of a victor, in the name of Jesus, Amen.

Daily Bread: Zechariah 5 – 8; Jude 1:1-25; Psalm 139:17-24

End of the Road
December 8

Scripture: "Let each of you look out not only for his own interests, but also for the interests of others."
~ Philippians 2:4

Spiritual Vitamin

Are you totally surrendered to God? When you were allowing your flesh to rule you, your choices and decisions were contrary to the will of God. You listened to the demands of the flesh and gave in to what it wanted, which was not the right thing to do. You followed the longings and desires of the flesh without giving much consideration to how what you were about to do would affect your spirit. You did not care about how anyone else, including God, felt about what you were doing. You were on a quest to please yourself. Now, all of that has changed. Because of the Presence of God in your life, you have the power to surrender selfishness. Selfishness is a very dangerous characteristic and when your desire is to please yourself, you can be certain that pride is in operation. Put an end to the destructive grip that selfish behavior has on your life and reclaim your power to include the wants and needs of others. Take time today to examine areas of your life where selfishness might be in operation. Tell selfishness that you and it have reached the end of the road.

Affirmation Prayer: Heavenly Father, on my journey with You, I have had some twists and turns, bumps and bruises. I know that many were a result of my selfishness. I was in the driver's seat and You were my copilot. I needed to make a switch. Thank You for convincing me to surrender my control. Now, you are the pilot and I am the copilot. Help me to stay in my rightful place, in the name of Jesus, Amen.

Daily Bread: Zechariah 9 – 11; Revelation 1; Psalm 140:1-5

Everything Must Change
December 9

Scripture: "Behold, I tell you a mystery; we shall not all sleep, but we shall all be changed."
~ 1 Corinthians 15:51

Spiritual Vitamin

Are you afraid of change? For the most part, human beings are afraid of change. When habits and routines are formed, we have a way of programming our minds to believe that the way something is now is the way it will be forever, which is not always true. When it's time for things to change, we resist out of a spirit of fear. It is time to surrender fear for faith because in reality, everything must change. Faith will move you forward while fear will hold you back. You can fight against change or you can go with the flow. Either way, change will occur. One day, Jesus is coming back. This will change everything that we currently know. Those who have accepted Him as Savior and Lord will be taken from the earthly realm to the heavenly realm. In order to be eligible to take this journey with Him, you must be willing to change. You must be in right relationship with Christ in order to see God. Take time today to get acquainted with change so that when it occurs, you will not be caught off guard.

Affirmation Prayer: Heavenly Father, thank You for making wonderful plans for my future. My earthly existence is not the only part of life for me. When my earthly time is done, I will be changed and taken into an eternal existence. Prepare me to spend eternity with You, in the name of Jesus, Amen.

Daily Bread: Zechariah 12 – 14; Revelation 2:1-17; Proverbs 30:1-10

I Can't Make You Love Me
December 10

Scripture: "Behold, I stand at the door and knock. If anyone hears my voice and opens the door, I will come in to him and dine with him and he with Me."
~ Revelation 3:20

Spiritual Vitamin

Are you enjoying unconditional love? God loves us unconditionally and freely shares His love with us without stipulations or demands. Yet we spend a great deal of our time trying to earn the love of other human beings. In some cases, we go to great lengths to hold on to relationships that we know are not bringing out the best in us, just to say we have a special someone. This type of behavior can lead to co-dependent relationships, which are extremely unhealthy for the human spirit. If you are in a co-dependent relationship, it's time to surrender your co-dependency of man for independence with God. Jesus died on the cross to set you free. *After that, why would you return to bondage of any kind?* Jesus saved you because He loves you. He wants you to love Him back, but He can't make you love Him. You should be willing to do that on your own. He has gone above and beyond to show you how much you mean to Him and He is more than worthy of your love. Take time today to let God know how much you love Him by relying and depending only on Him.

Affirmation Prayer: Heavenly Father, I don't have to try to make You love me, You already do. Thank You that there is nothing I can do to lose Your love. Show me the way I should go. I entrust my life to You, in the name of Jesus, Amen.

Daily Bread: Esther 1; Esther 2:1-18; Revelation 2:18-29; Revelation 3:1-6; Psalm 140:6-13

If Loving You Is Wrong
December 11

Scripture: "Love the Lord your God with all your heart, with all your soul and with all your strength and with all your mind."
~ Luke 10:27

Spiritual Vitamin

Are you loving the wrong things? It is implied by the title of this song, that there is some level of resistance between the one who loves and the one who is being loved. The one who loves is saying, "I am bound and determined to love you, even if it's the wrong thing for me to do." This seems to be the kind of love that is fixed on and directed toward someone without their acceptance or approval. In the secular sense, this kind of love was born out of an improper attraction, not a healthy and wholesome relationship. Love should not be mishandled and cheapened in this manner. From a Christian perspective, this is how you should feel about God. You should say "Father, if loving YOU is wrong, I don't want to be right". The enemy doesn't want you to love God and when you decide to do it anyway, he will try everything in his power to make this decision seem like the wrong one. It can never be wrong to love God. Take time today to surrender to God. Remove your loyalty from the enemy and give your loyalty and allegiance to God. Loving Him is not an obligation, but an opportunity as well as a privilege.

Affirmation Prayer: Heavenly Father, help me to love You more than anything and to develop a firm commitment to You, no matter what circumstances I face, in the name of Jesus, Amen.

Daily Bread: Esther 2:19-23; Esther 3 – 5; Revelation 3:7-22; Psalm 141:1-10

I Know I'll Never Love This Way Again
December 12

Scripture: "And above all things, have fervent love for one another, for love will cover a multitude of sins."
~ 1 Peter 4:8

Spiritual Vitamin

Are you a victim of past hurts? When someone you love hurts you, there is the temptation to build walls around your heart so that you will not be hurt again. In an effort to protect yourself, you decide that you will never allow yourself to love this way again. This is not the design of your heavenly Father. His message is that love covers a multitude of sins. In order to follow the will of God concerning love, you must surrender the desire to protect yourself because if you belong to God, He has promised to protect you. God's Holy Spirit guides you into truth. When you spend time in the Presence of God, He talks to you through His Spirit. When you love with the wrong motives, you are setting yourself up for failure but when you love without expectations, you allow others the freedom to be who they really are without the pressure to meet your standards. Allow people to experience your love without strings attached. You have freely received the love of God, now freely give love to others without expecting anything in return. Take time today to love, God's way. He will protect your heart from harm.

Affirmation Prayer: Heavenly Father, my love and faithfulness will never leave You. Help me to always remember that no one else can love me like You, in the name of Jesus, Amen.

Daily Bread: Esther 6 – 8; Revelation 4; Psalm 142:1-7

Selwyn B. Cox

I Look To You
December 13

Scripture: "I will lift up my eyes to the hills, from whence comes my help? My help comes from the Lord who made heaven and earth."
~ Psalm 121:1-2

Spiritual Vitamin

Who is your "go to" person? God wants you to trust Him to take care of you. He has promised to help you. *Have you learned how to depend on God?* He wants you to look to Him to provide the things you want and need. Surrender self-reliance and stop trying to do everything in your own strength. *When you need something, who do you turn to for help? When troubled times arise in your life, where do you go for support? Do you immediately look to God, or to some other source?* God has promised to be with you to lead and guide you into all truth. The more you look to Him for support, the more you will learn that everything you need is wrapped up in His Presence. Your ultimate goal should be to look to, love, learn from and lean on your heavenly Father for everything you need. Look to God to provide the house, the spouse, the job or anything else you desire. Take time today to look to God because if He provides the blessing, there will be no strings attached.

Affirmation Prayer: Heavenly Father, teach me the way I should walk because I look to You. You are my help and my support. I cannot make it without You. Keep my eyes focused on You, in the name of Jesus, Amen.

Daily Bread: Esther 9 – 10; Revelation 5; Proverbs 30:11-23

I Surrender
December 14

Scripture: "And those who know Your name will put their trust in You; for You, Lord, have not forsaken those who seek You."
~ Psalm 9:10

Spiritual Vitamin

What will it take for you to completely surrender to God? Anything that is not in the will of God for your life will not be good for you in the end. Surrender whatever it is that stands between you and God's best for you. If He does not want it for you, you should not desire it for yourself. If your highest goal is to please God, then you will willingly and freely let go of anything He does not want you to have. You will not fight and argue or kick and scream, trying to justify why you should have a particular thing that He has spoken against. You will want for yourself what He wants for you and you will be happy to accept whatever that is. *What or who will you have to leave behind?* Everyone that you have chosen may not be able to go with you to the destination God has in mind. *What are you willing to sacrifice for the will of God?* If you are having trouble with this, consider the fact that Jesus gave His very life to save you. That should make it a bit easier for you to make your choice. Take time today to surrender to the Lordship of Jesus Christ and start experiencing the wonderful blessings He is waiting to give.

Affirmation Prayer: Heavenly Father, help me to trust You with all my heart rather than leaning on my own understanding. Assure me that I have been crucified with Christ and as a result, must surrender my ways, in the name of Jesus, Amen.

Daily Bread: Malachi 1; Malachi 2:1-17; Revelation 6; Psalm 143:1-12

Kiss and Say Goodbye
December 15

Scripture: "As soon as he had come, immediately he went up to Him and said to Him, "Rabbi, Rabbi" and kissed Him."
~ Mark 14:45

Spiritual Vitamin

Are you prepared to deal with betrayal? This is something no one wants to deal with, but it has or will happen to everyone. Jesus experienced it prior to being crucified. He spoke of it to His disciples. When it happened to Him, He did nothing to retaliate. He allowed God to handle the person who decided to betray Him with a kiss. Betrayal can only happen at the hands of those who are close to you. This is why when it comes to your inner circle, you must choose wisely. Judas made a conscious decision to betray the Master as a result of his own greed. In hindsight, he saw that nothing was worth what he had done. Judas' act hurt him more than it hurt Jesus because Jesus had already planned to die. Jesus died because of love; Judas died because of guilt and shame. Jesus can turn betrayal into a blessing, hurt into healing and darkness into light. *Will you allow Him to do that for you?* Take time today to surrender the pain of betrayal and allow God to turn it into a blessing. Then, you can move forward in the purpose and destiny of God.

Affirmation Prayer: Heavenly Father, give me the strength to honor my word and to be a true friend and confidante to those You place within my circle of influence. Let me never betray another, in the name of Jesus, Amen.

Daily Bread: Malachi 3 – 4; Revelation 7; Psalm 144:1-8

Let It Be
December 16

Scripture: "But Jesus answered and said to him, "Permit it to be so now, for thus it is fitting for us to fulfill all righteousness." Then he allowed Him."
~ Matthew 3:15

Spiritual Vitamin

Are you able to let it be? As human beings, we waste a great deal of time trying to manipulate the details of situations that are really outside of our ability to control. There are some things not meant for us to handle and that is sometimes difficult to accept and understand. Sometimes, it's best to just let it be. It is time to surrender manipulation and the desire to control. One of the rewards of being connected to a loving and powerful God is not having to fight your own battles. Jesus invites you to cast your cares on Him and tells you that He cares for you. Jesus does not make promises that He cannot keep and He does not speak empty words and leave you with unmet expectations. Everything He says, He does. You must learn how to rest in Him and gain a desire to let His plan prevail. *How comfortable are you with giving God full and complete control?* Take time today to surrender the love of being in charge. God can handle the situations of life much better than you can and He's always working for your good.

Affirmation Prayer: Heavenly Father, I am sure that You have full knowledge of what is best for me. Make me willing to demonstrate this faith through my actions, in the name of Jesus, Amen.

Daily Bread: Ezra 1; Ezra 2:1-67; Revelation 8; Revelation 9:1-12; Psalm 144:9-15

(Sometimes You Gotta) Lose To Win
December 17

Scripture: "Do you not know that those who run in a race all run, but one receives the prize? Run in such a way that you may obtain it."
~ 1 Corinthians 9:24

Spiritual Vitamin

Can you trust God to give you something better than what you already have? Sometimes the things we cry about the loudest are the things that mean the least. We attempt to hold on to something we believe to be of value when God is trying to give us something worth much more. It is time to surrender the imitation for the authentic. Everything God has, satan has a counterfeit. You have to know which is which. This is where spiritual discernment comes into the picture. The enemy will cause you to believe that what you currently have is the real thing. He already knows that is a lie and he is hoping to keep you from discovering that fact. Sometimes, you will believe you are losing when in actuality, you are winning. What you are experiencing is in the plan of God. Some gifts come wrapped in sandpaper! Don't despair. Just learn the lesson and pass the test. This simple decision can change your life. Take time today to surrender the counterfeit. Trade in the cubic zirconia from the enemy for the rare and priceless diamonds from the Lord!

Affirmation Prayer: Heavenly Father, thank You for the provisions You have put in place that cause me to win, even when it looks like I'm losing. Keep my eyes on the prize, which is victory in Christ, in the name of Jesus, Amen.

Daily Bread: Ezra 2:68-70; Ezra 3; Ezra 4:1-5; Revelation 9:13-21; Revelation 10; Proverbs 30:24-33

My Heart Will Go On
December 18

Scripture: "Those who trust in the Lord are like Mount Zion, which cannot be moved, but abides forever. As the mountains surround Jerusalem, so the Lord surrounds His people from this time forth and forever."
~ Psalm 125:1-2

Spiritual Vitamin

Martin Luther said "I have held many things in my hands, and I have lost them all; but whatever I have placed in God's hands, that I still possess." *Can you identify?* You don't have to remain in a place of despair. Pain and sorrow are only meant to last for a season. When the season ends, God gives us the grace to move forward. Some pain makes you feel like you will never be able to do that. When this happens, you must summon the strength and courage of God. It is time to surrender the curse of being stagnant. Stagnant things stink because they have no current or flow. You must not allow this to define you or your circumstances. There is a song from a very successful movie and play called "Annie" with a very profound message – the sun will come out tomorrow! No matter what has happened to you and how devastating it was, there is something you can do to help yourself. Place your heart back into the hands of God. He will do what is necessary to heal you and empower your heart to go on. Take time today to surrender anything that attempts to hold you back from God's ultimate best for you.

Affirmation Prayer: Heavenly Father, I will trust in You with all my heart and my soul. You are my light of the morning when the sun rises. My daily walk with You shows me a morning without clouds. You are my strength and reason to go on, in the name of Jesus, Amen.

Daily Bread: Ezra 4:6-24; Ezra 5; Revelation 11; Psalm 145:1-7

Nearer My God To Thee
December 19

Scripture: "let us draw near with a true heart in full assurance of faith, having our hearts sprinkled from an evil conscience and our bodies washed with pure water."
~ Hebrews 10:22

Spiritual Vitamin

Are you and God close? God wants to be close to you. He has made His intentions clear all throughout scripture and the meaning is clearly understood. In order to be close to Him, you must put off worldliness and ungodly habits and behaviors. It is time to surrender carnality. The definition of the word carnal is "pertaining to or characterized by the flesh", so a carnal mind cannot understand spiritual things. At some point, a decision will have to be made. *Which one will win your devotion, the carnal or the spiritual?* God wants to draw you nearer but you must be in the proper position to be drawn. You must be willing to walk by the spirit rather than by the flesh and your soul must have a longing to be in the Presence of God. These disciplines will elevate your worship life and lead you to a place of greater peace. Practice being near to God now because the ultimate goal is to live with Him for eternity. Take time today to grow and develop your spirit man (woman). Your life will change in ways you never imagined.

Affirmation Prayer: Heavenly Father, I have put on the breastplate of righteousness and am drawing closer to You. Help me to continue to grow and to develop my spirit in the ways of Your Word, in the name of Jesus, Amen.

Daily Bread: Ezra 6; Ezra 7:1-10; Revelation 12; Psalm 145:8-13

Love Under New Management
December 20

Scripture: "and that you put on the new man which was created according to God, in true righteousness and holiness."
~ Ephesians 4:24

Spiritual Vitamin

The enemy of God was once in control of the way you thought and behaved. The enemy spoke and you listened; he gave instructions and you followed orders. It is time to transfer your allegiance and loyalty from the enemy and give it to God instead. Resign from your old position, change employers and work for someone new. God is offering you a position in the service industry. *Do you want to work for the best boss in the world?* If so, then you want to take this job. The benefits are better than you could ever imagine. Your new job description offers you the chance to practice the art of love under new management. You can learn what God's Word says about love and put those things into practice in your daily life. The best praise you can give to God is a surrendered life; one that is submitted to His will and obedient to His Word. Take time today to become familiar with your employee handbook, which is the Bible. It will teach you everything you need to know about your new job.

Affirmation Prayer: Heavenly Father, thank You for choosing me. I am now governed by You as my new boss. I am in love under new management. I know with You I can accomplish all things. Help me to always be willing to follow Your guidance and instruction, in the name of Jesus, Amen.

Daily Bread: Ezra 7:11-28; Ezra 8:1-14; Revelation 13:1-18; Psalm 145:14-21

On My Own
December 21

Scripture: "Then Jesus answered and said to them, "Most assuredly, I say to you, the Son can do nothing of Himself, but what He sees the Father do; for whatever He does, the Son also does in like manner.""
~ John 5:19

Spiritual Vitamin

Do you credit God with your success? It's easy to be deceived into thinking you are responsible for your own success. After all, you are the one who went to school to learn the skills that earned you the degree and helped you land that great paying job you are now privileged to have. Then you went out and purchased the car and home of your dreams. You married the perfect mate and you are now living what is known as the American dream. There is only one problem with this scenario. You did not do any of these things on your own. Nothing you have accomplished came solely by your own merits. It was all because of the grace and mercy of God. For this reason, it's time to surrender self-gratification. You do not have the knowledge or the power to sustain yourself. You have been kept by the power of God's Holy Spirit. You need Him to do everything and there's nothing you can do without His help. Even the air you breathe comes from God. Take time today to give up the notion that you are responsible for your current station in life. It was not you; it was God.

Affirmation Prayer: Heavenly Father, when I look at the credits of my life story, all Your names appear. I often think of you as Adonai (Lord, Master), El Olam (The Everlasting God), Jehovah-Raah (The Lord my Shepherd). Everything I am is because of You. Remind me that I am never on my own, in the name of Jesus, Amen.

Daily Bread: Ezra 8:15-36; Ezra 9:1-15; Revelation 14:1-13; Proverbs 31:1-9

Precious Lord
December 22

Scripture: "He restores my soul; He leads me in the paths of righteousness for His name's sake."
~ Psalm 23:3

Spiritual Vitamin

How do you respond during difficult times? As you may know, sometimes life will become difficult. There will be days when you will feel the pressures of life and it will seem as if the walls are closing in on you. On days like this, you will need to seek strength from a source higher and greater than yourself. It is time to surrender stubbornness and be willing to ask for help. You were not designed to make it all alone. You need the assistance of God and others. Put your hand in God's hand and let Him lead you down the path of righteousness to a place of restoration. You do not have super-human strength and you will get tired sometimes. Don't always feel that you have to push yourself past your physical limitations in order to accomplish your goals. Pray to your heavenly Father for guidance and wisdom concerning the proper method to employ to create a sense of balance in your life. There is time to do everything God wants you to do. Take time today to pray for strength and our precious Lord will meet your every need.

Affirmation Prayer: Heavenly Father, You are more precious to me than life itself. Thank You for ordering my steps day by day. Thank You for showing me the way. Thank You for allowing me to hear what You say. Continue to guide my hands and help me to carry out Your plans, in the name of Jesus, Amen.

Daily Bread: Ezra 10; Revelation 14:14-20; Revelation 15; Psalm 146:1-10

Shaky Ground
December 23

Scripture: "Therefore whoever hears these sayings of Mine, and does them, I will liken him to a wise man who built his house on the rock: and the rain descended, the floods came, and the winds blew and beat on that house; and it did not fall, for it was founded on the rock."
~ Matthew 7:24-25

Spiritual Vitamin

Are you standing on shaky ground? Solid ground provides a stable, firm and sure foundation on which to stand. When something is being built, it is wise for the builder to first establish that the foundation is secure. Shaky ground is dangerous ground. When you operate under the spirit of integrity, you are standing on solid ground. But when you operate under a spirit of lies and deceit, you are standing on shaky ground. When your reasons for helping people come from a place that is genuine and sincere, you don't have to toot your own horn. Those you help will do it for you. It's time to surrender self-promotion. You don't have to promote yourself; if the work you do is done with clean hands and a pure heart, God will promote you. If what you are doing is sincerely from your heart, others will give you recognition and thanks for the good deeds you do. Remember, God sits high and looks low and the things done in darkness and in secret are never hidden from His sight. Take time today to make sure you're standing on solid ground so that what God is building in you can stand.

Affirmation Prayer: Heavenly Father, I realize that I am on shaky ground if I do not heed to Your Word, Your will and Your way for my life. I know there is nowhere to run and nowhere to hide from You if my motives are not in tune with Your will. Search me and establish me so I am on a firm foundation, in the name of Jesus, Amen.

Daily Bread: Nehemiah 1 – 2; Revelation 16; Psalm 147:1-11

Haven't You Heard?
December 24

Scripture: "Have you not known? Have you not heard? The everlasting God, the Lord, the Creator of the ends of the earth, neither faints nor is weary. His understanding is unsearchable."
~ Isaiah 40:28

Spiritual Vitamin

There will be many things that will attempt to take your attention away from and your focus off of God. It has been said that satan has an arsenal of weapons of mass distraction. The enemy is the king of distraction so you must be intentional about staying focused. He is extremely good at throwing things in the way to keep you off course, in an effort to delay your arrival at the destination God intended for you. He knows he cannot abort your destiny but he also knows that if you are unsure about your place in God, that there is a good chance he can cause confusion. Confusion will aid in his plan to keep you off course. When you have taken a wrong turn and you find out that you have lost your way, don't despair. *God is looking for you; haven't you heard?* He will never let you end up somewhere too far to be rescued by Him. It is time to surrender distractions; do it today. Make a firm commitment to use discipline and stand your ground. Stop giving in to every trick and tactic the enemy throws your way. Take time today to put yourself in a position to be used by God and to hear His voice concerning His plans for your life.

Affirmation Prayer: Heavenly Father, the enemy has tried to trick me, telling me that he has a treat for me if I obey him. He tried that with Jesus when He was in the wilderness. It did not work then and it will not work now. Had he not heard? I am Your anointed one and am convinced that neither life nor death can separate me from Your love. Assure me that I am on a firm foundation, in the name of Jesus, Amen.

Daily Bread: Nehemiah 3 – 4; Revelation 17; Psalm 147:12-20

The Only Hope We Have
December 25

Scripture: "Therefore the Lord Himself will give you a sign: Behold, the virgin shall conceive and bear a Son, and shall call His name Immanuel."
~ Isaiah 7:14

Spiritual Vitamin

Today is the day we celebrate the birth of our Savior and Lord. Happy Birthday Jesus! On this day, Christians around the world set aside time to give thanks and praise to God for sending Jesus as a ransom for our sin. Jesus is the most precious gift any of us will ever receive. Everyone is looking for hope and in the birth, death and resurrection of Christ, we find that hope. Before you were even born, God was thinking of you. He knew that man would fall and be in need of a Savior. He gave Jesus as a gift to you. *How does that make you feel?* Because of the love of God, you have hope in a wonderful Savior. *In appreciation for the priceless gift of Jesus, what will you give God in return?* The best gift you can give Him is your whole heart, in humble submission to His will. You can give Him a made up mind, where there is no doubt about His supernatural ability to save, deliver and set free. You can give Him a mind that is determined to think God-centered thoughts for the purpose of carrying out His will. You can give Him your love, loyalty and devotion and make Him first in everything you say and do. Take time today to celebrate your King for unto us a child is born, in the person of Jesus Christ! On His birthday, give Him the gift of your obedience.

Affirmation Prayer: Heavenly Father, You are the real reason for this season. Help me to always acknowledge You on the day we celebrate Your birth, in the name of Jesus, Amen.

Daily Bread: Nehemiah 5 – 6; Revelation 18:1-17; Proverbs 31:10-20

The Beat Goes On
December 26

Scripture: "whereas you do not know what *will happen* tomorrow. For what is your life? It is even a vapor that appears for a little time and then vanishes away."
~ James 4:14

Spiritual Vitamin

Do you value time? Time is a precious commodity. It does not slow down or stop for any reason. Whether you do what you *should* do at any given moment in time or not, time itself will not wait for you. Ready or not, the beat goes on. This is proof positive that you must do everything within your power to avoid wasting time. The hourglass illustrates just how quickly time can get away from you. Because of this, it's time to surrender procrastination. The habit of wasting time is your enemy. You have no control over the clock. The number of seconds, minutes and hours of your life have been predetermined by God. He alone knows just how much time you have. This thought can be a bit intimidating but if properly processed, can also serve as inspiration to keep you grounded and focused. Every day, you should do the things that make the most of your time, rather than idly allowing precious moments to slip away. Take time today to evaluate areas where procrastination may be in effect and do what is necessary to eliminate it.

Affirmation Prayer: Heavenly Father, Your Word tells me that when You return, You will come quickly. I know that You are not pleased if I am lukewarm. I need to be hot or cold and if not, there is no place for me with You. Help me to accomplish all You have set my hands to do and be on fire for You, in the name of Jesus, Amen.

Daily Bread: Nehemiah 7 - 8; Revelation 18:17-24; Revelation 19:1-10; Psalm 148:1-6

Ain't No Stopping Us Now
December 27

Scripture: "Then Peter began to say to Him, "See, we have left all and followed You.""
~ Mark 10:28

Spiritual Vitamin

You are a survivor. There is strength in you that you did not know you possessed. God has shown you some surprising things about yourself and now you are learning that you're a resilient and powerful person. It's time to surrender the idea that you might not make it. This is one of satan's lies. Stop believing him and start trusting in the Word of God. You will make it because you have an Omnipotent God on your side. He has never been defeated and He never will be. The enemy knows that if you ever realize who and whose you are, that his days of manipulating and controlling you will be over. Once you totally surrender to God, the enemy will be fired and his influence in your life will come to a screeching halt. He knows that the only reason you listen to him is because you really don't know any better. Once you learn better, his ability to control your actions and thoughts will be greatly diminished. Take time today to celebrate. God has already predestined your victory. Because of this, you can declare, "ain't no stopping me now!"

Affirmation Prayer: Heavenly Father, victory is mine today and every day. Keep me mindful of this truth, in the name of Jesus, Amen.

Daily Bread: Nehemiah 9:1-38; Revelation 19:11-21; Psalm 148:7-14

No More Drama
December 28

Scripture: "And Jabez called on the God of Israel saying, "Oh, that You would bless me indeed, and enlarge my territory, that Your hand would be with me, and that You would keep me from evil, that I may not cause pain!" So God granted him what he requested."
~ 1 Chronicles 4:10

Spiritual Vitamin

Attention! Attention! Calling all drama kings and queens. I have an announcement to make. The announcement is --- no more drama; the party's over! You have the power to declare war on whatever it is that's hindering you from being the best you that you can be. Be it dramatic people or circumstances, they must be put in their proper place. In the scripture above, the name Jabez means pain. Drama causes pain. All year long, there have been instances when trivial, insignificant things have invaded your space, physically, mentally and emotionally. You fell for the nonsense and the drama when you could have simply prayed for God to take control and continued to move forward. You are on your way to a God-determined destination and you don't have time to get off course. Drama is not your friend and neither is anyone who continuously brings it to you. Along these lines, you must make sure that you're not creating undue drama for yourself. You have the right to a peace-filled life. Don't settle for anything less. Take time today to identify where there is drama in your life and do whatever is needed to get rid of it.

Affirmation Prayer: Heavenly Father, I have rid my life of people and events that bring about intense conflict. In other words, I am dead to and done with drama. Keep me alive, alert, and attentive to Your plans for my life, in the name of Jesus, Amen.

Daily Bread: Nehemiah 10; Nehemiah 11:1-21; Revelation 20; Psalm 149:1-9

Time To Say Goodbye
December 29

Scripture: "Surrender your heart to God, turn to Him in prayer, and give up your sins --- even those you do in secret. Then you won't be ashamed; you will be confident and fearless."
~ Job 11:13-15 (CEV)

Spiritual Vitamin

As the end of the month draws near, I want to encourage you to surrender, letting go of everything that is not conducive to a strong and thriving relationship with God. You are just days away from witnessing the start of a brand new year. One year is ending while another one is beginning. You are standing on the threshold of newness. A blank canvas is about to be unfolded before you. *What type of picture will you paint?* You should be excited about the prospective blessings that are on their way to you in the coming year. One thing you must do is surrender your devotion to and connection with sin. It's time to say goodbye. Anything that has not served you well in this current year has no business crossing over with you into the next. Sin and satan are enemies of the soul. Their intention is to remain with you throughout the balance of your life, causing you shame and misery each and every day. Surrendering your loyalty to sin will produce a dramatic impact on your life. Things once unattainable will become attainable and dreams deferred will begin to be realized. Take time today to break up with anything that is not for your ultimate good; it's time to say goodbye. Jesus makes all things new.

Affirmation Prayer: Heavenly Father, I have shed the estranged relationships of sin from the past. I have said goodbye. I have embraced a new life in You. Empower me to never look back, in the name of Jesus, Amen.

Daily Bread: Nehemiah 11:22-36; Nehemiah 12:1-47; Revelation 21; Proverbs 31:21-31

Try Jesus
December 30

Scripture: "Oh, taste and see that the Lord is good; blessed is the man who trusts in Him."
~ Psalm 34:8

Spiritual Vitamin

For the last 365 days, you have tried a number of things. Some of them worked while others did not. In many cases, the things you tried have failed you and left you feeling empty inside. This is the perfect reason for you to try Jesus because Jesus never fails. When all else fails, Jesus never fails. He holds a record that proves the fact that He's never lost at anything since the time of His birth right up until this very moment. What Jesus says He will do, He does. What Jesus starts, He finishes. Once you give Him a try, there will be no need to continue looking elsewhere for answers or solutions. Christ is the answer! *What is better than perfection?* He is perfection personified. Isn't it amazing that His greatest desire is to become your Savior and Lord? *Jesus is calling; will you answer the phone?* If you haven't already, take time today to try Jesus. Nothing else you know of can compare to the greatness of God.

Affirmation Prayer: Heavenly Father, You truly are good. Thank You for giving me the opportunity to try Jesus. Teach me that He's the best thing that will ever happen to me, in the name of Jesus, Amen.

Daily Bread: Nehemiah 13; Revelation 22; Psalm 150:1-6

Let Go & Let God
December 31

Scripture: "Do not remember the former things, nor consider the things of old. Behold, I will do a new thing, now it shall spring forth; Shall you not know it? I will even make a road in the wilderness and rivers in the desert."
~ Isaiah 43:18-19

Spiritual Vitamin

You've lost weeks, months and years of your life, consumed with the wounds of yesterday. You have replayed hurt tapes over and over again in your mind, rehashing what happened and how it made you feel. Now, it's time to surrender the pain. Let go of all of that negativity and come out of the darkness into God's marvelous light. Let go of anything that threatens your progress or your growth; let go of things like unforgiveness, bitterness, anger, hatred, slander, jealousy and maliciousness. You don't have any more time to waste. This is the last day of the year and there is at least one thing you have not accomplished up to this point. *Why don't you use the remaining hours to do something that will brighten your future instead of focusing on some negative or hurtful aspect from your past?* Don't take the baggage from this year across the threshold into the next. Take time today to let it all go and start the new year with a clean slate.

Affirmation Prayer: Heavenly Father, the time has come and I understand. The truth is, unless I let go, unless I forgive myself and others, unless I forgive the situation and know it is over, unless I let you have full control, I cannot move forward. Holding on is believing that there is no hope, letting go is knowing my future is secure in You. Help me to leave the old and to welcome the new, in the name of Jesus, Amen.

MONTHLY REFLECTIONS

Congratulations on your achievement! You Did It! You have completed the Believers 12 Step Plan.

The JAMS@Work 365 Devotional was designed to be tailor made to meet your spiritual needs. God inspired this devotional. It is my prayer that you will recycle the daily devotions on an as needed basis to uplift you and others for years to come.

Thank you for your purchase and for allowing me to share in your journey. I highly commend you for having the desire and discipline to strengthen your relationship with Jesus Christ.

Following are some ABC's to help keep this experience ALIVE.

A. Annotate - Keep a journal of your spiritual experience

B. Build - Create your personal playlist (use songs that hold special meaning to you)

C. Communicate - Tweet, Snap Chat, Instagram, and post on Facebook excerpts from Jesus' Amazing Miracles at work (JAMS@work) 365 Devotional and the goodness of God in your life.

May God be with you until we meet again!

About The Author

Selwyn Brian Cox grew up in the District of Columbia. He is the middle child in his family, but named himself the unofficial head of the family after the death of his mother. He graduated from Anacostia Senior High School and attended Howard University and the University of the District of Columbia, where he studied Business Administration.

Selwyn retired from the Environmental Protection Agency after 35 years of dedicated service. From April 2001 to December 2004, he served as the Vice President of Civil Rights in the AFGE Union Local 3331. In this role, he worked tirelessly to protect the rights of EPA bargaining unit employees and to develop accountability tools that would hold managers accountable for unfair treatment. Along with Marsha Coleman-Adebayo, he co-founded the EPA Victims Against Racial Discrimination (EPAVARD), a non-profit organization dedicated to ending discrimination. Selwyn's work was instrumental in securing a hearing which exposed racial injustice at EPA before the House Committee on Science. As a result, President George W. Bush signed into law the "No Fear" Act in May 2002, which holds Federal agencies accountable to provide a work environment free of discrimination and retaliation. Selwyn is a lifetime member of Blacks in Government (BIG) and also a member of the National Association for the Advancement of Colored People (NAACP).

Obeying the will and purpose of God for his life, Selwyn accepted the call into ministry and received his certificate of license in June 2014, after completing the comprehensive Minister in Training program at the Alfred Street Baptist Church in Alexandria, VA. Selwyn's new career is full-time service to others. His mantra is "Survived and Saved by the Savior to Serve." As a result of his love and dedication to God and his coworkers, Selwyn started a Bible study and fellowship ministry prior to leaving EPA in June 2012. The ministry is called "Jesus' Amazing Miracles Sessions @ Work (JAMS@WK). He still meets with the group once a month during their lunch hour. JAMS@WK is a love ministry, discussing and providing practical Christian principles.

Family is very important to Selwyn. He loved and cherished his mother and following her death, he founded a ministry called "Mothers in Mind." The ministry mission is caring for widows and elderly women. There are approximately 10 women in the ministry. Activities include social outings, shopping and home visits. In recent years, Selwyn also founded a ministry called "Brother to Brother", in tribute to the memory of his brother, who recently passed away. He mentors young men in the absence of their fathers, teaching them the importance of developing a personal relationship with God. He also engages them in meaningful discussions on topics dealing with conduct, courtesy and self-esteem. Selwyn is waiting with great anticipation to see what God has in store for him in the future.

If this book has encouraged you in any way, Selwyn would love to hear from you. You may contact him at the following email address: selwynbcox@gmail.com.

About Kingdom Journey Press

Kingdom Journey Press, Inc. is a full-service publishing company specializing in providing customized services to support our clients from the conception of an idea to getting your story to the masses! Since the time of inception and in conjunction with our umbrella organization, Kingdom Journey Enterprises, we have become recognized globally for our ability to establish a unique presence, while building relationships with partners and clients consisting of current and aspiring writers, and ministry, business, and community organizations.

Our services include:
- One-on-One Consultations
- Dedicated Service Representatives
- Manuscript Evaluation
- Coaching for current and aspiring authors
- Editing
- Cover and Print Layout Design
- Print and E-Book Format
- Copyright
- Worldwide Distribution
- Marketing and Sales Support

For more information, visit our website at www.kjpressinc.com.

www.ingramcontent.com/pod-product-compliance
Lightning Source LLC
Chambersburg PA
CBHW031306150426
43191CB00005B/98